Factors Related to the
Professional Development
of Librarians

by

Elizabeth W. Stone, Ph.D.

The Scarecrow Press, Inc.
Metuchen, N.J.   1969

© Copyright 1969, by

Elizabeth W. Stone

SBN 8108-0274-0

Acknowledgments

To the author's major professor, Dr. Charles H. Goodman, whose helpful guidance, thoughtful evaluation, and sound criticism during the preparation of the dissertation provided encouragement and inspiration;

To the Rev. James J. Kortendick, S. S., Ph. D., Head of the Department of Library Science, The Catholic University of America, for encouraging the writer to undertake further graduate study, for providing the invaluable aid of research assistants, and for his sustained interest in the project;

To Sarah Rebecca Reed, for personal interest, for early and continuing support, and for close attention in the progress of the study;

To John G. Lorenz for belief in the value of this undertaking and constructive suggestions concerning the presentation of the data;

To Dhirendra N. Ghosh, for instruction and counsel with regard to all the statistical aspects of this study;

To the fifteen librarians in the pilot study for their valuable and constructive suggestions;

To the Deans of the ALA accredited library schools in the United States for their one-hundred per cent cooperation in supplying the names of graduates for the population;

To Dr. Harlan Mills and Dr. Bronson Price for sharing their statistical skills and experience in questionnaire preparation and analysis;

To Dr. Mary Gaver for her interest in all research in librarianship and in appreciation of her personal encouragement to make these research findings visible to the profession;

To co-workers in the Department of Library Science and numerous graduate students for their interest and untiring efforts in checking the statistical and clerical work;

iii

To the members of the graduating classes of 1956 and 1961 of the accredited library schools for generously giving their time to completion of the questionnaire;

And especially to the members of her family for their patience, understanding, and steadfast support, the writer is deeply grateful.

Table of Contents

List of Tables

List of Figures

Figure   Page

Chapter I Introduction

Purpose of the Study

This study was undertaken to determine whether one could identify some of the factors that motivate librarians to continue their professional development after receiving the Master's degree in Library Science. Conversely, it also sought to identify some of the factors which might deter professional development activities.

The following questions were posed:

1. What do librarians regard as the most encouraging and most deterring forces that influence them to participate in professional improvement activities and in formal course work?

2. What activities do librarians consider to be most important for professional development? What are their actual practices and is there a gap between what they are doing and what they think they should be doing for maximum professional growth?

3. Does their background influence librarians' motivation?

4. Can special measurements or indexes be developed concerning librarians' professional attitudes, activities and aspirations that may be associated with their motivation toward continuing education?

5. Is it possible to develop devices that can determine approximately the degree and kind of motivation that librarians have for professional improvement and formal course work? If so, are degree and kind of motivation related to background characteristics or to the special indexes that measure professionalism and aspiration?

6. What do librarians perceive to be the attitudes of allied groups concerning their continuing professional development? Do these perceived attitudes of related groups affect librarians' motiva-

15

tion toward professional improvement and formal course work?

7. What do the librarians perceive to be the responsibility
of allied groups for their professional development? What does this
reveal about librarians' motivation for continuing education?

Justification for the Study

Change is the major concern in American librarianship today. Advancing technology, increasing volume of recorded knowledge, the population explosion, and manpower shortages are only a
few of the problems that assault the existing organization and administration of library services. Margaret Mead stated one of the
most vivid truths of the new age: "No one will live all his life in
the world into which he was born, and no one will die in the world
in which he worked in his maturity."[1]

Some members of the profession appear distressed, even a-
fraid, that the very identity of the profession may not be able to
survive these changes. Other library leaders, however, respond
that the most creative and effective solution is to develop a dynamic
program of continuing education which will assist the profession in
understanding, even anticipating, the stresses of rapid and radical
change. John Lorenz sensed the urgency of this need:

> The development of strong programs for the coming dec-
> ades demands from professional associations, library
> schools, and librarians a commitment to the ideas of self-
> renewal and excellence in professional education, and to
> willingness to adapt to change, to utilize the knowledge of
> other disciplines in designing new libraries and new ser-
> vices to meet new needs. [2]

The library profession has begun to assume its responsibility
for providing adequate programs of continuing education for its members. An example has been the increasing number of listings of informal library education opportunities in the annual publication, Continuing Education for Librarians. This register was started in 1964
by Sarah Reed in the Library Services Division of the U. S. Office

of Education, [3] and was continued for 1967-68 and 1968-69, by the American Library Association's Office of Library Education. [4] The opportunities listed each year vary widely and occur sporadically. In general, there is evidence of a need for long-range cooperative planning in order to achieve an adequate program for the profession as a whole.

A survey of the literature of the past twenty years revealed a dearth of studies related to the continuing education of librarians. Librarianship almost never appears in comparative studies of the professions and their self-development programs. Material that does discuss the factors associated with professional growth has rarely been based on research, [5] and no previous study has shown concern for the relationship of motivation to continuing education.

There have been a few exceptions, however, which are related in one way or another to some aspect of the present study. In a study of head librarians in the Mid-west, Robert Alvarez considered such factors as age, education and previous experience, relating them to the concept of career development. [6] Based on data found in the third edition of Who's Who in Library Service, John Harvey studied patterns of occupational mobility exhibited by 1316 chief public and college librarians. [7] Perry Morrison studied 676 academic librarians and presented a group profile based on use of the Ghiselli "Self-Descriptive Inventory," which covered the factors of sex, age, type of library school, and variety of experience. [8]

None of these studies was concerned primarily with continuing education or with what motivates a librarian to participate or not to participate in development activities.

In order to achieve cooperation in planning for long-range solutions, the actual needs of the librarians should be known. In order to implement plans, information is needed as to what actually motivates librarians to take advantage of opportunities. To date, these elements--knowledge of need and knowledge of motivational forces--have been largely lacking as sound bases for programming opportunities for continuing education.

Hypotheses Tested

The following hypotheses were examined in order to answer some of the questions pertinent to this study.

A. Degree and type of motivation:

1. There is no relationship between the degree of professional improvement motivation and each of the following variables:
    a. Age.
    b. Sex.
    c. Undergraduate major.
    d. Years between the Bachelor's degree and Master's in Library Science.
    e. Professional Index Score.
    f. Degree of aspiration.
    g. Type of aspiration.
    h. Years in present institution.
    i. Salary.
    j. Position in library.
    k. Perceived attitude of relevant group.
2. There is no relationship between the kind of professional improvement motivation and each of the variables (a through k) listed in Hypothesis 1.
3. There is no relationship between the degree of formal course work motivation and each of the variables (a through k) listed in Hypothesis 1.
4. There is no relationship between the kind of formal course work motivation and each of the variables (a through k) listed in Hypothesis 1.
5. There is no relationship between any of the following variables:
    a. Degree of professional improvement motivation.
    b. Kind of professional improvement motivation.

      c. Degree of formal course work motivation.
      d. Kind of formal course work motivation.

B. Positive and negative forces:

   6. There is no relationship between what the librarian re-
      garded as the dominant positive force on his efforts for
      professional improvement and any of the following vari-
      ables:
      a. Age.
      b. Salary.
      c. Undergraduate major.
      d. Formal course work since Master's degree in
         Library Science.
      e. Degree of aspiration.
      f. Professional Index.
      g. Career satisfaction to date.
      h. Degree of professional improvement motivation.
      i. Kind of professional improvement motivation.
   7. There is no relationship between what the librarian re-
      garded as the dominant negative force on his efforts for
      professional improvement and any of the variables (a
      through i) listed in Hypothesis 6.
   8. There is no relationship between what the librarian re-
      garded as the dominant positive force on his efforts for
      formal course work and any of the following variables.
      a. Age.
      b. Salary.
      c. Undergraduate major.
      d. Formal course work since Master's degree in
         Library Science.
      e. Degree of aspiration.
      f. Professional Index.
      g. Career satisfaction to date.
      h. Degree of formal course work motivation.
      i. Kind of formal course work motivation.

9. There is no relationship between what the librarian re-
    garded as the dominant negative force on his efforts for
    formal course work and any of the variables (a through i)
    in Hypothesis 8.

10. There is no relationship between the category of forces
    the librarian regarded as an encouraging influence on his
    efforts for professional improvement and the category he
    regarded as a deterring influence.

11. There is no relationship between the category of forces
    the librarian regarded as an encouraging influence on his
    efforts for formal course work and the category he re-
    garded as a deterring influence.

These hypotheses will not ordinarily be repeated in the chapters which discuss them.   For convenience they will be referred to
by number as Hypothesis 1-a, 1-b, and so on.

Definition of Basic Terms

The following definitions explain the meanings of terms as
used in the chapters that follow:

Motivation

Saul W. Gellerman's definition of motivation is used in this study
because it is broad enough to apply to motivation for professional
development as well as motivation on the job.

> The ultimate motivation is to make the self-concept real:
> to live in a manner that is appropriate to one's preferred
> role, to be treated in a manner that corresponds to one's
> preferred rank, and to be rewarded in a manner that re-
> flects one's estimate of his own abilities.   Thus we are
> all in perpetual pursuit of whatever we regard as our de-
> served role, trying to make our subjective ideas about
> ourselves into objective truths.   When our experiences
> seem to be confirming those ideas, we are likely to feel
> that life is good and the world itself is just, but when we

are denied the kinds of experiences to which we feel entitled, we are likely to suspect that something is drastically wrong with the world. [9]

Professional Development

Professional development, as used in this study, is equated
with professional growth and continuing education:

> In this study these three terms refer to all activities and
> efforts by the individual to upgrade his knowledge, abili-
> ties, competencies and understanding in his field of work
> or specialization so that he can become a more effective
> professional and be able to handle responsibilities of
> greater scope and accountability. This study is chiefly
> concerned with factors that may be associated with li-
> brarians' motivation to develop professionally through for-
> mal education and professional improvement activities.

The factors considered are those that may be associated with
the librarian's motivation to develop professionally through:

> 1. Professional improvement activities such as attending
> conferences, short courses, workshops and professional
> meetings; reading, writing and editing professional litera-
> ture; participation in in-service (on-the-job) training pro-
> grams; membership in informal study groups; conducting
> research, and many others.

> 2. Formal course work as a fully registered student in
> credit or non-credit courses after receipt of the Master
> of Library Science degree.

The term, professional development, as used in this study,
includes both professional improvement and formal course work.

Organization of the Study

The first part, Chapters I and II, sets the stage for the
study. It deals with background, literature, methods, and procedures.

The second part, Chapters III through VIII, deals with the findings, analyzes them, and relates them to each other in various ways.

The third part, Chapter IX, summarizes the findings, points to certain major implications, and makes several recommendations.

Notes

1. Mead, Margaret "Why Is Education Obsolete?" Harvard Business Review 36:34 November-December, 1958.

2. Lorenz, John G. "The Challenge of Change" PNLA Quarterly 29:13, October, 1964.

3. Reed, Sarah R. (ed.) Continuing Education for Librarians-- Conferences, Workshops and Short Courses, 1964-1965 (Washington: Office of Education, U.S. Department of Health, Education and Welfare, 1964); Reed, Sarah R. and Toye, Willie P. Continuing Education for Librarians--Conferences Workshops, and Short Courses, 1965-66 (Washington: Office of Education, U.S. Department of Health, Education, and Welfare, 1965); Reed, Sarah R. Continuing Education for Librarians--Conferences, Workshops, and Short Courses, 1966-67 (Washington: Office of Education, U.S. Department of Health, Education, and Welfare, 1966).

4. American Library Association, Office for Library Education, Continuing Education for Librarians--Conferences, Workshops, and Short Courses, 1967-68 (Chicago: American Library Association, March, 1967); Continuing Education for Librarians--Conferences, Workshops, and Short Courses, 1968-69 (Chicago: American Library Association, December, 1967).

5. There have been several doctoral and master's dissertations which related to some aspect of the present inquiry, dealing with characteristics of librarians, in-service training, and recruitment. A representative sampling of these two groups is given in the Bibliography.

6. Alvarez, Robert S. "Qualifications of Heads of Libraries in Cities of Over 10,000 Population in the Seven North-Central States" (unpublished Doctor's dissertation, Graduate Library School, University of Chicago, 1939).

7. Harvey, John Frederick The Librarian's Career: A Study of Mobility (ACRL Microcard Series No. 85.) Rochester, N.Y.: University of Rochester Press, 1957.

8. Morrison, Perry David "Career of the Academic Librarian: A Study of the Social Origins, Educational Attainments, Vocational Experience, and Personality Characteristics of a Group

of American Academic Librarians" (unpublished Doctor's dissertation, University of California, 1960).

9. Gellerman, Saul W. Motivation and Productivity (New York: American Management Association, 1963), p. 290.

Chapter II
Determination of the Sample and Development
of the Questionnaire

Once the general purpose and scope of this investigation were
determined, the methods and procedures to be used to obtain the
necessary data were developed.   These included: a) identifying the
sample; b) the nature of the survey sample design;   c) selection of
the variables to be measured by the questionnaire;   d) development
of the questionnaire as well as its format and the technique of presentation; e) organization and administration of the instrument; and
f) analysis of the data.

The Sample

Identifying the Sample to be Surveyed

One criterion in selecting representative librarians was the
recency of their graduation from library school.   This was done in
order to determine, as part of the study, whether or not the length
of time since graduation from library schools would make any difference in the factors affecting their professional growth.   The
graduating classes of 1956 and 1961 were then chosen for comparison.   This choice was based on the assumption that the 1961 graduates would have been out of graduate school long enough to recognize the need for professional growth.   The 1956 graduates would
probably have been working long enough to have established certain
patterns in development activities.   The five-year span was considered desirable since the survey would be taken only once.   The
time span between the two groups should not be so large that the

24

survey would indicate differences which were due to the greater maturity of one group rather than an intrinsic difference between them. If the survey were to be conducted at different intervals, it might have been worthwhile to take groups separated by a larger period of time.

Specifically, the study was limited to those librarians who had received a Master of Library Science degree from a school accredited by the American Library Association. [1] The term professional librarian embraces all librarians, administrators, and other specialists in public, school, academic, and special libraries, library associations, and in government agencies with responsibility in the field of librarianship.

Since it was necessary to have a precise record of all who would comprise the total population, all the library schools in the United States that were accredited in 1956 and 1961, were asked to provide lists of their 1956 and 1961 graduates. All responded with their lists of graduates for those years, a total of 2,781 names. [2] The names appearing on these lists were then checked against the 1966 edition of Who's Who in Library Service, which serves as a directory of professional librarians, not a list of selected members of the profession. [3] Of the names reported by the library schools, only 873, or 31.8 per cent, were in Who's Who in Library Service.

Biographical data for each name thus identified was then entered on a card. The information listed was: name and address, date of birth, year of attainment of the MLS degree, and title of current position. The criteria established for selection of the sample for this study eliminated 67 names, of whom 45 were not in library positions; and 22 lived outside the continental United States. This left 806 names.

Forty-seven per cent of the librarians who had graduated in 1956 and 51 per cent of those who had graduated in 1961 were employed in academic libraries. It is quite possible that this is a considerably higher proportion of academic librarians than would be found if the occupations of all of the 2,781 graduates were known. Based on the statistics that were available at the time of graduation, the Library Journal found that 27 per cent of the 1956 class[4] and

31 per cent of the 1961 class[5] were entering academic libraries.
While this difference might be accounted for by changes of positions
after graduation, it may well be that academic librarians are more
apt to return questionnaires in a survey than public or school librarians. This discrepancy, however, remains an unanswered question.

Despite these doubts regarding the uneven representation of
various types of librarians in the sample it seemed to be a reasonable basis for this first sample.

Nature of the Survey Sample Design

The probability sample was chosen as the method for conducting this study, in order to obtain a wide distribution of librarians
from all parts of the country and from all the accredited schools.
Francis Cornell, in his article on sample surveys in education, [6]
and Bronson Price, of the U. S. Office of Education, [7] had both
stressed two requirements that are basic for a true sample: (1)
each individual in the sample must have some known probability for
entering the sample; and (2) automatic selection must be made by
some predetermined means, such as an established table of random
numbers.

The first condition was met by making a separate card for
each of the 806 individuals in the list. Statistical tables especially
designed for a random sample were selected to fulfill the second requirement. [8]

The 806 cards were then classified by the type of library
with which each librarian was associated (academic, public, school,
or special) and by the year of graduation.

Although a sample of 15 to 20 per cent would normally be
more than adequate for a population of this size, it was determined
that a sampling of 25 per cent would compensate for some of the obsolete addresses in the 1966 edition of Who's Who in Library Service. [9]

It was also decided that the stratified random-sampling technique be employed, with the sample allocated proportionately to each

of the four types of libraries in each of the two sample years.

The Variables

Selection of the Variables

Since the basic purpose of the survey was to seek a better
understanding of factors that might affect the professional growth of
librarians, variables relating to motivation and professional improvement were selected for analysis. The system of scoring these variables is explained in Appendix A.

Variables Related to Background Characteristics

The variables that were selected for study of background
characteristics were: age, sex, marital status, number of children,
residence either east or west of the Mississippi River, undergraduate major, number of years between the Bachelor's degree and the
MLS, number of libraries that had been worked in and their types,
number of years in present institution, salary, number of employees
in library, present position in library and how long in it, number of
people supervised.

Variables Related to Special Measurements of Professional Development Characteristics

Each librarian's attitude was measured in relation to the attributes, knowledge, characteristics, and responsibilities connected
with his profession. A section of the questionnaire reflected the
12 criteria developed by Raymond Ranta[10] for measuring professional orientation to provide the basis for the Professional Index Score.[11]

The degree of aspiration was the librarian's relative desire
to achieve certain professional or personal goals. This score was
adapted from that used by Ranta.[12]

The type of aspiration was the librarian's ambition in li-

brarianship 10 years hence.   The librarians were separated by type
into those who indicated a desire to stay in the same general type
of job or library; and those who desired either an entirely different
type of job, or a position in a different type of library.

Satisfaction with career was determined by the librarian's
feelings about his career to date, with the respondents divided into
those satisfied and those dissatisfied.

The career desires determined the librarian's desire or lack
of desire to stay in the profession of librarianship, comparing librarians who had goals within librarianship and those who had goals
outside librarianship.

Variables That Were Encouraging or Discouraging

The positive factors that encouraged librarians to undertake
professional improvement and formal course work were studied.
Those negative factors that deterred the librarian from professional
improvement and formal course work were also considered.

Motivational Variables

The degree of professional improvement motivation was the
relative intensity of the librarian's motivation for improving himself
in his occupation through conferences, short courses, workshops,
reading, and other similar methods.   The kind of professional improvement motivation measured the types of motives that predomi-
nated in the librarian's reasons for improving himself.

The degree of formal-course work motivation was determined
by the relative intensity of the librarian's motivation for improvement through formal course work.   The kind of formal-course work
motivation measured the type of motives that prompted the librarian
to improve himself.

While most of the variables in this study were based on indexes that compared librarians with others in this study, these four
motivational variables were measured by a rating system that was
intrinsic in itself.   The score was based strictly on the responses

recorded in the questionnaire.   The motivational measurements were
adapted from methods used by Harold Swanson. [13]

A detailed explanation of these measurements and the way in
which they were scored is given in Appendix A.

The Questionnaire

The literature on development and construction of questionnaires was studied as the basis for developing the questionnaire used
in the study.   In addition, a large number of questionnaires was
studied.

Development and Pre-Test of the Questionnaire

An early step was that of eliciting perceived positive and
negative factors in professional development, and of ascertaining the
respondents' attitudes toward continuing education.   Another step was
to adapt devices for measuring four variables--the degree and kind
of motivation for professional improvement and the degree and kind
of motivation for formal course work.

Suggestions made by librarians and educators in personal
conferences were helpful in developing the investigation and in
weighting the items to be scored for the various indexes.   In all,
there were twelve revisions before the final questionnaire was sent
out to the sample population.

The literature had stressed the importance of pre-testing any
questionnaire.   Midway through the revisions, therefore, a draft
was sent to fifteen professional librarians in the Washington area
who were graduates of several different library schools.   The investigator followed the pre-test with personal interviews to discuss
alternate types of questions, instructions, operating procedures, and
arrangement.   This pre-test resulted in many revisions including
the decision to preface the questionnaire with definitions.   Most of
the suggestions were concerned with the positive and negative motivating factors.

The last draft was sent to six members of the original pilot
group for a second pre-test and suggestions from this round were
incorporated in the final format for the positive and negative factors
listed in Part 1 of the questionnaire.

Organization of the Instrument

A covering letter, the first page of the instrument, identified
the investigator and her address, gave the purpose of the study, as-
sured anonymity of the replies and promised the respondents a copy
of the results.   The entire instrument was printed on colored paper
in order to attract attention.   A chart on the verso defined the terms
used.   Along with the definitions, the terms professional development, professional growth, and continuing education were identified
as being synonymous in the study.

The questions were arranged in a psychological, rather than
a logical, manner to sustain the respondent's interest.   The approach was made as personal as possible, particularly in the word-
ing of the headings.   To facilitate answering the questions, a card
was devised as a guide to the symbols for the different column
headings.

The questionnaire was divided into seven parts, each containing variations of the more obvious and the more difficult questions.
These sections were entitled:

1. "Some of Your Ideas About Factors that Encouraged or
Discouraged You from Participating in Professional Growth Activities." This part comprised 43 positive and 43 negative questions
on the respondents' perception of forces involved in his professional
development.

2. "Some of Your Ideas About Yourself and Your Work."
This data measured professional orientation, level of aspiration, desire to remain in or leave the profession, career satisfaction, and
aspiration in librarianship.

3. "And Now About Yourself." This part asked questions a-
bout background.

4. "Your Activities Concerning Professional Growth." This

part compared what the respondent was actually doing with what he thought he should be doing for maximum professional development.

5. "Some of Your Ideas About Formal Course Work Following the MLS Degree." This part was concerned with the degree and kind of motivation for formal course work, as well as perceived attitudes of groups toward this work.

6. "Some of Your Ideas about Professional Development Activities." This section sought information about the degree and kind of motivation for professional improvement activities, as well as perceived attitudes of various groups.

7. "Lastly, Your Ideas and Proposals for Action." Here, recommendations were sought for library administrators, library associations, graduate library schools, library planners in the U.S. Office of Education, State Library Agencies, publishers of professional literature, and individual librarians.

Mailing of the Questionnaire

The questionnaire was preceded by a letter which outlined the need, the purpose and the general nature of the study. Three days later, on April 29, 1967, two copies of the questionnaire were sent to all those in the sample, along with a postpaid return envelope.

Of the 200 questionnaires mailed, 145 were answered, a response of 72.5 per cent of the total.[14] Some of these arrived too late to be included in the full tabulations, but were incorporated in the open-end and other special analyses. Since some of the forms returned were unuseable and some respondents were no longer employed in the library field, the final data in this study were based on the returns from 138 librarians, of whom 52 were from the 1956 class and 86 from the 1961 class.

Analysis of the Data

Routine procedures were used for coding, punching, and verifying the data obtained from the returned questionnaires.[15] The variables were analyzed by means of two 60 x 60 correlation tables,

one for the 1956 class and one for the 1961 class. These tables
allowed for the intercorrelation of 3,540 items. However, several
of the variables were approached in different ways: by actual score,
by high-low dichotomy, and by rank order, in order to discover all
possible relationships. In addition, correlation coefficients were
computed by machine for each of the double-entry answers in Parts
1 and 4 of the questionnaire (84 questions in Part 1; 37 questions in
Part 4).

Whether an association existed between the variables was determined by the chi-square. [16] In the section which compared involvement with the importance of professional development activities,
the gap between the two was measured by the matched or paired t-
test (Part 4 of the questionnaire). [17]

Reliability was judged by computing the 95 per cent confidence limits of the mean. These confidence limits used the sample
Standard Deviation. Ninety-five per cent confidence limits were
constructed for a few variables out of the 60 variables discussed a-
bove. These intervals were small, and since these intervals were
overestimates, the sample was considered reliable. [18]

The particular statistical methods used are outlined in each
section of this study. The percentages in the tables, although showing a total of 100, have been rounded off to the nearest one-tenth
of one per cent.

Notes

1. For the sake of brevity, the designation Master of Library Science will generally be abbreviated throughout this dissertation to MLS.

2. According to statistics published in the Library Journal, there
had been 1,059 graduates from accredited schools in the
United States placed in positions in 1956 and 1,413 graduates
placed in 1961, totalling 2,472. Donald R. Strout and Ruth
B. Strout, "Salaries Stronger: More Positions," Library
Journal, 82:1601 June 15, 1957; ----, "Story is the Same,"
Library Journal 87:2326 June 15, 1962.

3. Ash, Lee (ed.) Who's Who in Library Service: A Biographi-

cal *Directory of Professional Librarians in the United States
and Canada* (fourth edition; New York: Shoestring Press,
Inc., 1966). The criteria for inclusion in this directory is
best described by the stated requirement that all respondents
be "active members of the library profession, archivists, or
information scientists associated with all types of libraries
in the United States and Canada.... The norm of professional
education is a Bachelor's degree together with the Bachelor's
or Master's degree from a library school, received prior to
December 31, 1965. Five years of recognized and progres-
sive professional experience may be substituted by those who
do not possess one or more of these formal educational requirements."

4. Strout, loc. cit., 82.

5. ---- loc. cit., 87.

6. Cornell, Francis C. "Sample Surveys in Education" Review of
Educational Research 24:363 December, 1954.

7. Interview with Dr. Bronson Price, Education Survey Statistician,
U. S. Office of Education, on February 28, 1967.

8. Tippett, L. H. C. (ed.) Random Sampling Numbers (No. XV in
Tracts for Computers. London: Cambridge University
Press, 1952).

9. Decided after consultation with D. N. Ghosh, Statistical Laboratory, The Catholic University of America.

10. Ranta, Raymond "The Professional Status of the Michigan Cooperative Extension Service" (unpublished Doctor's dissertation, National Agricultural Extension Center for Advanced
Study, University of Wisconsin, 1960), p. 40, 45-46, 164-
167.

11. Chapter IV, p. 64.

12. Ranta, op. cit., p. 50, 169.

13. Swanson, Harold B. "Factors Associated with Motivation Toward Professional Development of County Agricultural Extension Agents in Minnesota" (unpublished Doctor's dissertation,
Graduate School, University of Wisconsin, 1965), p. 187-195.

14. Eleven of the questionnaires were returned by the Post Office,
not being deliverable.

15. The statistical procedures used throughout the study were care-
fully checked and supervised by D. N. Ghosh of the Statistical Laboratory of The Catholic University of America. The
cards were punched and the calculations made in the Univer-

sity's Computer Center.

16. Chi-square, (x^2), was a statistic used to test associations or
relationships when two variables were reduced to a 2 x 2
table.   In this study it was mainly used to test whether relationships between the two MLS classes, 1956 and 1961,
were significant, i. e. whether or not they might be the result of chance only.   All of the significant associations that
were found are listed as footnotes to the tables presented.
The formula was used with "fo" standing for observed frequency and "fe" standing for expected frequency.

$$x^2 = \sum \frac{(fo - fe)^2}{fe}$$

17. The paired t-test was used to test the significance of the difference between two observed means when the two samples
were not independent.   The formula used was the following:

$$t = \frac{Z - \mu}{S_{\overline{Z}}}$$

where:

$$Z_i = x_i - y_i$$

18. The 95 per cent confidence limits for the population mean is
$\overline{x} \pm 1.96 \sigma / \sqrt{N}$ where $\sigma / \sqrt{N}$ is the standard error of the
mean.   Strictly the formula for the stratified random sample
should be used, but this would give a fairly close approxi-
mation, and it is safe to use it since this is an overesti-
mate.

Chapter III

Background Characteristics of the Sample Librarians and Their
Perceived Attitudes of Relevant Groups

The library supervisor must understand his employees if he
is to motivate them. Charles Goodman recognized the importance
of adjusting professional development programs to the needs of the
individual when he stated:

> There is only one effective way to get the individual to
> participate in professional development activities--to influ-
> ence the individual to want to do so. It is the individual
> who must make the final decision to participate and he
> will determine how deeply he will be involved. If a su-
> pervisor is to be effective in motivating his employees he
> must have some understanding of the whole man or wom-
> an--his background, his levels of aspirations, goals, am-
> bitions, abilities, interests. [1]

It is important to examine the background characteristics of
the individual librarian in order to discover possible relationships
between these variables and motivation for professional development
activities. The variables selected for this study include age, sex,
marital status, education, place of employment, and certain employment characteristics.

This chapter also summarizes what the librarians perceived
to be the attitudes of various groups toward their continuing education. Questions were asked to determine whether motivation for
professional development activities depends on the immediate supervisor or on other groups such as the library's administration, the
governing board of the library, colleagues in the library, professional associates outside the library, respected associates in the
community, leaders in library associations, faculty of the graduate's
library school and family.

Only the significant positive or negative factors derived from
these findings will be discussed.   The statistics on the variables
are presented in the text as percentages and in the accompanying
tables.

Age, Sex, and Marital Status

Age

The librarians in the sample ranged in age from 28 to 64.
The average age of the 1956 MLS graduate was 43. 7 and of the 1961
graduate, 40. 2.   The mean and median age, standard deviation and
range of the 1956 and 1961 MLS librarians are shown in Table I.

Table I

Mean, Standard Deviation, Range of Age, and Number of
Children of the Librarians in the Sample: 1967

Descriptive Category	Mean		Standard Deviation		Range	
	1956	1961	1956	1961	1956	1961
Age	43. 7	40. 2	7. 8	9. 7	32-64	28-64
Number of children	1. 0	1. 0	1. 4	1. 2	0-6	0-4

These librarians are not so old that retirements will soon
deplete their numbers, which implies that motivation toward continuing professional development should be of vital concern to the sample
as a whole at a time when the profession needs to change with technological and societal requirements.

The greatest concentration of 1956 librarians, 53. 8 per cent,
was in the 35-44 age group.   In the 1961 group, the greatest concentration, 37. 2 per cent, occurred in the 25-34 range, but the next
age group, 35-44, was 30. 2 per cent of the total.

There was a significant difference (chi-square = 5. 42; P =
. 019) between the 1956 and 1961 graduates in the high-age bracket

and in the low-age bracket.   The 1956 group had 63. 5 per cent in
the older category (41 years or over), as compared with 43. 0 per
cent in the 1961 group.   See Table II.

Of those graduating in 1956, the school librarians had the
highest average age, 49. 2, as well as the highest median age, 47.
They also rated highest when the sample was totalled, with a mean
age of 44. 7 and a median age of 45.   In the class of 1961, special
librarians had the highest average age, 46, and the highest median
age, 47.

The data indicate a rise in the average age of those entering
librarianship, since there was only a 3. 5 year difference between
the average age of the two classes that graduated five years apart.
In the 1956 group only 2 librarians were over 60, while in the 1961
group 4 were 60 or over.   No graduates of the 1956 class received
their MLS after the age of 55, whereas 4 from the 1961 class were
55 or over.

For both groups there was a significant relationship between
age and the number of years between the Bachelor's degree and the
MLS.   There was evidence of an increasing gap between undergraduate study and graduate library study, rather than the converse.   For
example, the average number of years between degrees for the 1956
graduate was 9. 2 years while it was 10. 9 years for the 1961 graduate.

For both groups there was a significant correlation between
higher age and the number of years in the present job, which means
that older librarians found it harder to advance in the library organization than their younger counterparts.   Also, those who were
younger generally had been employed in more libraries, possibly
because they were more willing to risk security to seek better positions.   If this is correct, it would be an argument for emphasizing
younger recruits as a means of increasing professionalism generally.

Age tended to have an inverse relationship with salary for
the 1956 class; the older the librarian, the smaller the current salary and the less the salary had increased between the date of the
MLS and 1967.

Table II

Distribution of the Librarians in the Sample by Age,
Sex, Marital Status, Density of Population,
and Geographical Area: 1967

Variables	1956		1961		Total Sample	
	No.	%	No.	%	No.	%
Age[a]						
High (41+)	33	63. 5	37	43. 0	70	50. 7
Low	19	36. 5	49	57. 0	68	49. 3
Sex						
Male	21	40. 4	37	43. 0	58	42. 0
Female	31	59. 6	49	57. 0	80	58. 0
Marital Status						
Single	24	46. 2	35	40. 7	59	42. 8
Married	21	40. 4	40	46. 5	61	44. 2
Divorced or Separated	3	5. 8	7	8. 2	10	7. 2
Widowed	4	7. 7	4	4. 7	8	5. 8
Density of Population[b]						
In large city (100, 000+ and suburbs)	36	69. 2	40	46. 5	76	55. 1
In all areas less than 100, 000	16	30. 8	46	53. 5	62	44. 9
Geographical Area[c]						
West of Mississippi	12	23. 1	34	39. 5	46	33. 3
East of Mississippi	40	76. 9	52	60. 5	92	66. 7

[a]Chi-square = 5. 42; P = 0. 019

[b]Chi-square = 6. 76; P = 0. 009

[c]Chi-square = 3. 94; P = 0. 047

The age variable will be discussed in different sections of
the study as it relates to the factors of the professional index, the
degree of aspiration, sources of encouragement and determent, and
the motivational variables.

Sex

Of the 1956 graduates, 40. 4 per cent were men and 59. 6 per
cent were women.   The proportion for the 1961 sample was approximately the same: 43 per cent male and 57 per cent female.   (See
Table II, page 38) In the whole sample there were 16 per cent
more women than men.   At the time of the survey, the average age
of the 1956 male graduate was 39. 6 and of the female, 46. 3.   From
the 1961 class, the men were 2. 2 years and the women 3. 9 years
younger than their 1956 counterparts although the classes had graduated five years apart.   The average age for the female librarian in
the sample was 44, which was 5. 9 years older than the average
male.   For a more complete summary see Table IV.

Significant correlations for both classes indicated that women
tended to allow more years to elapse between the Bachelor's degree
and the MLS than men did.   This difference was especially high in
the class of 1956, with an average of 6. 8 more years between the
two degrees of the women than of the men.   The difference was
smaller for the 1961 class in which the women averaged 2. 0 more
years between degrees than the men.   Another indication that the
average age for the men entering librarianship was increasing was
that 1961 graduates averaged 2. 8 years older than 1956 graduates.
Women who graduated in 1961 averaged 1. 1 years older than 1956
graduates.

For both groups, the salary differential between the first
professional position and the current position was less for women.
When salaries were divided into high and low, a larger proportion
of women were in the low-salary range, especially for the 1956
graduates.

As indicated in Table III, of the 21 male librarians from the
1956 class, 42. 9 per cent were heads or assistant heads of libraries; of the 31 women, 38. 7 per cent were heads or assistant
heads of libraries.   Both sexes, therefore, were represented in
this top group with a difference of only 4. 2 per cent.   From the
1961 class, however, 35. 1 per cent of the 37 men were in this top
category, but only 18. 4 per cent of the 49 women--a difference of
16. 7 per cent.   Among the more recent graduates, men advanced

Table III

Number and Percentage of Librarians in the Sample
Occupying Top Administrative Positions, by Sex: 1967

| | 1956 | | | | 1961 | | | | Total Sample | | | |
| | Men (N=21) | | Women (N = 31) | | Men (N=37) | | Women (N = 49) | | Men (N=58) | | Women (N = 80) | |
	No.	%	No.	%	No.	%	No.	%	No.	%	No.	%
Head or Assistant Head Librarian[a]	9	42.9	12	38.7	13	35.1	9	18.4	22	37.9	21	26.3
Administrative[b]	18	85.7	23	74.2	27	73.0	31	63.3	45	77.6	54	67.5

[a] In the class of 1956 3 Assistant Heads were men; in the class of 1961 2 Assistant Heads were women.

[b] Administrative positions include Heads of Libraries, Assistant Heads, and Department and Division Heads. In the class of 1956, 78.8 per cent of the respondents were administrators; 67.4 per cent of the class of 1961 were administrators.

Background of the Sample   41
more rapidly than women.

Expanding the administrative group to include department and
division heads, 85.7 per cent of the men from the 1956 class held
administrative positions as compared with 74.2 per cent of the wom-
en.   From the 1961 class, 73.0 per cent of the men and 63.3 per
cent of the women were in such positions.   See Table III.

Some of the distinguishing characteristics of the men and
women from both classes, as compared with the total sample, are
indicated in Table IV.

Marital status

Table II, page 38, shows the percentage of librarians in the
1956 and 1961 groups who were single, married, divorced, separated, or widowed.   Approximately the same percentage of individuals were married as were unmarried. [2]   Since only 40.4 per cent
of the 1956 graduates and 46.5 per cent of the 1961 graduates were
married, the percentage married was low as compared with other
occupational groups.   A recent study by Corson and Paul of high-
level professionals in the Federal service revealed that 98 per cent
of the sample were married. [3]

In order to establish whether marital status was important
in relation to achievement of administrative positions, contingency
tables were constructed and the chi-squares computed.   At the 5
per cent level of significance the results showed no statistically significant association between marital status and top level library
positions.

The marital status variable will be discussed in different
sections of the study as it relates to the professional index, the degree of aspiration, and type and degree of motivation.

The 1956 group had from zero to 6 children and averaged
0.60.   The 1961 group had from zero to 4 children and averaged
0.49.   There was no significant relationship between the number of
children and any of the other characteristics in the study.   See
Table I.

Table IV

A Profile of the Male and Female Librarians in the Sample, by
Selected Variables: 1967

Selected Variables	1956		1961		Total Sample	
	Men	Women	Men	Women	Men	Women
Sex: Per cent	40.4	59.6	43.0	57.0	42.0	58.0
Average age at time of survey	39.6	46.3	37.4	42.4	38.1	44.0
Education: average age at which received Bachelor's degree	23.8	23.7	25.0	28.0	24.6	26.3
Education: average age at which received MLS degree	29.6	36.3	32.4	37.4	31.4	37.0
Education: average number of years between Bachelor's and MLS	5.8	12.6	7.4	9.4	6.8	10.7
Entry into librarianship: per cent entering from another occupation	42.9	61.3	45.9	59.2	44.8	60.0
Present responsibilities: per cent holding administrative positions	85.7	74.2	73.0	63.3	77.6	67.5
Present responsibilities: per cent Directors or Assistant Directors	42.9	38.7	35.1	18.4	37.9	26.3
Professional improvement activity: per cent listing workshops and short-term courses	66.7	74.2	81.1	67.3	75.9	70.0

Education and Professional Training

One important indication of continuing career development was
the amount of formal course work undertaken after completion of the
MLS degree.   The MLS was the highest degree for 94. 2 per cent of
the total sample of 138.   From the 1956 class, only 2 had received
another Master's degree following the MLS, one in the humanities
and one in the social sciences.   Two 1961 graduates had received
the Ph. D. , one in the humanities and one in the social sciences.
Four from this class had earned another Master's, 2 in the social
sciences and 2 in the humanities.[4]   Despite the recent development
of sixth-year certificates in library science, only one from the entire sample had participated in such a program.

After their MLS, 38. 4 per cent of the entire sample had
taken formal courses for credit.   The difference between the two
classes was significant at the one per cent level: 51. 9 per cent of
the 1956 graduates had taken courses for credit as compared to 30. 2
per cent of the 1961 class.   Five from the class of 1956 and 6 from
the 1961 class indicated that their courses were leading to a Ph. D.
degree.   Of these, 6 were working for doctorates in the humanities,
2 in library science, 2 in the social sciences, one in education.
The total number of courses taken for credit   was listed as follows:
17 in the humanities, 16 in the social sciences, 8 in library science,
7 in education, 3 in automation, and 2 in philosophy.

Whether or not the respondent had taken formal course work
seemed to bear little relationship to any of the other variables in
the study.

The two classes had markedly similar undergraduate special-
izations.   Of the 1956 group, 36. 5 per cent had majored in the humanities as did 37. 2 per cent of the 1961 group.   From the 1956
class, 36. 5 per cent had concentrated on the social sciences as compared to 31. 4 per cent in the 1961 class.   Of the total of 138,   70
per cent had majored in either the humanities or the social sciences
--37. 0 per cent in the former and 33. 3 per cent in the latter.   After
the humanities and social sciences, education accounted for 13. 0 per

per cent of undergraduate studies.

There were comparatively few graduates who had specialized
in the sciences: 7. 7 per cent from the 1956 class and 12. 8 per
cent from the 1961 class.

For the 1961 group there was a significant positive relationship between those who had majored in humanities and days spent at
workshops.

A summary indicating the education and professional training
of the 1956 and 1961 MLS graduates is presented in Table V.

Place of Employment

Density of Population

To investigate possible relationships between the size of the
general geographical area and various aspects of professional development, the questionnaire asked whether the respondent was now employed in:

1. A large city of 100, 000 population or more.
2. A suburb near a large city.
3. A small or middle-sized city of 10, 000-100, 000, but
   not a suburb of a large city.
4. A town of less than 10, 000.
5. The open country.

Placing these 5 categories into a dichotomy of larger and of
smaller population concentrations (large cities of 100, 000 or more
and population areas of 100, 000 or less) there was a significant difference at the 0. 009 level between the two classes.   The 1956 graduates were more concentrated in the larger population centers than
the 1961 graduates: 69. 2 per cent of the 1956 group, compared to
46. 5 per cent of the 1961 class.

In general, there was significant correlation of professional
development activity with residence in heavily populated areas.   The

Table V

A Profile of the Education and Professional Training
of the Librarians in the Sample: 1967

Variables Related to Education and Professional Training	1956	1961	Total Sample
Field of study for Bachelor's: percentage listing:			
Humanities	36. 5	37. 2	37. 0
Social Sciences	36. 5	31. 4	33. 3
Sciences	7. 7	12. 8	10. 9
Education	13. 5	12. 8	13. 0
Philosophy or religion	3. 8	3. 5	3. 6
Library Science	1. 9	2. 3	2. 2
Percentage with no advanced degrees beyond MLS	96. 2	93. 0	94. 2
Percentage earning another Masters' before MLS	19. 23	18. 6	18. 8
Percentage earning Masters' after MLS	3. 8	4. 7	4. 3
Percentage earning Ph. D. after MLS	0. 0	2. 3	1. 4
Percentage taking graduate work toward a Ph. D. (not yet completed)	9. 6	7. 0	8. 0
Percentage taking a 6th year program in library science after the MLS	0. 0	1. 2	0. 7
Percentage taking formal course work for credit after MLS[a]	51. 9	30. 2	38. 4
Field of study for non-degree course work after MLS: percentage of those taking courses, listing:			
Humanities	15. 4	10. 5	12. 3
Social Sciences	15. 4	9. 3	11. 6
Education	9. 6	2. 3	5. 1
Philosophy or religion	3. 8	-	1. 4
Library Science	5. 8	5. 8	5. 8
Automation	1. 9	2. 3	2. 2

[a]There was a significant difference between the class of 1956 and 1961 of those taking formal courses for credit: chi-square = 6. 45; $P = 0.01$.

1961 graduate who lived in the large city generally had read more
books, held more offices in associations, and had read more non-
library professional journals than had those in smaller communi-
ties.

The 1956 group also showed certain significant correlations
with density of population, but they were somewhat different.   The
1956 graduate who lived in a larger population concentration tended
to have worked in a greater number of libraries, more libraries of
different types, and consequently to have spent less time in his
present position than his counterpart in the medium-sized or small
city.   He also showed a greater increase in salary since receiving
the MLS degree.

Region of Residence

Of the 1956 class, 23. 1 per cent lived west of the Mississippi River as compared with 39. 5 per cent of the 1961 class. [5]

The librarian living west of the Mississippi published more
articles, belonged to more learned societies and professional associations generally and held more offices than did his counterpart
living east of the Mississippi.   Although a higher percentage of
1961 librarians lived west of the Mississippi, there were no significant correlations between this and other variables in the study.

In relation to geographical region, Reed observed in the
1966-1967 report on conferences, workshops and short courses for
that year: "A marked increase... is represented by the western
region which reported almost 50 per cent more activities than in
the previous year. "[6]

Employment Characteristics

Experience at Entry

When the librarians in the sample began their careers, age
and education were varied, and they had also had a variety of work

experiences.   Perhaps the most striking characteristic was that approximately 53 per cent of both classes had come from a previous occupation; and for 9. 5 per cent, librarianship was a third career rather than the second.   Before entering graduate library school, 25 per cent of the 1956 class and 38. 4 per cent of the 1961 class had had some library experience. [7]

Ascent on the Career Ladder

Since graduation from library school, the 1956 librarian had worked in an average of 2. 75 libraries. [8]   Nine (17. 3 per cent) were still in the library where they had started to work.   One had worked in 6 other libraries, and 2 had worked in 5 other libraries, but these were the exceptions.   The 1956 graduate had been employed in his current library an average of 7. 0 years and in his current position an average of 5. 27 years.   There was an average of 77 people working in his library and he supervised an average of 15 of these.

The comparative figures were substantially less for the 1961 graduate, perhaps because of the 5 year difference.   He had worked in an average of 1. 86 libraries. [9]   34. 9 per cent had worked in different types of libraries from the one currently served.   The 1961 graduate had been in his present library an average of 4. 39 years and in his present position an average of 3. 42 years.   The average number of employees in his library was 98, and he supervised an average of 11 of these, nearly as many as his 1956 counterpart.

The rapidity with which graduates achieved administrative positions was one of the striking revelations of this study.   Ten years after entry into librarianship, 78. 8 per cent of the 1956 group were in administrative positions; 5 years after, 67. 4 per cent of the 1961 group were administrators. [10]

Within this administrative category, 40. 4 per cent of the 1956 group had become either heads or assistant heads of libraries and 25. 6 per cent of the 1961 group had attained this position.

The following significant correlations between job characteristics and other variables in the study were found:

Contrary to expectations that professional activity would be increased through daily association with a larger number of professional colleagues, it was found that practicing in a large library had no relationship with other variables for the class of 1961, and the few significant correlations for the class of 1956 indicated that professional activity may be impeded rather than enhanced through close colleague associations.   Those in the class of 1956 working with a larger number of employees tended to belong to fewer non-library professional associations.   Two other significant correlations for the 1956 class indicating that motivation for professional activity might be impeded are discussed in Chapter VII.

Generally, the more libraries in which the 1956 graduate had had experience, the larger the number of people he was now supervising; the greater span of years between the Bachelor's degree and MLS, and the smaller the number of libraries in which he had been employed.

For the 1961 graduate, the more types of libraries he had worked in, the more library associations he belonged to; but he was also less likely to engage in research.

The longer the respondents had been in their current positions the more non-library professional associations they belonged to. The longer the period spent in one place by those from the 1961 class, the longer the span between the Bachelor's degree and MLS. Those in the 1956 class were more likely to live in an area with less than 100,000 population.

There were several significant correlations with the number of employees supervised: the more people supervised, the higher the salary and the larger the increase between the first professional salary and the current one.   The 1956 librarians supervising a larger number of employees had worked in more libraries.   They were also likely to be editors of a library journal, to hold more offices in associations, to have worked out a self-learning agenda, and to have the ambition to work in an entirely different type of library position or in a different type of library in order to advance.   Of the 1961 librarians, those who entered library school sooner after receiving the Bachelor's degree, rather than following other endeav-

ors, were also the ones who were supervising more people at the
time of the survey.

The significant correlation for all those who were heads or
assistant heads of libraries was that they belonged to more library
and non-library professional associations. The 1956 heads of libraries attended more days of workshops and took more formal
courses for credit.

Salary Data

There was a marked positive association between current
salary and number of years since receiving the MLS degree for librarians in both classes. The actual average increase since graduation for the 1956 librarian had been $5309, or $531 per year. The
range in increase was from $1600 to $9800. The average increase
for the 1961 librarian covering half as many years was $2995, or
$599 per year, ranging from no increase to $10, 700. Thus the
later graduate showed a greater average increase per year (an average of $68. 00 more per year) and also a higher increase for a 5
year span than the highest member of the 1956 graduates covering
a 10 year span. This would indicate that during the first 5 years
of employment the average librarian's salary showed greater yearly
increase than during the next 5 years, when the increases tended to
taper off.

The average salary in 1966 for the 1956 graduate was $9708,
with a range from $6500 to $14, 200; for the 1961 graduate the average was $8758, with a range from $5600 to $16, 900.

The highest salary reported was in the 1961 group. It was
interesting that this was not the salary of a head librarian, but of
an assistant head in a large university library. The top salary in
the 1956 group was for the head librarian of a university.

When the salaries were split into a dichotomy, 61. 5 per cent
of the 1956 class were in the high category as compared with 43 per
cent of the 1961 group. Since economic reward is a definite index
of advancement, the salary of the librarians was studied from two
angles: the salary received at the time of the study and the salary

difference between the first job after the MLS and the current position.   The relationships between these two variables and others
in the study were almost identical.

For both classes the following relationships were significant:
the higher the salary, generally the more people supervised.   This
was particularly true for the 1961 class; so even if he lacked the
experience it appeared that a more recent graduate could reach a
higher salary bracket if he supervised a larger number of employees.
The male graduates from both classes generally made a higher salary than the female.   Generally those with higher salaries read
more books in their special subject field.

Significant relationships that appeared solely in the 1961
group for those with a higher salary and a higher increase since
graduation were: more books read and published, more memberships in non-professional associations, more offices held in professional associations, and more research.

As noted earlier, the younger the 1956 graduate, the higher
his salary tended to be.   Those with the higher salaries from this
group were more likely to live in a city of 100,000 or more.

All of the background characteristics discussed so far--age,
sex, marital status, education, place of employment, entry into librarianship, and ascent of the career ladder--are summarized in
Table VI.   This profile compares the 1956 librarians with the 1961
librarians.

Perceived Attitudes of Relevant Groups

Among personal characteristics is the way in which a person
perceives the attitudes of relevant groups toward his professional development efforts.   This study tried to approach this in four ways:
(1) Parts 5 and 6 of the questionnaire asked the respondent what he
perceived to be the feelings of 9 groups toward his pursuits of continuing education.   (2) A dichotomy was made of those who felt their
supervisors were favorable and those who felt they were opposed to
their professional development.   Correlations were then computed

to see if this attitude related to any of the other variables in the study.   (3) The librarians ranked 42 items as sources of greatest encouragement or greatest determent to their professional development and 7 of these items related to relevant groups.   (4) In Part 7, final section of the questionnaire, the respondents were asked to make recommendations to these groups regarding continuing education.   In addition to expressing their own attitudes, they also revealed perceptions about the attitudes of others.

This section presents data collected in Parts 5 and 6 of the questionnaire.   Chapter V will discuss the relative influence of these groups as sources of encouragement and of determent.   Chapter VIII summarizes attitudes mentioned in the open-end questions.

In Parts 5 and 6 of the questionnaire the librarians indicated their perception of the attitudes of 9 groups toward professional improvement and formal course work.   Included were immediate supervisor, administration of the employing library, governing board of the library, colleagues where employed, professional associates elsewhere, respected associates in the community, library association leaders, library school faculty, and family.

Professional Improvement Activities

The librarians felt that the faculty of their library schools had been most favorably disposed toward their professional improvement.   At the other extreme, 16.6 per cent of the respondents sensed either mild or strong opposition from the administration of their library.   Opposition was felt by 15.2 per cent of the respondents from their immediate supervisors and by 8.7 per cent from their governing board.

A dichotomy was made of those who felt the administration or supervisor were favorable (or neutral) toward their professional improvement activities and of those who perceived a negative attitude.   Of the 1956 graduates, 23.1 per cent regarded their superiors as being mildly or strongly opposed to such participation; 22.1 per cent of the 1961 graduates perceived opposition.   These data are shown in Table VII.

Table VI
A Summary Profile of the Librarians in the Sample,
Relative to Background Characteristics: 1967

Selected Variables	1956	1961
Background Characteristics		
Average age at time of survey	43. 7	40. 2
Age group concentration: the 10-year age span in which there was largest number	35-44 (53. 8%)	25-34 (37. 2%)
Age: per cent in high age bracket (41 years or over)[a]	63. 5	43. 0
Marital status: per cent married	40. 4	46. 5
Children: average number	1. 0	1. 0
Sex: per cent who were men	40. 4	43. 0
Education		
Education: per cent with no advance degrees beyond the MLS	96. 2	93. 0
Formal course work: per cent taking courses for credit, but not toward degrees after MLS[b]	51. 9	30. 2
Field of study for Bachelor's degree: per cent listing--		
Humanities	36. 5	37. 2
Social Sciences	36. 5	31. 4
Field of study for formal course work following MLS: per cent of those taking courses listing--		
Humanities	15. 4	10. 5
Social Sciences	15. 4	9. 3
Place of Employment		
Density of population: per cent living in cities of 100, 000+ and their suburbs[c]	69. 2	46. 5
Geographical area: per cent living West of the Mississippi[d]	23. 1	39. 5
Entry into Librarianship		
Per cent entering from another occupation	53. 8	53. 4
Per cent entering with some previous library experience	25. 0	38. 4
Ascent of Career Ladder		
Number of other libraries worked in: per cent worked in 2 or more[e]	44. 2	19. 8
Number of other types of libraries worked in: per cent who worked in other types	46. 2	34. 9
Length of service in present institution: per cent who worked in six years or more[f]	67. 3	45. 3
Length of service in present job: per cent who worked four years or more	48. 1	44. 2
Number of employees in library: average no.	77	98
Number of employees supervised: average no.	15	11

Table VI (cont.)

Selected Variables	1956	1961
Number of heads of libraries: per cent who were heads	40. 4	25. 6
Number in administrative positions: per cent who were administrators	78. 8	67. 4
Sex of those holding administrative positions:		
Per cent of the men	85. 7	73. 0
Per cent of the women	74. 2	63. 3
Salary: average at time of study	$9, 708	$8, 758
Salary: per cent in high category ($9, 000 and over)	61. 5	43. 0
Salary: average yearly increase	$531	$599

[a]Significant difference between class of 1956 and 1961: chi-square = 5. 42; P = 0. 019.

[b]Significant difference between class of 1956 and 1961: chi-square = 6. 45; P = 0. 011.

[c]Significant difference between class of 1956 and 1961: chi-square = 6. 76; P = 0. 009.

[d]Significant difference between class of 1956 and 1961: chi-square = 3. 95; P = 0. 047.

[e]Significant difference between class of 1956 and 1961: chi-square = 9. 42; P = 0. 02.

[f]Significant difference between class of 1956 and 1961: chi-square = 6. 28; P = 0. 012.

Table VII

Attitude of Management Toward Professional Improvement Activities
and Formal Course Work of Librarians, as Perceived
by the Librarians in the Sample: 1967

Attitude of Administration and/or Supervisor as perceived by Librarians	1956 No.	%	1961 No.	%	Total Sample No.	%
Toward professional improvement						
Favorable or neutral	40	76. 9	67	77. 9	107	77. 5
Opposed	12	23. 1	19	22. 1	31	22. 5
Toward formal course work						
Favorable or neutral	29	55. 8	50	58. 1	79	57. 2
Opposed	23	44. 2	36	41. 9	59	42. 8

For both classes if the administration and supervisor favored
participation in professional improvement activities, they also tended
to favor formal course work. Those 1956 librarians who perceived
a positive attitude also tended to be receiving higher salaries. The
1961 graduates who perceived a favorable attitude generally participated in more research activity. Since these were the only significant correlations, the positive attitudes of relevant groups appear
to have minimal influence in motivation. This finding is discussed
further in Chapter V.

Formal Course Work

In general, the respondents perceived more opposition to
their formal course work than to professional improvement activities.

The librarians felt that their library school faculty had been
the most favorable toward their taking formal course work beyond
the MLS degree. At the other extreme, 33. 4 per cent of the respondents sensed either mild or strong opposition from the immediate supervisor. Opposition was sensed by 31. 2 per cent of the re-

spondents from their administration and by 18.8 per cent from their governing board.

When a dichotomy was made of those who found the administration or supervisor favorable (or neutral) toward their formal course work and of those who perceived opposition, 44.2 per cent of the 1956 graduates regarded their superiors as being mildly or strongly opposed to such participation; 41.9 per cent of the 1961 respondents perceived this opposition.

Approval of participation in formal course work and approval of professional improvement activities showed high positive correlation. There were no significant correlations with other variables in the study for the 1956 graduates who reported a favorable attitude from their superiors. The 1961 graduates who perceived a positive attitude from their superiors tended to have read more books and journals in library science and to have engaged in some research.

Conclusion

The data obtained indicate that certain background characteristics should be considered when attempting to motivate librarians toward professional development activities. The knowledge of the relative importance of these characteristics offers insight into the personal reasons behind the variables that will be discussed in the next chapter.

Notes

1. Goodman, Charles H. "Employee Motivation" (paper read at Seminar on Middle Manager Development in Libraries, The Catholic University of America, Washington, D.C., June 17, 1964).

2. In this study, those who were not married included the single, the divorced or separated, and the widowed.

3. Corson, John J. and Paul, R. Shale Men Near the Top (Balti-

more: Johns Hopkins Press, 1966), p. 82.

4. One of the respondents received an additional Master's in phi-
    losophy, plus the one reported above in the humanities.

5. Chi-square = 3.95; P = 0.05.

6. Reed, Sarah R.   Continuing Education for Librarians--Confer-
    ences, Workshops, and Short Courses, 1966-1967   (Wash-
    ington: Office of Education, U.S. Department of Health,
    Education, and Welfare, 1966), p. 1.

7. It should be noted here that in order to confine the questionnaire,
    inquiries about previous occupation experience were omitted.
    These particular percentages and statistics were based on an
    analysis of each respondent's listing in Who's Who in Library
    Service.   Lee Ash (ed.), Who's Who in Library Service:
    A Biographical Directory of Professional Librarians in the
    United States and Canada.   (4th ed.: New York: Shoestring
    Press, Inc., 1966.)

8. This includes the present library in which the respondent was
    working.

9. This figure includes the present library in which the 1961 gradu-
    ate was working.

10. This category included heads, assistant or associate heads, and
    heads of departments and divisions of libraries.   Supervisors,
    coordinators, and heads of one- or two-man libraries were
    excluded.   They, however, would also require administrative
    know-how for effective operation.

        This figure is higher than the statement made in 1946 by
    Wheeler who wrote: "Half the graduates who stay in library
    work five years have been put into positions of administra-
    tive responsibility to direct the work of others in a depart-
    ment, a branch, a school library, if not as head librarian."
    Joseph L. Weeler   Progress and Problems in Education for
    Librarianship   (New York: The Carnegie Corporation of New
    York, 1946), p. 63.

Chapter IV

Special Measurements of
Professional Development Characteristics

Special measurements were devised for studying several composite variables, such as the degree and the type of aspiration, satisfaction with career, and future career desires. The respondents' sense of professionalism was charted by a professional index score.

The librarians were distributed according to their scores and each of the composite variables was correlated with the background variables previously discussed; then the elements that make up the composite variables were correlated with each other and again with other variables. [1]

Some of the questions asked in developing the scoring systems were: What had the respondents done to prove their interest in the profession since graduating from library school? Did they belong to professional associations, read professional literature, publish articles or books? Did they conduct research; participate in independent study groups or in training programs; develop a self-learning agenda? What were their career aspirations?

The answers to these and similar questions not only provided the data for the measurements of motivation toward professional development, but helped to clarify the professional nature of librarianship. These measurements also provide an objective norm for evaluating an individual in terms of his professionalism.

I.   Measurement of Career Attitudes

Career attitudes were approached from three aspects: (1) aspirations, both degree and type; (2) satisfaction with career; and (3) future desires. This section will measure the distribution of

57

these attitudes and explore associations with other variables.   A
summary profile of the 1956 and 1961 MLS graduates is given in
Table VIII.

Career Aspirations:

Degree of aspiration

        The desire to achieve certain professional goals or objectives
was graded in relation to other librarians in the sample.   The highest possible score was 14 and was based on the respondent's answers to 7 questions. [2]   The average score for the 1956 graduate
was 5. 6, with the scores ranging from 1 to 11.   For the 1961 graduate the average score was 5. 8, and the range was from 0 to 12.
        When the Degree of Aspiration Scores were divided arbitrari-
ly, 34. 6 per cent of the 1956 librarians and 37. 2 per cent of the
1961 class were in the high category, with a score of 6 and above.
The 1961 class had a slightly higher degree of aspiration than the
1956 class, whether the data were analyzed by actual scores or by
the high-low dichotomy.
        An examination of the degree of aspiration of the two classes
and of selected variables, revealed many more relationships for the
1961 class than for the 1956 class, as shown in Table IX.   Of these
significant correlations, perhaps the most important are that generally those who were younger and those who had a shorter time span
between the Bachelor's degree and MLS had a higher degree of aspiration.   This indicated a definite association between age and degree of aspiration.   The statistics also showed the 1961 graduate
to be motivated toward formal course work although he felt that his
superiors opposed his participation in this activity.   The relationship between aspiration and professional activity, also indicated in
this Table, will be discussed in the next section of this chapter.
        In order to establish whether marital status was an impor-
tant factor in relation to the degree of aspiration score, a contingency table was constructed comparing marital status with high and
low degree of aspiration scores.   No significant difference in as-

Table VIII

A Summary Profile of the Librarians in the Sample by the
Measurement of Their Career Attitudes: 1967

Measurement of Career Attitudes	1956	1961
Degree of Aspiration Score:		
Average score (highest possible score was 14)	5. 6	5. 8
Per cent in high category (score of 6 and above)	34. 6	37. 2
Type of aspiration--culmination of ambitions in librarianship 10 years from time of survey:		
Per cent wanting administrative positions or higher administrative positions	51. 9	58. 1
Per cent desiring same type of job and library	71. 2	81. 4
Per cent desiring different type and/or library	28. 8	18. 6
Career satisfaction:		
Per cent indicating good progress; satisfied	80. 8	86. 0
Per cent indicating general dissatisfaction	19. 2	14. 0
Career desires:		
Per cent desiring to stay in librarianship	82. 7	82. 6
Per cent desiring to leave librarianship	17. 3	17. 4

sociation was found between marital status and degree of aspiration score that could be detected by chi-square at the 5 per cent level of significance.

Type of Aspiration

The librarians in the sample were asked what position would represent the culmination of their ambitions in librarianship 10 years from now. Administration was the most popular, chosen by 51. 9 per cent of the 1956 class and 58. 2 per cent of the 1961 class. Specifically, the position of head librarian was mentioned most often by the 1956 group and that of department or section head by the 1961 graduates. Of the total sample, 7. 3 per cent indicated a desire to teach library science.

Table IX

Relationship Between Degree of Aspiration of the Librarians
in the Sample and Selected Variables: 1967

Relationship	Correlation Coefficients			
	Not Significant		Significant at 5% Level[a]	
	1956	1961	1956	1961
The relationship between the Degree of Aspiration and:				
Respondent's age	-.23	--	--	-.40
Number of years between BA and MLS degrees	-.24	--	--	-.31
Number of other types of libraries in which the respondent had been employed	-.15	--	--	.23
Respondent's perception of his supervisor's attitude toward formal course work	-.07	--	--	-.29
Respondent's Formal Study Motivation Type Score	.01	--	--	.25
Respondent's Formal Study Motivation Degree Score	.06	--	--	.41
Professional Index Score	--	--	.28	.22
Occupations Characteristics Index Score	--	.21	.29	--
Total number of professional associations to which respondent belonged	--	.15	.31	--

[a]Significant: 1956--Correlation coefficient of 0.273 and above;
1961--Correlation coefficient of 0.213 and above.

The librarians were separated by the type of their aspirations: those who indicated a desire to stay in the same general type
of job or library; and those who desired either an entirely different
type of job, or a position in a different type of library.   Of the
1956 graduates, 28.8 per cent wanted to advance to something quite
different; 18.6 per cent of the 1961 group gave this response.   In

the whole sample, 22. 5 per cent of the librarians apparently wanted
to advance to a different type of job or type of library situation.

Those 1956 graduates who aspired to something different
tended to be younger, to have worked in more different libraries,
to have been fewer years in the present job and present institution,
to be supervising more employees, to hold more offices in associations, to have read more books in library science, and to have majored in the humanities.

Generally the 1961 graduate who aspired to a different type
of job situation had a higher Professional Index Score, had published more articles, belonged to more non-professional library associations, had held more offices in library associations, had read
more library and non-library professional journals, was likely to
have a self-learning agenda, had taken formal courses for credit
since the MLS, and lived in a city with a population of 100, 000 or
more.

It appeared that the librarian ambitious for a different situation engaged in more professional development activities than the librarian who was content with his current situation.

Satisfaction with Career

Each respondent was asked to indicate his feelings about his
career to date. Of the 1956 group, 19. 2 per cent expressed dissatisfaction with their current situations and of the 1961 group 14
per cent.

For the 1956 group, some interesting associations with other
variables were discovered. Rather than being individuals who had
done little about their professional development, they tended to have
read more books in library science, as well as in their subject
area; and had published more articles and books. The 1961 respondents who expressed dissatisfaction were generally women. Those in
the class of 1961 who had made greatest increase in salary since
the MLS generally thought they had made good progress in their careers to date.

Career Desires

The majority, 82.6 per cent of the total, indicated a desire
to remain in their profession: the percentage was practically identical for both classes, 82.7 per cent for 1956 and 82.6 per cent for
1961.

The librarians were asked if they had plans to:

leave librarianship for a job in another profession that
would make fuller use of particular capabilities and potential.

leave librarianship for a higher paying job in another profession.

The response from both groups was again almost the same: 17.3
per cent of the 1956 class and 17.4 per cent of the 1961 class
wanted to leave the profession. A detailed analysis was then made
to ascertain any common characteristics of these respondents.

Of the 24 individuals who expressed some desire to leave librarianship, 23 indicated a desire to make fuller use of their capabilities and potential. Ten of these respondents were also interested
in a higher salary. Only 1, a graduate of 1956, listed a higher
salary as the sole incentive for leaving the profession.

Most of these respondents mentioned the profession they
would enter in order to make fuller use of their abilities. The
most popular was college or university teaching of a subject specialty, with 8 in this category (1 from 1956 and 7 from 1961); next
was writing, with 4 from the 1961 class and 1 from 1956. Five
single choices were for data processing, priesthood, geology, social work, and building and design. Five from the class of 1956
and 1 from the class of 1961 did not specify a choice.

Certain distinctions were noted between the 1956 librarians
who wished to leave librarianship and the others: they had published more articles, belonged to more learned societies, had done
more research, had a higher sense of professionalism, and had
worked in more types of libraries. The 1961 respondents desiring
to leave were generally heads of libraries, male, who had published more books and articles.

Those who expressed a desire to leave librarianship were viewed in relation to their perceptions of the attitudes of relevant groups. This analysis revealed that 41.6 per cent of the group felt strong opposition from their administration, their supervisor, or their library board if they took formal courses. Only 12.5 per cent perceived strong favor from these groups toward their formal course work.

Although these respondents observed less opposition toward professional improvement activities, still 25 per cent had perceived opposition, either slight or strong, from the administration, supervisor, or library board.

Probably the most important factor that appeared in this analysis was that all but one respondent said they felt their abilities were not being fully utilized in librarianship and that another profession would probably make better use of their potential.[3]

II. Indexes of Professionalism

In order to qualify as a professional, an individual must satisfy the standards established by the profession which includes the requisite education and specialized skills and knowledge. He is also distinguished from non-professionals by additional criteria which generally include social understanding, ethical or altruistic behavior, and scholarly concern, which includes continuing education and the ability to conduct or interpret research.

This section will attempt: (1) to ascertain the professional position of each librarian, in relation to the total sample, based on an index of professionalism; (2) to determine the association between this index of professionalism and other variables in the study; (3) to ascertain the distribution of the librarians in the sample in relation to each of the component parts of the professional index; and (4) to determine the association between each of the component parts of the professional index and other variables in the study.

The Professional Index

One of the variables in this study was the Professional Index, which identified each librarian's personal attitude toward his occupational attributes, knowledge, characteristics, and responsibilities. It also measured the degree of participation in professional development activities.

After an extensive survey of the literature of professionalism, a list of 12 criteria that had been developed by Raymond Ranta was selected which could be used to measure a professional and could therefore serve as the basis for an index.

Ranta stated that a profession is comprised of individuals who:

1. Place service to others higher in importance than personal gains.

2. Have a strong sense of public responsibility.

3. Are particularly skillful and proficient in their work.

4. Are especially dedicated to their job and what it stands for.

5. Work in setting where they must basically direct their own programs of work independently; in a sense practicing autonomy in decision-making.

6. Try to continually improve themselves. They have a never-ceasing quest for learning.

7. Are concerned about, and work toward, the improvement of their colleague's welfare.

8. Work within acceptable ethical standards.

9. Have a knowledge of and familiarity with professional literature in their field.

10. Will change methods of job procedure when new information based on research is received.

11. Believe in the interchange of information.

12. Utilize and understand the specific language employed in their field of work.[4]

To this list was added a qualification established by the National Education Association for a professional in any field: "Actively participate with his colleagues in developing and enforcing standards fundamental to continuous improvement of his profession and, abide by those standards in his own practice."[5]

Seventeen questions in the instrument reflected these 13 criteria and scoring systems were established for each question, providing a Professional Index Score for each respondent. [6] For purposes of analysis, the correlation coefficients were computed for the scores in three different ways: by using the actual scores for each individual; by dividing the scores into high and low groups; and by using the rank order with relationships that had a 0.05 correlation coefficient.   The results were related to the other variables in the study.

Of the 17 components, 14 had a significant correlation with the Index Score for the 1956 class; 11 with that of the 1961 class. Since all the relationships were positive, and those which were not significant at the 0.05 level were nearly so, the Professional Index Score was considered a valid measurement.

Each librarian in the sample population was assigned a score. This ranged from 6.5 to 38.5 for the 1956 class, and from 6.5 to 38.0 for the 1961 class.   The average score was 20.6 for the 1956 class and 19.2 for the 1961 class.   The median for the two classes was also similar: 21.5 for the 1956 class and 18.3 for the 1961 class.   The highest possible score was 52 points.

When, however, the sample librarians were divided into two categories, high (Index Score of 20 and above) and low (Index Score under 20), 51.9 per cent of the 1956 group were in the high group in comparison with 45.3 per cent of the 1961 class, as shown in Table X.   But the average of those in the high group was nearly the same in each class: 26.0 in the 1956 group and 24.9 in the 1961 group.   The mean of the low scores for each group was also similar: 14.4 for 1956 and 14.5 for 1961.

The 5-year span between graduations made little difference in the score of the two classes in regard to mean and median.   But when a profile of each class was made of the significant correlations for the Professional Index Score and its constituent variables, certain distinctions become apparent.

Those with a high Professional Index in the 1956 class generally had published more articles and books, belonged to more learned societies, had attended more days of workshops, and had done more research than lower scoring members of the class.

Table X

Distribution of the Librarians in the Sample According
to Professional Index Scores: 1967

Professional Index Scores	1956			1961			Total		
	No.	%	Mean	No.	%	Mean	No.	%	Mean
Combined Distribution									
High (20 and above)	27	51.9	26.0	39	45.3	24.9	66	47.8	25.3
Low (under 20)	25	48.1	14.4	47	54.7	14.5	72	52.2	14.4

The 1961 graduates with a high Index had emphasized other
factors. Proportionately they had read more books in their area of
specialization, belonged to more professional associations--both library and non-library, and scored higher on the question concerning
attitude toward problems of fellow workers. [7]

Partial analyses were also made of the variables in the study
(not component parts of the Professional Index Score) having significant correlations with the Index to determine the combination of
variables associated with a high Professional Index.

First, comparisons on the Professional Index Scores indicated that most of the 1956 librarians with a high Index also had a
high level of aspiration and high type and degree of motivation for
professional improvement. Second, on the high-low scores, the
1956 graduates with the highest Professional Index Score tended to
want to leave librarianship for another profession. Finally, on the
rank order listing, the other factors already listed were reinforced
with an additional significant correlation. The 1956 librarians with
the high ranks tended to be younger than those with low Professional
Index Score ranks.

The same methods of comparison indicated that most of the
1961 librarians with a high index of professionalism also had a high
level of aspiration and a high degree of motivation for professional
improvement. Though they tended to be the heads or assistant heads

of their libraries, they seemed at the same time to aspire to quite a different type of job or library situation.

There were no significant relationships between the Professional Index and salary for either group, either to the exact amount received or to the increase made since the MLS degree. There were no correlations between the Index Scores and sex, undergraduate major, or years between the Bachelor's degree and MLS.

Marital status as a factor in the amount of professional development activities was measured on a contingency table constructed to compare the Professional Orientation Score for each of 4 categories. The results showed no statistically significant difference. In the total sample, 54.1 per cent of those who were married had a high Professional Index; 44.2 per cent of those who were not married had a high Index.

The Professional Index Score was also used to analyze data of those who felt opposition from their supervisor, administration, or board. A dichotomy of high and low scores showed no statistically significant difference. Respondents in both groups perceived the opposition; however, some continued to participate and some were discouraged. This is significant because it indicates that these groups were not criticized simply as a means of shifting the blame from the individual.

Each variable that constituted the Index was also studied to determine its relationship to other variables in the study. The following components will be discussed: Occupations Characteristics Index, attitude toward problems of fellow workers, membership in professional associations, offices held in professional associations, workshops and other short-term training programs, professional reading, publications, research activity, participation in small voluntary study groups, and development of a self-learning agenda.

Constituent Parts of the Professional Index Score

This section analyzes the 17 component parts of the Professional Index Score. Table XI presents a summary profile of the two classes in relation to the Index Score and its elements.

Table XI

A Summary Profile of the Librarians in the Sample by the
Indexes of Professional Development: 1967

Indexes of Professional Development	1956	1961
Professional Index Score: Average Score (out of a possible 52 points)	20. 6	19. 2
Professional Index Score: Median Score	21. 5	18. 3
Professional Index Score: Per cent in high category (20 points and above)	51. 9	45. 3
Professional Index Score: Mean within the high category (20 points and above)	26. 0	24. 9
Professional Index Score: Mean within the low category (under 20 points)	15. 2	14. 5

Constituent Parts of the Professional Index Score

	1956	1961
Occupational Characteristics Index: Average weighted Score (out of a possible 20 points)	11. 8	11. 5
Occupational Characteristics Index: Per cent in high category (13 points and above)	57. 7	43. 0
Concern for problems of fellow workers: Per cent making a score[a]	59. 6	38. 4
Membership in library associations: Average number	2. 5	1. 4
Membership in library associations: Per cent in high category (3 or more associations)	48. 1	47. 7
Membership in non-library professional associations: Average number	1. 0	1. 1
Membership in non-library professional associations: Per cent belonging to none	44. 2	48. 8
Membership in learned societies: Average number	0. 3	0. 2
Membership in learned societies: Per cent belonging to none	78. 8	82. 6
Offices in professional associations: Average number held since MLS	2. 1	1. 6
Offices in professional associations: Per cent who had held no offices since MLS	38. 5	43. 0
Attendance at workshops, institutes, seminars: Per cent attending during last 5 years	71. 2	73. 3
Average number of days attended during last 5 years	6. 3	7. 8
Median number of days attended during last 5 years	3. 0	3. 0

Table XI (cont.)

Indexes of Professional Development	1956	1961
Library journals read regularly: Average	3.5	3.6
Library journals read regularly: Per cent in high category (4 or more journals)	55.8	53.5
Non-library professional journals read regularly: Average	1.1	.7
Non-library professional journals read regularly: Per cent reading none[b]	44.2	62.8
Books read in librarianship during the past year:		
Per cent reading no books	25.0	24.4
Average number of books read	6.1	3.8
Median number of books read	3.0	2.0
Books read in area of subject specialization:		
Per cent reading no books	21.2	22.1
Average number of books read	9.7	13.6
Median number of books read	4.0	4.0
Articles published during last 5 years:		
Per cent publishing no articles	57.7	58.1
Average number published	5.5	1.9
Median number published	1.0	0.0
Library journals edited:		
Per cent editing no journals	78.8	86.0
Average number edited	.7	1.9
Median number edited	0.0	0.0
Research activity since MLS:		
Per cent doing no research	71.2	80.2
Per cent doing one research project	23.1	12.8
Per cent doing two research projects	5.8	7.0
Participation in voluntary study groups since MLS:		
Per cent participating in no group	71.2	81.4
Per cent participating in one group	26.9	17.4
Per cent participating in two groups	1.9	1.2
Use of a self-learning agenda:		
Per cent having a self-learning agenda	30.8	33.7

[a]Difference between two classes: chi-square = 5.88; P = .01

[b]Difference between two classes: chi-square = 4.53; P = .03

Occupations Characteristics Index

The first 23 questions in Part 2 of the questionnaire, "Some
of Your Ideas About Yourself and Your Work, " sought to identify certain attributes and attitudes that characterize a professional person.
By design, 13 of the questions did not apply to the information
sought and were omitted from the tabulations. [8] But 10 questions
were given weighted scores. These were concerned with: service
to others over personal gain, sense of public responsibility, skill
and proficiency in work, dedication to job, desire to direct own program and to work independently, ethical standards, willingness to
change methods and procedures based on research findings, belief
in the free interchange of professional information, utilization and
understanding of the specific language employed in the profession.
These questions covered criteria that were not related to librarianship specifically, but are characteristics of occupations in general.
They will therefore be referred to as the Occupations Characteristics Index.

The mean weighted scores for these questions were nearly
identical for both classes: 11. 8 for 1956 and 11. 5 for 1961.   The
score for each class ranged from 2 to 20--the highest possible
score.

There was a substantial difference (although not statistically
significant) between the 1956 graduates (57. 7 per cent) and the 1961
graduates (43 per cent) who made a high score on the Occupations
Characteristics Index.   Those who had been in the profession longer
evidently recognized the importance of these professional criteria
more than those who had graduated 5 years later.

In addition to having a high Professional Index, those respondents of the 1956 class who had a high Occupations Index also
tended to have a higher degree of aspiration.

Attitude Toward Problems of Fellow Workers

One question sought to determine the degree of association

the respondent wished to have with his colleagues.   Points were
given for one answer only: "I should be primarily concerned with
personal problems and on-the-job problems of fellow workers. "
This query reflected the criterion that a professional should be interested in the whole person and that the actions of one influence
others.

The 1956 graduates made a significantly higher score on this
question than the 1961 group (59. 6 per cent as compared to 38. 4
per cent). Of all the criteria that made up the Professional Index
Score, this item showed the greatest difference between the two
classes.

The 1956 respondents who showed concern for the problems
of their colleagues had generally worked in fewer libraries and had
spent more years in their present institution.   In addition, they
tended to come from the less populated areas of the country.   It is
possible, therefore, that this group's greater interest in the other
employees was based on a closer association over a longer period
of time rather than on more abstract concepts, since there was no
significant correlation with reading, self-study, or participation in
workshops.

Membership in Professional Associations

Active membership in organizations germane to the librarian's needs may, in itself, be an indication of professionalism.

Mary L. Bundy and Paul Wasserman stated that a significant
hallmark of the librarian is the nature of his relationships.

> The professional constantly expands upon his circle of
> contacts and reinforces and strengthens existing colleague
> relations, pursuing an active role by continuing his growth
> through self-study and associating himself with the local
> and regional and national activities in librarianship and in
> other special disciplines with which his work puts him in
> contact.   For him, keeping up with professional trends
> and advances through the journals and monographs is a
> matter of fact...   This is in contrast to the librarian who
> confines his relationship to those which are merely com-
> forting, reassuring, and reinforcing of his prejudices and
> limitations. [9]

The 1956 graduate belonged to an average of 2.5 library associations, as compared with 1.4 for the 1961 graduates.[10] The
median of 2.5 for the 1956 graduates was also higher than the 2.0
median of the 1961 class. The 1956 range was from zero to 6; the
1961 range was from zero to 5. When the population was split into
a high-low dichotomy, 48.1 per cent of the 1956 and 47.6 of the
1961 graduates were in the high group of 3 or more memberships.

Both classes showed a few significant correlations between
number of library association memberships and other variables in
the study. Those who belonged to more library associations tended
to have held more offices, read more library journals, and to desire a library position different from the one they were holding.

Although the current emphasis in library literature is on
inter-disciplinary communication, 47.1 per cent of the librarians
did not belong to non-library professional organizations. The American Association of University Professors and the National Education
Association had the highest membership with 21 and 15 members,
respectively, from the total sample.

Graduates of both classes belonged to an average of one non-
library professional association. Those with membership in more
than one had generally spent more years in their present position,
had read more books during the last year in library science, held
more offices in associations, and had a higher salary.

The sample belonged to a still smaller number of learned
societies: 21.2 per cent of the class of 1956 and 17.5 per cent of
the 1961 class. This meant that each individual from the 1956 group
belonged to 0.3 societies and the average for 1961 was 0.2.

In evaluating college faculties, M. E. Haggerty postulated
that the most significant evidences of an intellectually active teacher
were membership in learned societies and production of scholarly
publications.[11] These tokens of scholarship, as he termed them,
were superior to advanced degrees, graduate study, or experience
as indexes of an individual's competence. Those librarians in both
classes who did belong to more learned societies had also published
more books, thus giving some support to Haggerty's theory.

Offices and Committee Service in Professional Associations

Another indication of professionalism is holding office or serving on committees for these associations. The study showed that the 1956 graduate had held an average of 2. 1 offices since his entry into the profession. This included service as chairman of a committee. The 1961 graduate averaged 1. 6 offices. The range for the 1956 class was zero to 10 and for the 1961 class, zero to 9. Of the 1956 graduates, 20 librarians, or 38. 5 per cent, had not held offices or served as committee chairmen; of the 1961 graduates, 38, or 44. 2 per cent, had not held offices or chairmanships.

Those librarians who had held the greater number of offices tended to have a higher Professional Index Score; had read more books in library science; belonged to more library and non-library associations; and had read more professional journals, including more library journals.

Workshops and Other Short-term Training Programs

Workshops and other short-term training programs have been growing in number.[12] They will probably continue to expand because they adapt readily to special needs, and the Federal government has been increasing grants for this type of continuing education.

Seventy-five per cent of the 1956 group and 72 per cent of the 1961 group had participated in some type of supplementary training of this type during the last 5 years. Since the duration of these informal training programs varies greatly, the most precise measurement was the number of days spent in workshops. The 1956 graduate had attended an average of 6. 3 days of such training programs; and the 1961 graduate, an average of 7. 8 days. When the number of days was divided into high and low, 42. 4 per cent of the 1956 graduates and 47. 6 per cent of the 1961 graduates were in the high group. The median for both classes was 3 days for the last 5 years, or three-fifths of a day per year.

The popularity of the different subject areas was rated by the number of days spent in attendance. Automation was the substantial

leader, both for days in attendance and for the number of times
listed by subject area.   The next most popular subject was special
librarianship; the third, administration and management; the fourth,
school librarianship; and the fifth, work with children and young
people.

Each respondent was asked to evaluate his workshop experience in relation to his current job situation.   Of the 174 different
workshops listed, 44. 3 per cent were rated "very helpful;" and 4. 6
per cent were of "no help. " Nearly 20 per cent of the workshops
received a negative reaction from the librarians who attended them.
Reed emphasized "that workshops and institutes are a waste of time
and money unless they represent sound educational planning and programming. " [13]

Using the evaluations given in the questionnaire, the subject
areas were ranked by their helpfulness.   Automation, buildings, and
administration were rated first, second, and third, respectively, by
the 1956 class.   The top ratings for the 1961 class were automation, administration, and work with children and young people.
Rated as most useful by the entire sample were automation, administration, work with children and young people, and buildings, in
that order.

Only one significant correlation was common to both classes
for the time spent in workshop.   Those who had attended more days
of workshops tended to have read more books in library science
than the librarian who had less workshop participation.

Professional Journals Read

The 5-year difference in graduation from library school had
little effect on the number of library journals that were read regularly.   The mean for the 1956 class was 3. 5 and for 1961, it was
3. 6.   When the group was divided into high and low there was still
little difference: 55. 8 per cent of the 1956 class were in the high
category (4 and over), while 53. 5 per cent of the 1961 class were
in the high group, as indicated in Table XI, p. 68.   Heading the
list of periodicals read regularly were the Library Journal, the ALA

Bulletin, and the Wilson Library Bulletin. Librarians who read more
library journals regularly generally belonged to more library and non-
library professional associations, and had held more offices in them.

For non-library professional journals read by librarians in
the sample, there was a significant difference (P = 0.03) between
the two classes when each was divided into high (one or more) and
low (none) read regularly. Of the 1956 class, 55.7 per cent were
high, as compared with 37.3 per cent of the 1961 class. The mean
for the 1956 class was 1.1 and the median 1.0. For the class of
1961, the mean was 0.7 and the median zero.

Bundy commented on the lack of interest in non-library professional journals when she surveyed public library administrators'
opinions of professional periodicals:

> As people whose business is the dissemination of informa-
> tion, one might have expected librarians to make more use
> of printed information from other fields. One suggestion
> afforded by this study is that the library periodicals might
> help to broaden the view of the library administrator by
> calling his attention to outside literature which has appli-
> cations to librarianship--and library schools might do
> more to introduce students to the literature in these
> areas. [14]

Professional Books Read

It would seem that one of the best measures of professional
interest would be the number of books read in librarianship. A librarian may join professional associations, attend meetings and workshops, and hold offices for personal reasons, but only a real interest in professional matters and a desire to increase one's knowledge
and skill would prompt the reading of books on library work. Alvarez stressed the relatively small amount of professional reading
done by librarians in his study. [15]

He found that during a 2-year period, 25 per cent of his select group of head librarians in the Mid-West had not read any books
in library science and 40 per cent had read no more than 2 books.
In the present study, 25 per cent of the 1956 class had not read any

books and 44. 2 per cent had read no more than 2 books.   Of the
1961 graduates, 24. 5 per cent had not read any books and 52. 3 per
cent had read no more than 2.   This would indicate that the reading
habits of librarians have not changed in the last thirty years.[16]
     The mean for the 1956 class was 6. 1 and the mean for the
1961 class was 3. 8.   The median number of books read by the 1956
group in library science was 3. 0 and by the 1961 group, 2. 0.
These statistics supported Alvarez's thesis that a small group read
a great many books, thus bringing up the average.

     There was a significant correlation for both classes between
those who had read the greatest number of books in library science
and the number of non-library association memberships, the number
of offices held in associations, and the number of days spent at
workshops.

     The entire sample had read more books in their area of sub-
ject specialization.   The median for both classes was 4 books, as
compared with 3 in library science by the 1956 class and with 2
books in library science by the 1961 class.   Of the 1956 graduates,
21. 2 per cent had not read any books in their area of special interest; 36. 6 per cent had read no more than 2 books.   The 1961 graduates showed similar statistics: 22. 1 per cent had read nothing;
38. 4 per cent had read no more than 2 books.   A few respondents
reported reading a large number of books in their specialty.   The
means, therefore, were quite high: 9. 7 for the 1956 class and 13. 6
for the 1961 class.

     Those respondents who had read more books in their area of
interest tended to have a higher salary and to have aspired to a different type job or library within the profession.

Publications

     Flexner pointed out over a half century ago that every profes-
sion must have a journal which provides more than just news, propa-
ganda, and agitation:
>   ... it is important to remember that we do not thus rise
>   above the journalistic to the scientific or professional

level. A profession must find a dignified and critical means of expressing itself in the form of a periodical which shall describe in careful terms whatever work is in progress; and it must from time to time register its more impressive performances in a literature of growing solidity and variety. To some extent the evolution... towards professional status can be measured by the quality of publication put forth in its name. [17]

He indicated that this was not solely the responsibility of publishers, but the joint responsibility of all members of a profession to provide a record that was scientific rather than journalistic.

Mary Lee Bundy surveyed a group of library administrators in 1961 and learned that library periodicals were an important means of influencing and guiding their day-to-day decisions and operation. 42.6 per cent of her respondents felt that library literature could be improved; 6.2 per cent felt it badly needed such improvement. [18] She concluded that "It is worth emphasizing once again that as the library periodical literature goes, so goes the library profession." [19]

Despite the importance given to publishing, 58 per cent of the respondents in this study had not published any articles during the past 5 years. The median number of articles published by the 1956 graduate was 1.0 and by the 1961 graduate, zero; 42.3 per cent of the 1956 class had published articles as compared with 41.9 per cent of the 1961 class. On the other hand, because of the unusually high number of articles reported by a few in the sample, the mean for 1956 was 5.5 and for 1961, it was 1.9.

Within each group, different correlations appear between the number of articles published and other variables in the study. Only one was found common to both classes; those who had published more articles tended to be dissatisfied with their current careers in librarianship and felt that they would need to move to another type of job in the profession.

Twenty-one per cent of the 1956 graduates had edited one or more library periodicals, compared with 14 per cent of the 1961 group. 1956 librarians who had engaged in this activity generally

had a higher Professional Index Score and held more offices in professional associations.   Those 1961 graduates who had edited journals also seemed to have published more books and engaged in more
research.

Only 5 of the 1956 and 6 of the 1961 graduates had written
a book, either in library science or in their area of specialization;
that was 7.9 per cent of the total sample of 138.   Two significant
relationships were common to both classes: those who had published books were more likely to have engaged in research and to
have belonged to learned societies.

Research Activity

Although many leaders have emphasized the need for librarians to engage in research, it has been characteristic of the
profession to invite specialists from other fields to study the nature
and needs of librarianship.   These specialists do research, state
their views and depart; rarely does sustained research ensue on the
part of the librarians themselves.   Wasserman and Bundy have
pointed up an essential difference between librarianship and some of
the more scholarly disciplines.   "Prestige in the professional society typically comes from office holding and work in the organization,
while in a scholarly discipline, prestige more usually follows upon
academic productiveness reflected in the form of articles and mono-
graphs."[20]

In the present study, 71.2 per cent of the class of 1956 and
80.2 per cent of the class of 1961 reported no research.

Of a total of 41 projects, 18 were reported by the 1956
class, and 23 by the 1961 class.   No one had engaged in more than
2 research projects.

Most of the activity was in reference and bibliography where
13 projects were listed, 2 from the 1956 class and 11 from the 1961
class.   The next most popular was library technology, with 4 reported by the 1956 respondents and 3 by the 1961 group.   The third
category identified was library administration, with 4 projects listed,
3 by the 1956 class and 1 by the 1961 group.

Despite the general increase in government and foundation grants, the individual was the most frequent initiator of research projects. Six graduates of 1956 and 9 of 1961 had sponsored their own work. Universities were next, having sponsored 6 for the 1956 researchists and 4 for 1961; and employing libraries, 2 public and 4 university, had initiated 6 projects. Only 3 research problems had been undertaken through the sponsorship of library associations, all by graduates of 1961. Of the 41 projects reported, 15 were of 6-months duration, 8 were from 7- to 12-months, and 8 were 19 months or longer.

There were two significant correlations common to the respondents who had engaged in research. They tended to have a high Professional Index Score and also to have published books.

Participation in Voluntary Study Groups

In recent years, small study groups have become an important extension of the principle of self-instruction. The American Psychological Association has viewed them as loosely knit groups of people who meet together, correspond with one another, read papers to each other, circulate reprints, and generally stimulate one another through mixed collaboration and competition. They have been termed "invisible colleges."[21]

At the 1967 Midwinter Meeting on Continuing Education, Cyril Houle stated that "these groups exert an extraordinary importance, not only on their own participants but also on other alert people who aspired to membership."[22]

In the present sample, 26.9 per cent of the 1956 group and 18.6 per cent of the 1961 group had participated in such voluntary study groups since receiving their MLS. Thirty-one study groups were reported with 29 respondents involved in one, and 2 respondents reporting membership in two groups. Nine of the 31 groups were composed of members from a library association, 4 were made up of fellow employees, and 15 were composed of librarians from the same geographical area with similar interests, regardless of association, employment, or other group affiliations.

Ten, or nearly one-third of the total number, concentrated
on administration which indicates the need in this area.

All respondents who participated in voluntary study groups
had a high Professional Index Score. Participants from the 1956
class were more likely to have a self-learning agenda, to belong to
more non-library professional associations, and to have published
more books. Participants from the 1961 class generally supervised
more employees, belonged to more library associations, and read
more non-library professional journals than those who did not participate in such groups.

Self-learning Agenda

John Gardner emphasized that "the ultimate goal of professional education is to shift to the individual the burden of pursuing
his own education."[23]

William Dill and his colleagues made this hypothesis the basis of a research study in which they emphasized the importance of
each individual having a self-learning agenda in order to ensure using his time efficiently and concentrating his efforts in a few key
areas at a time.[24] In making his survey, Dill asked his respondents if they had clearly thought through what they were preparing for,
knew what they wanted to learn, how they wanted to change, what
part of their self-education had the highest priority, and if they had
developed specific strategies for learning.

Nearly one-third of the sample, 32.6 per cent, indicated they
had such an agenda. By class: 30.8 per cent of 1956 and 33.7
per cent of 1961 had self-learning programs.

Those who had a self-learning agenda also tended to have a
relatively high Professional Index Score. The 1956 graduates also
had a higher degree of motivation for professional improvement,
generally read more library journals, and were more likely to belong to individual study groups than those who had not worked out
such a plan.

Those from the 1961 class who had developed a self-learning
agenda generally had published more articles, belonged to more non-

library professional associations, read more non-library journals, and seemed to desire advance in the same type of library or in the same type of job.

III.   Conclusion

The distribution of the librarians in the sample according to certain indexes that may affect the librarian's motivation toward professional development have been reviewed in this chapter. A sensitive administrator, aware of the need for professional development, might use the objective norms presented in this chapter as a possible means of identifying those employees who require particular stimulation.

Notes

1. Significant differences from zero correlation at the 0.05 level are reported.   That is, for these relationships there is a 95 per cent probability that the correlation coefficient will not be zero.

2. For a detailed description of how the Degree of Aspiration Score was computed, see Appendix A, Scoring Systems.

3. The one (a 1956 graduate) who listed salary as the only reason for wanting to leave had shown the least salary increase since entering the profession and was earning the lowest salary of all 24 in the group.

4. Ranta, Raymond R.   "The Professional Status of the Michigan Cooperative Extension Service" (unpublished Doctor's Dissertation, National Agricultural Extension Center for Advanced Study, University of Wisconsin, 1960), p. 40.

5. National Education Association.   National Commission on Teacher Education and Professional Standards   What You Should Know About New Horizons: A Condensation of New Horizons for the Teaching Profession, a Report of the Task Force on New Horizons in Teacher Education and Professional Standards (Washington: National Education Association, 1962), p. 7.

6. A detailed account of the 17 items that made up the scoring system and how each was devised is given in Appendix A, Scoring Systems.   One part (the Occupations Characteristics Index) was made up of 23 questions but is here considered as

only one component. There were, then, 16 questions plus the
Occupational Index Score, which totalled 17 components.

7. Discussion of this question and significant differences in answer-
    ing it between the two classes is given on p. 70, 73, 75-76.

8. Details on the individual questions asked and the weighted scores
    used are described in Appendix, Scoring Systems.

9. Bundy, Mary L. and Wasserman, Paul   "Professionalism Recon-
    sidered" College and Research Libraries, 29:23 (January,
    1968).

10. The American Library Association and its state chapters were
    by far the most popular, with memberships of 87 and 93
    respectively. The regional associations and the Special Li-
    braries Association were next, each with 23 members.

11. Haggerty, M. E. The Faculty (Vol. II of The Evaluation of
    Higher Institutions   Chicago: The University of Chicago
    Press, 1957), p. 66-67.

12. In 1966-1967, 288 activities of this type were reported for li-
    brarians, compared with 259 the previous year. This was
    an increase of about 10 per cent. Sponsorship has been by
    institutions of higher education, library associations, state
    library agencies, individual libraries, or combinations of
    these. Sarah R. Reed, Continuing Education for Librarians
    --Conferences, Workshops, and Short Courses, 1966-67.
    (Washington: Office of Education, U. S. Department of Health,
    Education and Welfare, 1966), p. 1.

13. Reed, op. cit., p. 4.

14. Bundy, Mary Lee "Public Library Administrators View Their
    Professional Periodicals" Illinois Libraries 43:418 (June,
    1961).

15. "No one can study the professional reading of librarians without
    immediate realization of two salient facts: (1) the surpris-
    ingly large number of recent publications in the library field,
    and (2) the surprisingly small number of librarians who actu-
    ally read these volumes. One need not send out question-
    naires to become aware of the latter situation; he need only
    step into the stacks of any large library and examine the
    book cards of some of the more important books which fill
    the shelves in the library science section... Furthermore...
    what little professional reading was done was accounted for
    by a small group who, out of the entire library staff, were
    the only ones with sufficient interest and ambition to look
    over some of the new books in their field." Robert Smyth
    Alvarez, "Qualifications of Heads of Libraries in Cities of
    Over 10,000 Population in the Seven North-Central States"

(unpublished Doctor's dissertation, Graduate Library School, University of Chicago, 1939), p. 101-102.

16. Differences in the two statistical bases should be noted, however.   Alvarez asked for reading over a two-year period and asked his respondents to actually list the books read.   The present study asked for reading during the past year, and asked only for a number.   It did not request the listing of actual books read, which might have lead to a greater number given than if actual titles were requested.   This tended to equalize the difference between the two time spans.

17. Flexner, Abraham "Is Social Work a Profession?" School and Society 1:911 (June 26, 1915).

18. Bundy, Mary Lee op. cit. , p. 412.

19. ----, op. cit. , 420.

20. Bundy and Wasserman op. cit. , p. 22.

21. de Solla Price, Derek J. and Beaver, Donald De B. "Collaboration in an Invisible College" American Psychologist 21: 1011 (November, 1966).

22. Houle, Cyril O. "The Role of Continuing Education in Current Professional Development" ALA Bulletin 41:265 (March, 1967).

23. Gardner, John W. Self-Renewal (New York: Harper & Row, 1963), p. 12.

24. Dill, William R. ; Crowston, Wallace B. S. and Elton, Edwin J. "Strategies for Self-Education" Harvard Business Review 43:119-130 (November-December, 1967).

Chapter V

Sources of Encouragement and Determent Relating to the
Librarian's Motivation Toward Professional Development

This chapter will seek to identify both the sources of encouragement and of determent that the librarians felt were significant in
their professional development. It will determine whether they
looked at different aspects of the same factors as being both encouraging and deterring or whether the encouraging factors are of a different kind than the discouraging factors. This study also attempts
to identify the dominant force which motivates a librarian to engage
in development activities. Hypotheses 6 through 11, reviewed in
Chapter I, are also tested.

I. Procedure

Theoretical Framework

One of the conventional assumptions of psychological practice
has been to regard factors that measure values as operating in a
bipolar continuum, "in which opposites are contrasted which are different in their own right. "[1] In the field of industrial relations, for
example, it was often assumed that job satisfaction and dissatisfaction were opposites, with one the mere negation of the other. This
theory of convertible bipolarity was challenged by Frederick Herzberg (1959)[2] and Frank Friedlander (1964)[3] who developed a theory
of dual motivation.

This more recent theory states that satisfaction and dissatisfaction are, for the most part, unrelated and noncomplementary
functions, rather than negatively related extremes of a single bipolar continuum. In industrial relations, it considers factors that

cause job satisfaction as different from those that cause dissatisfaction instead of simply opposites of the same factor.

This study has adapted the theoretical framework developed by Herzberg, the positive-negative type of questionnaire used by Friedlander,[4] and Harold Swanson's application of the concept of dual motivation in regard to continuing education within a profession,[5] and applied it to seeking the factors which motivate librarians toward or away from professional development activities.

Nature of the Instrument

To use this positive-negative technique in determining motivation, the questionnaire asked the same questions twice, first in a positive and then in a negative manner. The respondents were asked to measure the importance of 42 variables as sources of encouragement. Then these same variables were reworded negatively to determine reasons for discouragement from professional development activities.

Each respondent was asked to think of his own past experience and to indicate the extent to which each qualitative element had been encouraging or deterring. This follows the method of Herzberg and Friedlander in referring to conditions of the past, but it differs from the Swanson study which attempted to determine what present and potential conditions or factors might influence their motivation toward professional development.

Directions for the first of these measures were as follows:

> As you consider your reasons for having undertaken formal course work or participating in informal professional improvement activities, which of the following factors were important to you in making your decision? The following is a list of some factors which may have contributed to your decision at the time. Please react to each factor or condition in two ways: (a) How important was each one of these in encouraging you to participate in professional improvement activities? (b) How important was each one of these in encouraging you to take additional formal course work?

Directions for the second section were almost identical except that the words "discourage" or "deterring" were substituted for "encouraged" or "encouraging."

In the first section on sources of encouragement and the second section on sources of determent, the respondent was asked to consider factors under two categories, "professional improvement activity" and "formal course work." There were three degrees of importance to choose from:

This factor was of major importance.
This factor was fairly important.
This factor was present but was not important.

If a specific factor were not present or did not influence his decision to participate at all, the respondent was asked to leave the pertinent boxes blank.

Responses were rated "3" for major importance, "2" for fairly important, or "1" for a present, though unimportant, factor, and were then converted into weighted scores for interpretive and statistical treatment. Tied ranks were each assigned the average of the ranks included in the tie.

Classification System

The scope of these measures is similar to the classification system developed by Swanson (1965),[6] but the items were adapted to librarianship by the investigator for Pre-test Number 1 and were further modified in the final form of the questionnaire through suggestions made by those in the pilot group. Although similar to the Herzberg and Swanson schemes, they were determined in a different way. Herzberg used the critical-incident technique and Swanson asked the participants to name what they considered to be positive and negative forces. This investigator followed Friedlander's method by asking each respondent to ascribe the importance of the variables listed as sources of encouragement or determent.[7]

The 42 qualitative elements were separated into: (1) indirect forces, consisting of factors related to the development opportunities themselves, group-centered forces, and situation-centered forces; and (2) direct forces, made up of work-study forces, incentives, and internal-individual centered forces. The division of the elements by major categories, classes, and areas is outlined in Table XII.

II. Identification of Sources of Greatest Encouragement
and Greatest Determent to Professional Improvement

The results of the study will be discussed from two main points of view: a vertical analysis of the data--comparisons among sources of encouragement and sources of determent, and a horizontal analysis--a comparison between the 42 individual factors of encouragement and, separately, a comparison among the 42 individual sources of determent. The vertical analysis was done by means of (1) vertical rankings of the sources of encouragement and sources of determent using weighted scores and (2) an analysis of variance.

First, all of the positive and negative responses of the 138 librarians in the sample were reviewed and the sources of encouragement and determent were ranked according to the weighted scores. Table XIII summarizes the rankings for both professional improvement activities and for formal course work. The rank order coefficients of correlation were then computed to show relationships between the 12 columns in Table XIII. These results are given in Table XIV, and indicate the degree of agreement among the librarians concerning their perceptions of important factors encouraging or deterring them.

Professional Improvement Activities

Encouraging (Positive) Forces

The highest ranking factors that encouraged the total sample to become involved in professional improvement were:

Rank 1. The professional improvement activity was of
high quality.

Table XII

Summary of System Used to Place Sources of Encouragement and Sources
of Determent into Major Categories, Classes, and Areas

Major Categories	Classes	Areas	Item No. in Questionnaire
1. Indirect Influences	1. Professional Development Opportunity Itself	1. Professional Improvement or graduate work opportunities themselves: quality, convenience, publicity, requirements, leadership.	1-5
	2. Group forces	2. Group factors: library personnel, professional associates; family.	6-12
	3. Situation forces	3. Situation factors: changing body of knowledge, clientele needs, role of library.	13-17
2. Direct Influences	4. Work-study forces	4. Work-study factors: staff to cover job; costs, finances, time.	18-23
	5. Incentive forces	5. Incentives: promotion, challenging assignments, new knowledge, work easier, salary, ideas, specialization.	24-31

Table XII (cont.)

Major Categories	Classes	Areas	Item No. in Questionnaire
	6. Internal forces	6. Internal--general: service, community welfare.	32-33
		7. Psychological factors: needs, motives.	34-38
		8. Attitudinal factors: enjoyment, ability to study.	39-40
		9. Physiological: age, health.	41-42

Table XIII. Sources of Encouragement and Sources of Determent Related to Professional Development Ranked According to Relative Importance by Librarians in the Sample: 1967

Major Cate-gories	Grouped Forces	Abbreviated Items	Professional Improvement Activities						Formal Course Work					
			Encouragement Rankings			Determent Rankings			Encouragement Rankings			Determent Rankings		
			Sample Total (1)	1956 (2)	1961 (3)	Sample Total (4)	1956 (5)	1961 (6)	Sample Total (7)	1956 (8)	1961 (9)	Sample Total (10)	1956 (11)	1961 (12)
Oppor-tunity Itself		1. Quality	1	1	1	1	3	2	2	1.5	2	3	2	3
		2. Location	7.5	12	7	2	2	2	11	7.5	13	2	3	2
		3. Publicity/planning help	14.5	19	14	6	11	8	25.5	24	25.5	15.5	15	13
		4. Reasonable require'ts	24	24	22.5	31.5	26.5	33.5	13	17.5	10	13.5	8.5	20
		5. Leadership	5	4	5	5	11	4	5	3	7	5	15	4
Indirect Influ-ence	Group Forces	6. Supervisor	16.5	21	16	15.5	9	16.5	24	33.5	21	7.5	6	16.5
		7. Administration	14.5	19	14	7.5	5	11.5	28	27.5	28	4	5	8
		8. Governing Board	40.5	39	41	26	20.5	30	38	36.5	37	23	11	29
		9. Professional associates	26	16.5	26	23	26.5	23.5	30	25.5	31.5	38	38	37
		10. Library school faculty	33	37.5	32	37	38.5	36	36.5	33.5	36	34.5	38	34
		11. Library association	27	14.5	28	20	20.5	20.5	41	42	41	41	33.5	40.5
		12. Home situation	19.5	29	18	13	11	11.5	14.5	14.5	14.5	7.5	7	13
Situa-tion Forces		13. Changing body of knowl'ge	9	8	8	36	29.5	40	14.5	10	19	38	28	40.5
		14. Read for techn'l knowl'ge	11	10	11	38	38.5	38	8.5	7.5	8	25.5	25	27
		15. " for behavioral "	28	23	27	21	23	20.5	20	20	22	19.5	20	18.5
		16. Clientele/spec. needs	34	33	34	34	29.5	35	33.5	36.5	33	38	41	34
		17. Changing role of library	16.5	16.5	17	27.5	35.5	25	27	30	23	25.5	26	24.5

Table XIII (cont.)

		(1)	(2)	(3)	(4)	(5)	(6)	(7)	(8)	(9)	(10)	(11)	(12)
Work Study Forces	18. Leave given	13	14.5	12	10.5	13	9	31	36.5	29	12	20	6.5
	19. Staff avail. to cover job	23	22	24	14	8	16.5	35	40	31.5	6	4	18.5
	20. Costs reasonable	22	25.5	20.5	17	15.5	14	17.5	21	14.5	10	8.5	13
	21. Financial help	42	42	42	24.5	22	27	36.5	32	38	15.5	20	9
	22. Help on transport. costs	21	13	25	7.5	4	18	42	41	42	21.5	10	22
	23. Available time	18	25.5	19	3	1	5	21	14.5	27	1	1	1
Incentives	24. Meet other librarians	6	6	6	29	29.5	28	32	27.5	34	32.5	28	39
	25. Promotion likely	31.5	35.5	30	39	40	38	23	22	25.5	34.5	35.5	37
	26. Challenging assign'ts.	29	30	29	24.5	32.5	23.5	16	16	16	27	33.5	22.5
	27. Use of new knowledge	3	3	4	19	14	19	1	1.5	1	13.5	12.5	10.5
	28. Work easier/more ef'tive	7.5	7	10	18	17.5	15	8.5	5	11	21.5	12.5	21
	29. Salary increases	35.5	37.5	35.5	33	35.5	30	17.5	17.5	17	32.5	41	29
	30. New & creative ideas	2	2	2	4	7	3	3	4	4	17	15	15
	31. Chance to specialize	25	27	22.5	10.5	19	6	6.5	10	6	11	17	6.5
Direct Influence	32. Better service to others	10	9	9	15.5	15.5	13	10	10	9	19.5	23.5	16.5
	33. Promote comm'ty welfare	31.5	31	33	40.5	41.5	38	39	36.5	39	38	41	34
	34. Security	35.5	32	40	30	24.5	32	25.5	25.5	24	36	38	37
	35. Acceptance by coworkers	38	35.5	39	31.5	32.5	30	33.5	30	35	30.5	31	29
Internal Individual	36. Use of best abilities	30	28	31	27.5	29.5	26	19	19	18	29	35.5	24.5
	37. Realize ambitions	19.5	19	20.5	22	24.5	22	6.5	13	5	18	23.5	10.5
	38. Involvement	12	11	14	10.5	10	10	40	39	40	24	20	31.5
	39. Enjoyment	4	5	3	10.5	17.5	7	4	6	3	9	20	5
	40. Can study effectively	39	40	35.5	40.5	35.5	41	12	12	12	30.5	28	31.5
	41. Age	40.5	41	37	42	35.5	42	22	30	30	42	31	42
	42. Good health/energy	37	34	38	35	41.5	33.5	29	23	30	28	31	26

Table XIV

Rank Order Correlation Coefficients for Sources of Encouragement and Sources of Determent Related to Professional Development for Librarians in the Sample: 1967

Reference Columns in Table XIII[a]	Category of Librarians			Type of Professional Development		Sources of		Coefficient
	Total	1956	1961	Professional Improvement	Formal Courses	Encouragement	Determent	
(1)	(2)	(3)	(4)	(5)	(6)	(7)	(8)	(9)
1, 4	x			x		x	x	.64
7, 10	x				x	x	x	.41
2, 5		x		x		x	x	.53
3, 6			x	x		x	x	.65
1, 2	x	x		x		x		.95
1, 3	x		x	x		x		.99
8, 11		x			x	x	x	.25
9, 12			x		x	x	x	.49
4, 5	x	x		x			x	.94
4, 6	x			x			x	.97
2, 3		x	x	x		x		.92
5, 6		x	x	x			x	.87
7, 8	x	x			x	x		.96
7, 9	x		x		x	x		.99

Table XIV (cont.)

(1)	(2)	(3)	(4)	(5)	(6)	(7)	(8)	(9)
8, 9		x	x		x	x		.90
11, 12		x	x		x		x	.74
10, 11	x	x			x		x	.89
10, 12	x		x		x		x	.94
1, 7	x			x	x			.52
4, 10	x			x	x	x	x	.80
2, 8		x	x	x	x	x		.43
3, 9				x	x	x		.54
5, 11		x		x	x		x	.82
6, 12			x	x	x		x	.80

a Identification of column numbers in Column #1 (Reference to Table XIII)

#1 - Professional improvement--Encouragement rankings--All librarians
#2 - Professional improvement--Encouragement rankings--1956 MLS librarians
#3 - Professional improvement--Encouragement rankings--1961 MLS librarians
#4 - Professional improvement--Determent rankings--All librarians
#5 - Professional improvement--Determent rankings--1956 MLS librarians
#6 - Professional improvement--Determent rankings--1961 MLS librarians
#7 - Formal course work--Encouragement rankings--All librarians
#8 - Formal course work--Encouragement rankings--1956 MLS librarians
#9 - Formal course work--Encouragement rankings--1961 MLS librarians
#10 - Formal course work--Determent rankings--All librarians
#11 - Formal course work--Determent rankings--1956 MLS librarians
#12 - Formal course work--Determent rankings--1961 MLS librarians

Rank 2. I thought it would give me a chance to be exposed to new and/or creative ideas.
Rank 3. I felt I would be able to use the new knowledge
in my job.

The first two factors were ranked in the same order by the 1956
and the 1961 MLS librarians. In fact, the 1956 group agreed exactly with the total, whereas the factor "I felt I would be able to use
the new knowledge in my job" was ranked fourth by the 1961 graduates. They ranked "I thought I would enjoy it" as third.

The least important factors to all the librarians in the sample
were:

Rank 42 Financial assistance was available through fellowships, scholarships, or loans.
Rank 40. 5 The governing board of my library encouraged
continuing education as a matter of policy.
Rank 40. 5 I felt I was never too old to start.

Table XIV presents the rank order coefficient of correlation
between importance of sources of encouragement--professional improvement activities--indicated by the 1956 MLS librarians, and importance indicated by 1961 MLS librarians. The result (. 92 denotes
a very high positive correlation) reveals that in general the perceptions are the same among librarians of these two classes.

Closer examination of individual differences in rankings, however, discloses, in spite of this high positive correlation, some disagreement in specific areas. For example, a dynamic library association, one that gave the individual an opportunity to become involved, was ranked 14. 5 by the 1956 group and 28 by the 1961 group.
The 1956 graduates also ranked the influence of professional associates higher, 16. 5; it was 26 for 1961 graduates. Whether the employing library paid part or all of the transportation costs was rated
13 by the 1956 group, 25 by the 1961 group. Desire for more security on the job was ranked 32 by the 1956 group and 40 by the
1961 group.

The 1961 graduates showed the highest positive difference
from the 1956 graduates in home situation, which ranked 18 for 1961
and 29 for 1956. Available time ranked 19 for the 1961 group and
25. 5 for the 1956 group.

Deterring (Negative) Forces

Tabulation of the weighted scores for factors deterring professional improvement showed that the most influential for all the librarians were:

Rank 1. The professional improvement activity was of inferior quality.

Rank 2. The opportunity was remote and/or inconveniently located.

Rank 3. I had little available time and it would have been difficult to fit into my schedule.

The 1956 MLS librarians reversed this order and listed the time factor first, inconvenient location second, and inferior quality third. The 1961 group ranked as first and second the same two items as the total sample, but considered as third "I didn't think any new or creative ideas would be presented."

The factors which were least important in deterring all the librarians in the sample were:

Rank 42.   I felt I was too old to start.

Rank 40. 5 I believed I couldn't study effectively.

Rank 40. 5 I felt there would be no opportunity to promote community welfare.

The 1956 group considered other factors as least important. "I was not in good health and had no extra energy to use" tied with the lack of opportunity to promote community welfare with a score of 41.5 for both. A score of 40 made "I felt there was poor chance that it would help me get a promotion" next. The 1961 graduates agreed with the total sample for the least important--age. Inability to study effectively was considered next and "I felt the total body of knowledge was increasing so fast that there was too much material for me to grasp" was rated 40.

The complete list of the rankings of deterrents is given in Table XIII, columns 4, 5, and 6 page 90. The rank-order coefficient of correlation was high (0. 87) between the rankings of the 1956 and the 1961 librarians in what constituted the greatest determents in professional development. (See Table XIV.) There was also a high correlation between the total sample and the 1956 graduates (0.94) and the total sample and the 1961 graduates (0.97).

As with the encouraging factors, there were some interesting comparisons between various rankings of the two groups. The 1956 librarians were more deterred by their library's refusal to pay part or all of the transportation costs, ranking this 4; the 1961 graduates ranked this item 18. The 1956 group ranked as 5, "the administration of my library did not encourage me to participate," whereas the 1961 rated this 11.5. The 1956 librarians rated "no staff was available to cover my job" as 8; the 1961 group considered this as 16.5; "my immediate supervisor did not encourage me to participate" was 9, compared with 16.5 by the 1961 group.

The greatest difference for 1961 graduates over 1956 was with "there was no opportunity to gain knowledge in my area of subject specialization." They ranked this 6 as opposed to 19 by the 1956 group. The next greatest variation was the rank of 7 by the 1961 group for "I didn't think I would enjoy it," as opposed to 17.5. The 1961 group considered the lack of "acknowledged leaders" as 4; the 1956 group rated this 11.

Formal Course Work

Encouraging (Positive) Forces

The reasons that ranked highest in encouraging the sample to take additional formal course work beyond the MLS degree were:

Rank 1.   I felt I would be able to use the new knowledge in my job.
Rank 2.   It was of high quality.
Rank 3.   I thought it would give me a chance to be exposed to new and/or creative ideas.

Among the 1956 graduates, the first two items tied for first place and "it was conducted by acknowledged leaders" was considered third. The 1961 group agreed with the total sample in first and second place but ranked as third "I thought I would enjoy it."

The factors listed as least important by all the librarians were:

Rank 42.   My library paid part or all of my transportation costs.

Rank 41.   My library association was dynamic and gave
a chance to be involved.

Rank 40.   Involvement.

The 1956 group rated a dynamic library association as least important; next, help with transportation costs; and "there was staff available to cover my job in my absence" was rated 40.   The 1961 rankings coincided with the sample for the two least important items.
"I was involved and had some responsibility in connection with it,"
was rated 40.

The complete list of rankings of sources of encouragement of
formal course work is given in Table XIII, columns 7, 8, and 9,
page 90.   The rank-order coefficient of correlation (see Table XIV)
was high (0. 90) between the rankings of the 1956 and the 1961 groups
in what constituted the greatest encouragement toward formal course
work.   There was also a high correlation between all the librarians
and the 1956 group regarding formal course work (0. 96); and a 0. 99
correlation between the 1961 group and the total sample.

The greatest discrepancies in ranking are noted in the following: (a) "my immediate supervisor encouraged me to participate"
which was ranked 21 by the 1961 graduates, but 33. 5 by the 1956
graduates; and (b) "I had available time and could fit into my schedule" which the 1956 group ranked 14. 5 as compared to 27 by the
1961 graduates.

The 1961 group, however, was found to place greater importance on: (a) reasonable requirements (rank 10 as compared to
17. 5 with the 1956 group);   (b) "my library gave me some leave so
I could participate" (rank 29 as compared with 36. 5);   (c) "there was
staff available to cover my job in my absence" (rank 31. 5 as compared with 40).

Deterring (Negative) Forces

The factors that all librarians in the sample felt discouraged
them the most from doing formal course work beyond the MLS
were:

Rank 1.   I had little available time and it would have been difficult to fit into my schedule.
Rank 2.   It was remote and/or inconveniently located.
Rank 3.   It was of inferior quality.

The 1956 graduates listed the same three, but reversed the order of inferior quality and inconvenience. The 1956 group coincided exactly with the total sample.

The factors listed as least important in deterring the librarians in the sample were:

Rank 42.   I felt I was too old to start.
Rank 41.   My library association was a closed group.

The next ranking consisted of 5 items which received identical scores and are jointly listed as 38. They were: lack of encouragement by professional associates; body of knowledge was changing so fast there was too much material to grasp; it wouldn't help clientele with special needs; there would be no chance to promote community welfare; and it would not contribute to security on the job.

The 1956 graduates considered 3 items as least important: "it wouldn't help clientele with special needs;" "I didn't see how it would help me get a salary increase;" and "I felt there would be no chance to promote community welfare." Age was the least deterring item with the 1961 graduates. The next lowest was a tie of "my library association was a closed group," and the "total body of knowledge was increasing so fast there was too much material to grasp."

The complete list of rankings for determents to formal course work is given in Table XIII, columns 10, 11, and 12, page 90. The rank-order coefficient of correlation between the rankings of the 1956 and the 1961 group was fairly high (0. 74), but it was significantly lower than the relationships reported for professional improvement, both encouragement and determent, and for formal course work, encouragement. This lower correlation would account for the greater number of individual discrepancies that were noted here. The correlation coefficient relating the 1956 graduates to the total response was 0. 89; for the 1961 group it was 0. 94. In addition, there were fewer responses to this section than to any other part of Question 1. One respondent may have partially explained this: "If I think formal courses are important--nothing deters me, so this doesn't apply."

Up to this point the analysis has concentrated on differences found through weighted vertical rankings. Further vertical analysis was made by means of variance, which takes into account all factors together and gives an overall picture.[8] The F ratios that were obtained clearly indicate significant differences between the positive factors, as sources of encouragement, and the negative factors, as sources of determent. Of those items related to professional improvement, the analysis of variance showed the following results:

1. There was a very distinct difference between the positive and negative factors, as shown by the F ratio of 1467.5, which was significant at the 0.01 level. This supports the hypothesis that the reasons one engages in professional development activities differ from, and are not merely opposite to, the reasons for which one might be deterred from engaging in such activities.

2. There was a significant difference between the classes of 1956 and 1961 within the positive category and within the negative category.

3. There was a significant difference between the respondents of each class, at the one per cent level, within the positive and negative categories.

4. There was a significant difference between the individual factors as sources of encouragement and sources of discouragement within the positive category and the negative category at the one per cent level.

5. There was interaction between the year of graduation and the factors within the positive and negative categories, but it was significant only at the 5 per cent level.

Of those items related to formal course work, the analysis of variance showed similar results:

1. There was a very significant difference between the positive and negative factors, as shown by the F ratio of 1010.7, which was significant at the 0.01 per cent level.

2. There was a significant difference between the classes of 1956 and 1961 within the positive category and within the negative category.

3. There was a significant difference between the individual factors as sources of encouragement and sources of discouragement within the positive category and the negative category at the one per cent level.

4. There was not a significant interaction between the year of graduation and the factors within the positive and negative categories. This means that the reaction of the classes to the various factors tended to show similarity rather than dissimilarity.

In summary, for both professional improvement activities and formal course work the analysis of variance clearly indicated significant differences among the various factors as sources of encouragement, and significant differences among the same factors as sources of determent related to professional development activities. For both formal course work and professional improvement activity, the hypothesis was substantiated that the reasons librarians engage in professional development activities differ from, and are not merely opposite to, the reasons for which they might be deterred from engaging in such activities.

Item by Item Comparison of Encouraging and Deterring Factors

Whereas the previous sections compared data vertically, by columns, resulting in comparisons among sources of encouragement and sources of determent, first by means of rankings based on weighted scores and second by means of an analysis of variance, this section will compare the data horizontally, item by item. To compare the individual sources of encouragement and determent, correlation coefficients were computed for each of the 42 items. Table XV indicates the degree of relationshp between the positive and negative aspects of each item.[9] The following paragraphs examine the findings in Table XV, pages 102 and 103.

Of the 42 possible correlations between the positive and negative aspects of each item in Part I of the questionnaire concerning professional improvement activity, 27 in the 1956 class and 19 in the 1961 class were not significant. For formal course work, 29 of these correlations were not significant for the 1956 group and 14

were not for the 1961 group.   This indicates that few accurate predictions of factors causing determent can be made from a knowledge
of the specific items causing encouragement relative to professional
development activity.

At the one per cent level, the 7 negative correlations in the
1956 class and the 15 negative correlations in the 1961 class regarding professional improvement, and the 9 negative correlations for
1956 and the 17 for 1961 regarding formal course work indicate that
if these factors were important to encouragement they would not be
important to discouragement in 99 cases out of 100.

The negative correlations at the 5 per cent level indicate that
in 95 cases out of 100 a factor that is important to encouragement
would not be important to discouragement.   There are 8 significant
negative correlations at this level for the 1956 class and 7 for the
1961 class regarding professional improvement; 4 for 1956 and 11
for 1961 regarding formal course work.

The correlation coefficients in Table XV indicate that none
of the 42 sources of encouragement and determent, when compared
item by item, have significant positive relationships.   All of the 42
correlations, both for formal course work and professional improvement activity, are either not significant at all, or have negatively
significant correlations, indicating that encouragement and determent
are unrelated and are thus not bipolar.   This supports Herzberg's
and Friedlander's findings that satisfiers and dissatisfiers are not
opposite ends of a common set of dimensions.   As this concept has
been applied to this study, it means that the reasons one engages in
professional development activities differ from (and are not merely
opposite to) the reasons for which one might not participate.

Relationship Between Motivations Regarding Professional
Improvement Activity and Formal Course Work

The relationships discussed so far have been concerned with
the positive and negative factors that influenced respondents to engage in professional improvement or in formal course work.   From
the data collected relationships were also observed between formal

Table XV

Correlations Between Sources of Encouragement and Sources of Determent Related to Professional Improvement and Formal Course Work as Perceived by the Librarians in the Sample: 1967

Abbreviated Items from the Questionnaire	Professional Improvement				Formal Course Work			
	1956		1961		1956		1961	
	coeff. (1)	(N) (2)	coeff. (3)	(N) (4)	coeff. (5)	(N) (6)	coeff. (7)	(N) (8)
1. Quality of opportunity	-.15	42	-.25*	74	-.22	32	-.24	47
2. Convenience	.01	36	-.20	68	-.33	30	-.22	45
3. Publicity/planning help	-.18	29	-.22	56	-.03	19	.27	31
4. Reasonable requirements	-.45	26	-.00	38	-.10	22	-.11	39
5. Acknowledged leaders	-.12	36	-.15	61	-.06	29	-.03	40
6. Supervisor	-.31	31	-.19	49	.34	22	-.73**	33
7. Administration	-.73**	33	-.34*	49	.67**	22	-.72**	28
8. Governing Board	-.59*	16	-.56**	21	-.58*	16	-.70**	16
9. Professional associates	-.51**	28	-.27	34	-.41	13	-.47*	22
10. Library school faculty	-.62*	16	-.24	23	-.59*	12	-.59*	17
11. Library association	-.51**	26	-.33	31	-.68	7	-.71*	8
12. Home situation	-.56**	28	-.50**	51	-.76**	26	-.72**	38
13. Changing body of knowledge	-.11	31	-.07	44	-.35	22	-.15	28
14. Need for technical knowledge	-.28	30	-.02	37	-.18	23	-.38*	33
15. Need for behavioral knowledge	-.06	23	-.49**	28	.04	15	-.29	27
16. Clientele with special needs	.03	16	-.74**	19	.29	9	-.62**	20
17. Changing role of library	-.09	22	-.39*	38	.28	10	-.33	26
18. Leave given	-.23	31	-.35**	54	-.03	11	-.72**	23
19. Staff available to cover job	-.24	29	-.62**	47	-.71**	20	-.52*	23
20. Costs reasonable	-.46*	29	-.29*	46	-.69**	21	-.42**	43
21. Financial help	-.52	11	-.62*	16	.25	13	-.68**	25
22. Help on transportation cost	-.37*	32	-.61**	42	.15	10	-.67*	13

Table XV (cont.)

	(1)	(2)	(3)	(4)	(5)	(6)	(7)	(8)
23. Available time	-.20	32	-.48**	52	-.29	27	-.63**	43
24. Meet other librarians	.09	37	-.20	61	-.24	13	-.70**	17
25. Promotion likely	-.60*	13	.05	23	-.31	14	-.54**	23
26. Challenging assignments	-.29	17	-.70**	33	-.29	16	-.55**	30
27. Use of new knowledge	.07	36	-.33*	59	-.24	28	-.29*	48
28. Work easier/more effective	-.19	32	-.55**	75	-.56**	26	-.66**	53
29. Salary increases	-.74**	16	-.08	25	-.43	16	.32	32
30. New and creative ideas	-.39*	36	-.21	68	-.44*	24	-.08	39
31. Chance to specialize	-.40*	25	-.57**	40	.10	20	-.11	37
32. Better service to others	-.20	29	-.26	49	-.78**	22	-.43**	36
33. Promote community welfare	-.32	17	-.72**	20	-.42	9	-.69**	14
34. Security	.26	16	-.61**	21	.03	13	.06	23
35. Acceptance by coworkers	-.75**	16	-.60**	23	-.75**	14	-.22	19
36. Use of best abilities	.20	21	-.50*	24	-.39	17	-.28	27
37. Realize ambitions	-.49*	24	-.22	37	-.55*	19	-.37*	42
38. Involvement	-.54**	33	-.67**	51	-.92**	13	-.68**	13
39. Enjoyment	-.07	37	-.14	63	-.33	26	-.35*	47
40. Can study effectively	-.22	9	-.27	18	-.56**	21	-.45**	34
41. Age	-.62	10	-.31	18	-.44	13	-.45*	27
42. Good health/energy	-.22	14	-.64**	25	-.37	15	-.58**	25

** Significant at 1% level.
* Significant at 5% level.

course work and professional improvement activities.

Professional Improvement and Formal Course-
work--Positive Relationships

There was a correlation coefficient of 0.52 for rankings of
encouragement sources to professional improvement and formal
course work for all librarians in the sample.   This indicates significant differences between the reasons that a respondent would be
encouraged to engage in professional improvement as opposed to the
reasons why he would be encouraged to take formal courses.

The greatest differences in the ranking of sources of encouragement related to professional improvement activities and the ranking of sources of encouragement related to formal course work are
shown in Table XVI.   All differences in rank of over 5 places are
noted in the table.   Some of these differences are accounted for by
the nature of the questionnaire itself, since it was necessary to use
one standard list in asking librarians about professional improvement
activities and formal course work.   It was to be expected, for example, that items concerning library associations would rank higher
in professional improvement than in formal course work.   Ability to
study effectively would be more applicable to course work than to
professional improvement; but workshops and short-term courses are
included under professional improvement so the difference is not as
great as might first appear.

For the administrator or educator it is important to realize
that some items have a stronger drawing power than others.   For
example: the attitudes of the administration and supervisor were
more important to professional improvement activities than to formal course work; leave given and transportation were relatively important for professional improvement activities, but not for formal
course work; while financial help did not rate very high in either
category, it was more important to formal course work.   Publicity
and planning help were considered more important to professional
improvement activities than to formal course work.

There was also a fairly low correlation coefficient (0.43)

Table XVI

Main Differences in Ranking Sources of Encouragement
Related to Professional Improvement and
Formal Course Work: 1967[a]

Question Number	Abbreviated Item	Professional Improvement Rank	Course Work Rank	Difference
	Higher Ranking for Professional Improvement			
38	Involvement	12	40	28
24	Meet other librarians	6	32	26
22	Transportation provided	21	42	21
18	Leave given	13	31	18
12	Library association	27	41	14
7	Administration	14. 5	28	13. 5
19	Staff available to cover	23	35	12
3	Publicity/planning help	14. 5	25. 5	11
17	Changing role of library	16. 5	27	10. 5
33	Promote community welfare	31. 5	39	8. 5
6	Supervisor	16. 5	24	7. 5
13	Changing body of knowledge	9	14. 5	5. 5
	Higher Ranking for Formal Course Work			
40	Can study effectively	39	12	27
41	Age	40. 5	22	18. 5
31	Chance to specialize	25	6. 5	18. 5
20	Possible salary increases	35. 5	17. 5	18
37	Realize ambitions	19. 5	6. 5	13
26	Challenging assignments	29	16	13
4	Reasonable requirements	24	13	11
36	Use of best abilities	30	19	11
34	Security in job	35. 5	25. 5	10
25	Promotion likely	31. 5	23	8. 5
42	Good health/energy	37	29	8
15	Need for behavioral knowledge	28	20	8
21	Financial help	42	36. 5	5. 5

[a]Over-all association between positive rankings regarding professional improvement and formal course work has a correlation coefficient of 0. 52.

between the way 1956 graduates rated encouraging factors to formal
course work and professional improvement.   In general their reactions reflected the same patterns as shown in Table XVI for the
whole group, but there were some variations.   For example, influence of professional associates ranked 16. 5 in encouraging professional improvement as opposed to 25. 5 in formal course work.
Home situation was a greater encouragement to formal course work
(rank 14. 5) than to professional improvement activities (rank 29).
The librarians also saw a greater opportunity to promote understanding of the changing role of the library through professional improvement activities (rank 16. 5) than through formal courses (rank 30).

The correlation coefficient for the 1961 graduates was almost
identical to the total sample--0. 54.   In general the differences were
also similar.

Professional Improvement and Formal Course-work--Negative Relationships

When the reasons for not engaging in professional improvement activities and formal course work were compared, there was
a high correlation between the over-all rankings of 0. 80.   The chief
differences in rankings are indicated in Table XVII.

Thus, lack of encouragement by professional associates, lack
of help on transportation costs, lack of opportunity for involvement,
lack of the presentation of new and creative ideas, poor publicity
and lack of planning help were more important deterring factors relative to professional improvement than to formal course work.

On the other hand, the following discouraging factors were
considered more important to formal course work than to professional improvement activities: rigid and unreasonable requirements,
new technical knowledge offered beyond comprehension, inability to
study effectively, lack of encouragement by supervisor and administration, lack of staff to cover job, unreasonable costs, lack of energy and poor health, difficult home situation, and inability to use
new knowledge on the job.

In using this information as an aid to planning, however, it is

Table XVII

Main Differences in Ranking Sources of Determent
Related to Professional Improvement and
Formal Course Work: 1967[a]

Question Number	Abbreviated Item	Professional Improvement Rank	Course Work Rank	Difference
	Higher Ranking for Professional Improvement			
11	Library association gave little chance for involvement	20	41	21
9	Professional associates did not encourage participation	23	38	15
22	No help on transportation costs	7. 5	21. 5	14
38	I wasn't involved	10. 5	24	13. 5
30	Lack of new and creative ideas	4	17	13
3	Lack of publicity and planning help	6	15. 5	9. 5
34	Didn't feel it would make me more secure in my job	30	38	8
	Higher Ranking for Formal Course Work			
4	Requirements were rigid and unreasonable	31. 5	13. 5	18
14	New technical knowledge I needed beyond my understanding	38	25. 5	12. 5
40	Didn't think I could study effectively	40. 5	30. 5	10
21	No financial assistance available	24. 5	15. 5	9
6	My immediate supervisor did not encourage me to participate	15. 5	7. 5	8
19	No staff available to cover my job	14	6	8
20	Costs were unreasonable	17	10	7
42	I was not in good health and had no extra energy	35	28	7
12	Home situation made participation difficult	13	7. 5	5. 5
27	Didn't feel could use new knowledge on the job	19	13. 5	5. 5
7	My administration did not encourage	7. 5	4	3. 5

[a]Over-all association between negative rankings regarding professional improvement and formal course work had a correlation coefficient of 0. 80.

important to relate these higher rankings to the actual position of
the item, as indicated in Table XIII, page 90. For example, inability to study effectively was ranked ten places higher in relation
to formal course work, but it was only rated 30. 5 out of the 42
items, so was not considered a major determent.

There was a high correlation (0. 82) between rankings by 1956
librarians for determents to professional improvement activities and
formal course work. The 1961 graduates' correlation of 0. 80 was
identical with that for the total sample.

III. Dominant Forces of Motivation

Conceptual Framework

The conceptual framework suggested by Herzberg was concerned not only with the dichotomy of satisfiers and dissatisfiers but
also with the dichotomy of intrinsic and extrinsic job characteristics. He sought a way to classify the factors by which an employee
found job satisfaction, improved in performance, and reached his
goal as opposed to the job factors which merely helped him avoid
unpleasant situations:

> This is a basic distinction. The satisfiers related to the
> actual job. Those factors that do not act as satisfiers
> describe the job situation. [10]

He found that the satisfiers dealt mostly with indexes of personal
growth and self-actualization, while the dissatisfiers involved environmental and physical characteristics, such as working conditions,
supervision, administrative practices, salary. He labeled the factors related to the content process of the job "motivators," as opposed to extra-job factors, which he called the factors of hygiene.
He felt the "motivators" revolved "around the need to develop in one's
occupation as a source of personal growth." The hygiene group
"does not motivate the individual to high levels of job satisfaction...
All we can expect from satisfying the needs for hygiene is the pre-
vention of dissatisfaction and poor job performance."[11] He postu-

lated that the lack of understanding of this distinction accounted for
much of the failure in motivating employees.

A few years later Friedlander and Eugene Walton, in seeking
the factors which will cause a worker to continue or to leave a job,
distinguished two sets of reasons and classified them into work-
process (intrinsic job characteristics) and work-context (extrinsic job
characteristics) categories. They concluded:

> In summary, the degree to which an individual is satis-
> fied would seem contingent upon the intrinsic content and
> process of the work itself, while the degree to which he
> is dissatisfied is influenced by the contextual and environ-
> mental setting of the job. Work-process and work-con-
> text characteristics are thus capable of appealing to dif-
> fering motives and, in turn, will tend to elicit differing
> behaviors. [12]

In trying to make a basic distinction between positive and
negative motivations in professional development, Swanson divided
his findings into two dominant forces: (1) indirect influences and
(2) direct influences. The indirect influences included the opportunity itself, group forces, and situation forces. The direct influences included work-study forces, incentives, and internal individual forces. [13]

Indirect-Direct Classification

In the present study the Swanson classification scheme was
adapted but a different method was used to obtain the data. In the
Swanson study, open-end questions were asked about the most important positive and negative factors in motivation. Then the answers were consolidated and placed into the class of factors that
the answers represented most accurately. In the present study the
42 questions were arranged by six classes: development opportunity (Questions 1 through 5); group forces (Questions 6 through 12);
situation forces (Questions 13 through 17); work-study forces (Questions 18 through 23); incentives (Questions 24 through 31); and internal-individual forces (Questions 32 through 42).

To determine what they regarded as the prime motivators in

their professional development, each respondent was asked to isolate the one factor most significant as an encouragement and the one
factor most significant as a determent for professional improvement
and for formal course work. The purpose of this procedure was to
fit the answers into one of the six classes and thereby determine the
dominant force for each respondent in each of the following: (1)
positive influence in formal course work; (2) negative influence in
formal course work; (3) positive influence in professional improvement; and (4) negative influence in professional improvement. Table
XVIII gives a summary of the responses by the six classes.

Further consolidation followed: the first three classes (development opportunity, group forces, and situation forces) were combined as indirect influences; the remaining categories (work-study
forces, incentives, and internal-individual forces) were combined as
direct influences. Since the sample was small, it was necessary to
use this indirect-direct dichotomy for all the statistical computations
made in relation to the other variables in the study. By using this
major division it was also possible to determine if such a division
of factors helped to identify a primary type of motivator toward professional development.

There was a wide range of elements signified as "most important" by the respondents. For example, 25 factors were thus
designated for professional improvement, positive; 22 for professional improvement, negative; 23 for formal course work, positive; and
23 for formal course work, negative.

Many of the respondents added a note in the margin indicating that a "most significant" factor had not been checked because several factors had determined their participation or their lack of participation and, therefore, they could not isolate the one prime factor. Thus, for professional improvement, 83 per cent of the sample
population isolated one "most significant" encouraging factor and 67
per cent a "most significant" negative element. For formal course
work, 59 per cent indicated one most important encouraging element
and 62 per cent one most discouraging. A summary breakdown showing differences in rating between the 1956 and 1961 MLS graduates
is shown in Table XVIII, page 112, but because of the relatively

small numbers involved the discussion of the findings in the following paragraphs is based on data that pertained to the whole sample
population.

Professional Improvement

Of the total sample, 44 per cent ranked incentives as the
dominant positive force toward professional improvement.   This
group of forces was found to be 32 per cent more important as a
positive factor than as a negative factor.   Only 12 per cent considered the incentives group as a major type of determent.   This supports the contention that positive and negative forces differ.

Within this incentives category, all the items checked except
two (meeting other librarians and possibility of increased salary)
related to the work process and the content of the work, namely:
opportunity to use new knowledge on the job, exposure to new and
creative ideas, the chance to specialize, the possibility that it might
lead to a more challenging or responsible assignment.   It is also
significant that the items pertaining to a possible salary increase
and opportunity for promotion were rated as a dominant force by only one per cent of the total of 138.

Work-study forces ranked sixth and last as a source of encouragement, with only 3 per cent of the sample choosing an item
from this section.   No one considered reasonable costs, available
time, or staff available to cover the job as a prime motivation.
Help on transportation costs, financial help, and leave given to participate in activities were each checked only once.   It should be
noted that these are environmental factors relating to the job, and
are not concerned with the content or process of the job itself.

Situation forces (changing body of knowledge, need for technical knowledge, changing role of library, etc.) were considered the
dominant motivators by 16 per cent of the total population, whereas
they were last as major determents with only one per cent of the
sample ranking them the most significant.

Two classes of factors were of almost equal importance as
determents to professional improvement: 31 per cent of the sample

Table XVIII

Encouraging and Deterring Factors Regarded by the Librarians in the Sample as Most Important in Professional Improvement Efforts and Formal Course Work: 1967

	Distribution of Librarians Regarding Factors Most Important[a]											
	Professional Improvement						Formal Course Work					
	1956		1961		Total		1956		1961		Total	
Dominant Classes of Forces	No.	Rank	No.	Rank	No.	Rank	No.	Rank	No.	Rank	No.	Rank
Encouraging (Positive)												
Indirect												
I. Professional development opportunity itself	7	3	10	4	17	3	4	4	4	4.5	8	4
II. Group forces	1	5	8	5	9	5	1	5.5	4	4.5	5	5
III. Situation forces	3	4	11	2.5	14	4	5	3	8	3	13	3
Total, Indirect	11		29		40		10		16		26	
Direct												
IV. Work-study forces	0	6	3	6	3	6	1	5.5	0	6	1	6
V. Incentives	22	1	29	1	51	1	16	1	18	1	34	1
VI. Internal-individual	9	2	11	2.5	20	2	6	2	15	2	21	2
Total, Direct	31		43		74		23		33		56	
Total	42		72		114		33		49		82	

Table XVIII (cont.)

	Professional Improvement						Formal Course Work					
	1956		1961		Total		1956		1961		Total	
Deterring (Negative)	No.	Rank	No.	Rank	No.	Rank	No.	Rank	No.	Rank	No.	Rank
Indirect												
I. Professional development opportunity itself	10	3	17	1	27	1	8	3	12	2.5	20	2
II. Group forces	11	2	10	3	21	3	9	2	5	4	14	4
III. Situation forces	0	6	1	6	1	6	1	5	1	6	2	8
Total, Indirect	21		28		49		18		18		36	
Direct												
IV. Work-study forces	13	1	13	2	26	2	12	1	19	1	31	1
V. Incentives	3	4	8	4	11	4	3	4	12	2.5	15	3
VI. Internal-individual	1	5	6	5	7	5	0	6	4	5	4	5
Total, Direct	17		27		44		15		35		50	
Total	38		55		93		33		53		86	

aThe statistics reflect the answers the respondents made in answer to the question as to which item checked was the "most significant" in regard to professional improvement and formal course work.

ranked the professional opportunity itself as the most important; 30
per cent chose work-study forces as the most important. A close
third was the group-force class with 24 per cent considering unfav-
orable attitudes of the library administration, supervisor, and family as the chief determent. Here again, notable differences showed
that positive and negative forces differ. Compared with the 3 per
cent who chose work-study as a prime motivator, 30 per cent rated
this class of factors as chief determent. Although 24 per cent found
group forces a prime determent, only 10 per cent found them as the
dominant positive force. Generally the individual items in each of
the dominant categories center on environmental or context factors
rather than work process or opportunity content. For example, in
Group 1, remoteness and inconvenient location emerged as a determent. In Group IV, work-study factors, time and leave given
emerged as important deterrents, while they were insignificant as
sources of encouragement.

Formal Course Work

        The librarians regarded the incentive factors as the most im-
portant in influencing formal course work. Forty per cent of the
138 librarians indicated that this class represented the most positive
encouragement in formal course work, while 17 per cent considered
it the most significant negative influence. Next in importance were
the factors in the internal-individual class. This class was ranked
first as a dominant positive force by 24 per cent, while only 5 per
cent rated it a prime negative force. These are additional examples
showing that positive and negative prime motivators differ.
        Work-study factors reappeared as chief determent group to
36 per cent; they were regarded as encouragement to only one per
cent of the 138 respondents. Lack of available time was rated as
a chief determent by 22 per cent, whereas time did not appear as
a prime motivator for any one. All of these work-study factors related to the job environment.

Table XIX

Summary of Significant Relationships Between Dominant Encouraging and Deterring Forces and Selected Variables as Perceived by the Librarians in the Sample: 1967[a]

Hypotheses 6, 7, 8, 9	Variables	Direct versus Indirect Forces							
		Encouraging (positive) Forces				Deterring (negative) Forces			
		Professional Improvement		Formal Course Work		Professional Improvement		Formal Course Work	
		1956	1961	1956	1961	1956	1961	1956	1961
	Background Characteristics								
a	Age								
b	Salary					-.37*		.40*	
c	Undergraduate major							-.32*	
d	Formal course work vs. none								
	Special Indexes								
e	Degree of aspiration								
f	Professional Index					-.31*			
g	Career satisfaction	-.28*							
	Motivational Variables								
h	Degree of professional improvement motivation								
i	Type of professional improvement motivation				.34*				
j	Degree of formal course work motivation								
k	Type of formal course work motivation								

[a]Significant relationships relative to Hypotheses 5-9 presented in Chap. 1, p. 19. *Significant at the 5% level.

Relationship Between Positive and Negative Forces and Selected Variables

By determining what each librarian regarded as the dominant class of forces in his professional development activities, it was possible to test Hypotheses 6 through 9 advanced in Chapter I.[14]

With a few exceptions, the results showed no relationships between the direct or indirect categories and most of the individual variables. Furthermore, the summary of significant relationships shown in Table XIX reveals that these significant correlations are not very high and that the tendencies of association are nowhere marked. Of the 5 significant relationships, 4 applied only to the 1956 respondents who represented 38 per cent of the total sample. This evidence indicates that the division of all the factors considered into direct and indirect categories did not produce a dichotomy in which the motivating qualities and the focus of interrelationship among themselves were different. To be of practical help to an administrator, a classification scheme would have to reflect the fact that the motivating qualities included in each type were made up of kinds of factors that were essentially different in some one concept.

Positive Forces--Professional Improvement

Hypotheses 6-a, b, c, d, e, f, and i were accepted for the entire sample. That is, there was no significant relationship between what the librarian regarded as the dominant positive force toward professional improvement and any of the following: age (6-a); salary (6-b); undergraduate major (6-c); formal course work since MLS degree versus none (6-d); degree of aspiration (6-e); Professional Index (6-f); and type of professional improvement motivation (6-i).

Hypothesis 6-g was accepted relative to the 1961 MLS graduates, but rejected for the 1956 librarians. For the 1956 graduates there was a significant relationship between career satisfaction to date and dominant positive force relative to professional improve-

ment.   Proportionately more librarians with high career satisfaction
tended to select factors relating to the indirect category--develop-
ment opportunity itself, situation, and group forces.   Although the
correlation is small, this indicates that for these librarians better
work or study conditions and financial help would not be highly important in encouraging professional improvement activities.

Hypothesis 6-h was accepted relative to the 1956 MLS graduates, but rejected for the 1961 librarians.   For the 1961 graduates
there was a significant association between the librarian's degree of
professional improvement motivation score and the dominant positive
force he chose.   Librarians with a high degree of professional improvement motivation tended to select factors relating to direct
forces (work-study-incentives and internal factors) as more important in encouraging their professional improvement activities.   This
indicates that for those librarians who had the most intense desire
to improve their competencies and position in the profession, better
work or study conditions and incentives would be important in encouraging their professional improvement activities.

Negative Forces--Professional Improvement

Hypotheses 7 a, c, d, f, g, h, and i were accepted for the entire sample.   There was no significant relationship between the category of forces the librarian regarded as the major negative determent toward professional improvement and any of the following:
age (7-a), undergraduate major (7-b), formal course work since
MLS versus none (7-c), Professional Index (7-d), career satisfaction
(7-g), degree of professional improvement motivation (7-h), and type
of professional improvement motivation (7-i).

Hypothesis 7-b was accepted relative to the 1961 MLS librarians, but rejected for the 1956 librarians.   For the 1956 group
there was a significant relationship between salary and dominant negative force.   Librarians with a higher salary were more likely to
select factors from the indirect influences, professional improvement
activity itself, situation and group forces, as dominant negative
forces toward professional improvement than those with lower sal-

aries.   This relationship may mean that for the librarians in this
category more financial help or better work-study conditions would
not be strong motivating factors toward professional improvement
activities.

Hypothesis 7-e was accepted relative to the 1961 MLS librarians, but rejected for the 1956 group.   There was a significant
relationship between the 1956 librarians' level of aspiration and the
dominant negative force.   Proportionately more librarians with high
levels of aspiration tended to select factors relating to indirect
forces (professional opportunity itself, group forces, and situation
forces) as being more important in deterring their professional improvement activities.

Positive Forces--Formal Course Work

Hypotheses 8-a, b, c, d, e, f, g, h, and i were accepted for
the entire sample.   There was no significant relationship between
what the librarian regarded as the dominant positive force and any
of the following: age (8-a), salary (8-b), undergraduate major (8-
c), formal course work since MLS versus none (8-d), level of aspiration (8-e), Professional Index (8-f), career satisfaction (8-g),
degree of formal course work motivation (8-h), and type of formal
course work motivation (8-i).

Negative Forces--Formal Course Work

Hypotheses 9-c, d, e, f, g, h, and i were accepted.   There
was no significant relationship between what the librarian regarded
as the dominant negative force and any of the following: undergraduate major (9-c), formal course work since MLS versus none (9-d),
level of aspiration (9-e), Professional Index (9-f), career satisfaction (9-g), degree of formal course work motivation (9-h), and type
of formal course work motivation (9-i).

Hypothesis 9-a was accepted relative to the 1961 graduates,
but rejected for the 1956 librarians.   For the 1956 group there was
a significant relationship between the librarian's age and the domi-

nant force he chose.   Proportionately more librarians with a higher
age tended to select factors relating to direct forces, namely work-
study, incentives and internal factors, as being more significant determents to taking formal course work after graduation from library
school.   This may mean that the degree to which an older graduate
is discouraged from taking formal course work is chiefly influenced
by the environmental setting of the job-study situation.

Hypothesis 9-b was accepted relative to the 1961 MLS librarians, but was rejected for the 1956 librarians.   For the 1956
group there was a significant relationship between salary and dominant negative force for formal course work.   Librarians with a
higher salary were more likely to select factors from the indirect
influences, formal course work itself, situation and group forces,
as dominant negative forces than those with lower salaries.   This
relationship may mean that for these librarians more financial help
or better work-study conditions would not be strong motivating factors toward formal course work.   The same relationship occurred
with respect to professional development activity.

Relationship Between Dominant Positive and
Dominant Negative Categories of Forces

        This section will review the results of testing Hypotheses 10
and 11 from Chapter I.   The hypotheses are repeated here.

Hypothesis 10

        There is no relationship between the category of forces the
1956 and 1961 MLS librarian regarded as a dominant positive, or
encouraging, influence on his efforts toward professional improvement and the category he regarded as a dominant negative, or deterring, influence.

Hypothesis 11

        There is no relationship between the category of forces the

1956 and 1961 MLS librarian regarded as a dominant positive, or encouraging, influence on his efforts toward formal course work and the category he regarded as a dominant negative, or deterring, influence.

Hypothesis 10 was accepted for the entire sample. There was no significant relationship between the category of forces the librarian regarded as most important as a positive influence on his efforts toward professional improvement and the category he regarded as most important as a negative influence.

Hypothesis 11 was accepted relative to the 1961 librarians, but rejected for the 1956 librarians. For the 1956 graduates there was a significant association between the category of forces the librarian regarded as most important as a positive influence on his efforts toward formal course work and the category he regarded as most important as a negative influence. The 1956 librarians who chose direct factors (work-study, incentives, and internal forces) as more important in encouraging formal course work also tended to select factors relating to direct forces as more important in deterring them from formal course work.

In Table XX, 3 of the 4 correlations were not significant, indicating that few accurate predictions of sources of discouragement can be made from a knowledge of sources of encouragement. These non-significant correlations indicate that encouragement and discouragement are unrelated, and thus not bipolar.

The one positive correlation indicates that to the extent that direct influences (work-study, incentives, and internal factors) are important to encouragement of the 1956 librarian in formal course work, the lack of these influences is also important to discouragement. In this instance, the assumption of some bipolarity of the encouragement-determent continuum seems to be partially substantiated. However, the item by item analyses in this chapter which compared the positive and negative associations of each of the 42 sources of encouragement and determent indicates that the positive factors which influence formal course work and professional improvement are different from those that are negative.

Table XX

Summary of Association Between the Category of Forces the Librarians in the Sample Regarded as a Dominant Encouraging
Influence on Their Efforts Toward Professional Improvement and Formal Course Work and the Category They
Regarded as a Dominant Deterring Influence: 1967[a]

Dominant Class of Forces: Direct Versus Indirect	Dominant (Encouraging) Positive Influence			
	Professional Improvement		Formal Course Work	
	1956	1961	1956	1961
Dominant Deterring Negative Influence				
Professional Improvement				
1956	.06			
1961		.19		
Formal Course Work				
1956			.47*	
1961				-.09

[a]Significant relationships relative to Hypotheses 10 and 11 presented in Chapter I, p. 20.

*Significant at the 5% level.

Classification by Content and Context of Sources of Encouragement and of Determent in Professional Development

Earlier in this chapter it was found by means of correlation-
al and variance analyses that encouragement and determent generally are not complementary functions. Further, division of motivating elements into direct and indirect influences did not show any essential difference between the two kinds of factors in each category.

The investigator then decided to adapt a hypothesis proven
by Friedlander and Walton in 1964 in order to determine a more
helpful and accurate way of categorizing positive and negative motivations. They had stated their hypothesis as follows:

> The reasons an employee remains with a current organi-
> zation (positive motivations) are concerned primarily with
> work-process factors; the reasons an employee leaves an
> organization (negative motivations) deal primarily with
> factors peripheral to the work process itself or with fac-
> tors related to the community environment. [15]

This theoretical framework is closely related to the study by Herzberg which concluded that the satisfiers deal with the actual job;
non-satisfier factors describe the job situation. Adapting these concepts to the present study and using the data collected resulted in a
new concept.

The reasons why a librarian becomes involved in professional
development (positive motivations) are concerned primarily with the
content of the professional development opportunity and its relation
to the work process. The reasons why a librarian is deterred from
professional development activities (negative motivations) are peripheral to the content of the development opportunity, but are related
to context or environment of the development opportunity and to extra-job factors.

The basic question to be answered from the data collected
was: Did positive motivations deal with one type of element, and
negative motivations with a different type? In order to answer this
question, the positive and negative factors were categorized as to
content and context. Elements central to content focused on the development opportunity and its relation to the work process, on doing
the job better, on success in doing the job, on moving upward as an
indication of professional growth, on value of the content of the development opportunity for the job situation or work process. Elements central to context were peripheral to the content of the development opportunity and its relationship to the work process:
costs, financing, available time, inconvenience of location, home
situation, attitude of supervisors and administration toward professional development--extrinsic factors related to the environment.
The realignment of the 42 factors into 2 categories--content-ori-
ented and context-oriented--then took the pattern shown in Table
XXI. [16]

Table XXI

Classification of Positive and Negative Motivations for Professional Development into Content and Context Categories as Compared to Classification into Direct and Indirect Categories: 1967

Item No.	Abbreviated Items from the Questionnaire[a]	Classification by Indirect and Direct Influences[b]						Classification by Content and Context Influences			
		Indirect			Direct			Content		Context	
		I	II	III	IV	V	VI	Work	Activity	Work	Activity
	I. Opportunity Itself										
1	Quality	x							x		
2	Convenience	x									
3	Publicity and planning help	x									x
4	Reasonable requirement	x									x
5	Leadership	x									x
	II. Group Forces										
6	Attitude of supervisor		x							x	
7	Attitude of administration		x							x	
8	Attitude of governing board		x							x	
9	Attitude of professional associates		x							x	
10	Attitude of library school faculty		x								x
11	Opportunity for involvement in library association		x						x		
12	Home situation		x								x
	III. Situation Forces										
13	Changing body of knowledge			x				x			
14	Need for technical knowledge			x				x			
15	Need for behavioral knowledge			x				x			
16	Clientele with special needs			x				x			

Table XXI (cont.)

Item No.	Abbreviated Items from the Questionnaire[a]	Classification by Indirect and Direct Influences[b]						Classification by Content and Context Influences			
		Indirect			Direct			Content		Context	
		I	II	III	IV	V	VI	Work	Activity	Work	Activity
17	Changing role of library			x				x			
	IV. Work-study Forces										
18	Leave given				x				x		
19	Staff available to cover job				x				x		x
20	Costs reasonable				x						x
21	Financial help				x						
22	Help on transportation costs				x				x		
23	Available time				x						x
	V. Incentives										
24	Meet other librarians					x		x			x
25	Promotion likely					x		x			
26	Challenging assignments likely					x		x			
27	Able to use new knowledge on job					x		x			
28	Work made easier or more effective					x			x		
29	Salary increase likely					x				x	
30	New and creative ideas					x		x			
31	Chance to specialize					x		x			
	VI. Internal-individual Forces										
32	Better service to others						x	x			
33	Promote community welfare						x	x			
34	Security						x			x	
35	Acceptance by coworkers						x		x		
36	Use of best abilities						x		x		

Table XXI (cont.)

Item No.	Abbreviated Items from the Questionnaire	Classification by Indirect and Direct Influences[b]						Classification by Content and Context Influences	
		Indirect			Direct			Content Work Activty	Context Work Activity
		I	II	III	IV	V	VI		
37	Realize ambitions						x	x	
38	Involvement						x	x	
39	Enjoyment						x	x	
40	Ability to study effectively						x		x
41	Age						x		x
42	Good health and energy						x		x

[a] The importance to encouragement and the importance to determent of various factors relating to professional development were compared in the questionnaire by means of two sets of questions; the first stated items 1 through 42 in a positive form; the second stated items 1 through 42 in a negative form.

[b] I = Opportunity itself
II = Group forces
III = Situation forces
IV = Work-study forces
V = Incentives
VI = Internal-individual forces

Table XXII

Relationship Between Individual Motivations and Characteristics of Professional Improvement
Activities as Perceived by the Librarians in the Sample: 1967

Type of Motivations	Characteristic of Professional Improvement Activity		
	Content Oriented	Context Oriented	N
Positive motivations--sources for encouragement (reasons for engaging in professional improvement)	90 (79%)	24 (21%)	114 (100%)
Negative motivations--sources of determent (reasons for not engaging in professional improvement)	37 (39%)	56 (61%)	93 (100%)
Totals	127	80	207

Table XXIII

Relationship Between Individual Motivations and Characteristics of Formal Course Work
Activities as Perceived by the Librarians in the Sample: 1967

| Type of Motivations | Characteristic of Formal Course Work Improvement Activity | | |
	Content Oriented	Context Oriented	N
Positive motivations--sources for encouragement (reasons for engaging in formal course work)	71 (87%)	11 (13%)	82 (100%)
Negative motivations--sources of determent (reasons for not engaging in formal course work)	26 (30%)	60 (70%)	86 (100%)
Totals	97	71	168

Only the influences checked as most significant were considered in this particular analysis, which accounts for the different
values for N in the summary tables.

Results

Tables XXII and XXIII indicate the relationship between type
of motivations and type of characteristics of the development activity. To the extent that the continuing education opportunity involves factors related to the content of the activity and its relation
to the work process it will generally appeal to positive motivations,
serve as a potential source of encouragement, and may well influence the librarian to participate in professional development activities. On the other hand, to the extent that the activity involves
factors peripheral and extrinsic to content that is related to the work
process, it will appeal to negative motivations, serve as a potential
determent, and may well influence the librarian not to engage in the
continuing education opportunity.

The positive and negative motivations to professional improvement activities and formal course work will be discussed in further
detail.

Professional Improvement Activities--
Positive Motivations

Seventy-nine per cent of the responses were concerned with
the content of the work process or the content of the opportunity itself. In these responses there is an intrinsic involvement of the librarian. Conversely, 21 per cent of the responses were concerned
with the context, or the environment, in which the professional improvement activity is performed or with its relationship to the context of the job situation.

Formal Course Work--Positive Motivations

The results are even more striking when categorized for

formal course work.   Eighty-seven per cent of the responses were
concerned with content of the work process or the content of the opportunity itself.   Only 13 per cent were concerned with the context,
or the environment.

Professional Improvement Activities--
Negative Motivations

When asked what factors deterred them from engaging in professional improvement activities, the librarians concentrated their
reasons in the context of the professional improvement activity or
the context of the work situation.   Sixty-one per cent of the choices
involved determent with context items, while 39 per cent were content factors.   The investigator feels that the context category would
have been higher in this comparison had the questionnaire been more
specific.

Formal Course Work--Negative Motivations

The librarians also considered elements in the work context
or opportunity context as major determents to formal course work.
Seventy per cent of the responses were concerned with context; 30
per cent with content.

Summary

In general the evidence from this section indicates that the
degree to which an individual librarian was encouraged to participate in development opportunities depended upon the intrinsic content
of the development opportunity and its relation to the work process.
The degree to which he was deterred was influenced by the context
of the development opportunity and its relation to the environmental
framework of his job.

IV. Conclusion

This chapter has reviewed what the librarians sampled regarded as the major forces affecting their efforts toward professional improvement and formal course work. In general, both classes,
1956 and 1961, showed a high degree of correlation in their rating
of encouraging and deterring factors, but there were some differences.

Generally the evidence supported the conclusion that the theoretical framework developed by studies in industrial psychology,
dealing with the double dichotomy of satisfiers versus dissatisfiers
and intrinsic versus extrinsic job characteristics, was relevant to
librarianship and could be adapted to a study of factors which encourage or deter professional development efforts.

The positive and negative aspects of these factors showed
that, to a considerable degree, the reasons a librarian engages in
professional development activities differ from, and are not merely
opposite to, the reasons for which he might not engage in these activities. It was also found that sources of encouragement were
mainly related to one type of element, content and indexes of personal growth. Sources of determent generally involved another type
of element, context.

The findings in this chapter would seem to have some important implications for managerial strategy which are discussed in
the final chapter of this study.

Notes

1. Thompson, J. W.   "The Bi-Polar and Undirectional Measurement
   of Intelligence" British Journal of Psychology 52:17 (1961).

2. Herzberg, Frederick; Mausner, Bernard and Snyderman, Barbara The Motivation to Work (ed. 2; New York: John
   Wiley & Sons, 1959), p. 59-83.

3. Friedlander, Frank "Job Characteristics as Satisfiers and Dissatisfiers" Journal of Applied Psychology 48:388-392
   (December, 1964).

4. ---- "Two Questionnaires, Two Analyses of Variance Tables, and Two Multiple Range Test Tables" American Documentation Institute, Document No. 8027. Washington: ADI Auxiliary Publication Project, Photoduplication Service, Library of Congress.

5. Swanson, Harold B. "Factors Associated with Motivation Toward Professional Development of County Agricultural Extension Agents in Minnesota" (unpublished Doctor's Dissertation, University of Wisconsin, 1965), p. 81-121.

6. Swanson, op. cit., 84-85, 200-208.

7. Friedlander, loc. cit.

8. An analysis of variance uses as its basic statistic the average of the squares of all the deviations from the mean.

9. There is a different N for each correlation since those items in the questionnaire which the respondent did not check as either positive or negative were eliminated. The results, therefore, are based only on those respondents for whom the factor was present. The decision to eliminate those individuals for whom a particular factor was not present was based on the hypothesis that the results would be more meaningful and accurate if they were based on factors that actually influenced the respondents, rather than including data which were not present at all.

10. Herzberg, op. cit., 63.

11. Ibid., 114-115.

12. Friedlander, Frank and Walton, Eugene "Positive and Negative Motivations Toward Work" Administrative Science Quarterly 9:207 (September, 1964).

13. Swanson, op. cit., 92.

14. Chapter I, p. 19.

15. Friedlander and Walton, op. cit., 197-98.

16. In order to verify the new classification by content and context, the investigator asked Dr. Friedlander to check the categorization of the questionnaire items. Opinions expressed by Dr. Frank Friedlander in a personal letter, dated October 9, 1967, p. 2.

Chapter VI

Perceptions and Practices of Librarians in the Development of Responsibility for Professional Growth

What the librarians thought they should be doing for maximum professional development and what they were actually doing in the area of continuing education are compared in this chapter.

The following questions were considered:

1. What did the librarian perceive as the activities that would help him most in his professional development and how deeply should he be involved? How important should they be?

2. What were his actual practices--how deeply was he involved with these activities in expenditure of time, energy, and effort? How important were they at the present time?

3. What was the gap between what he was doing and what he thought he should be doing?

I.   Procedure

Theoretical Framework

Various professions have tried to discover the relationship stated above. In 1956 Samuel Blizzard used sociological theory to analyze the roles of Protestant clergymen. He identified six major activities and asked clergymen to evaluate them from three perspectives: importance, effectiveness, and enjoyment. He found that clergymen were spending the major part of their time at tasks they considered least important, least enjoyable, and least effective. His general conclusion was that "no matter how different ministers' ideas of what is important in the ministry, all wind up doing substantially the same thing."[1]

In 1961 Beryl Dillman varied this concept and applied it to a study of teachers.[2] He compared the practices that teachers were actually engaged in for their professional growth with what the teachers thought their practices should have been. He found that many of the activities they deemed important received relatively little of their time and energy. He found, too, that regardless of how different the teachers' ideas might be of what they should be doing, they all spent time on generally the same activities.

In general, this study has adopted the method used by Dillman in his analysis of teacher perception regarding professional growth,[3] but some different statistical methods are used, particularly in the measurement of the gap between present involvement and perceived importance of the activity under consideration.

Nature of the Instrument

The part of the questionnaire germane to this study was composed of 37 activity items that have often been claimed to be related to professional growth. Each librarian was asked to indicate the importance of each activity to him. In the first section, which listed individual activites, he was asked to evaluate his present involvement (amount of time, energy, and effort expended) under the following headings: (1) I am very much involved; (2) I am somewhat involved; and (3) I have little involvement. In a second column, he checked how important he thought each activity should be to him for achieving his maximum professional growth; (1) it should be of major importance to me; (2) it should be fairly important to me; or (3) it should be of little importance to me.

In the second section, which listed group activities, each participant was asked to check in the first column the degree of his involvement: (1) I am a leader (which would include holding offices, teaching, being chairman of committees, etc.); (2) I am an active member (which would include regular attendance, membership on committees, etc.); and (3) I am a member, but not active. In a second column, he checked how important he thought each of these group activities should be to him for maximum growth: (1) it should

be of major importance to me; (2) it should be fairly important to
me; (3) it should be of little importance to me.

Statistical Analyses Used

Responses to each of the 37 activities were separated into
different categories: 1956 and 1961 MLS graduates and total sample;
type of librarian (academic, public, school, or special); male and
female librarians; librarians living in population centers of 100,000
and over, medium-sized cities of 10,000 to 100,000, and towns of
less than 10,000 and open country.

Frequencies of response on "degree of involvement" (relative
amount of time, energy, and effort expended) were assigned one of
three weights (with 3 for the greatest involvement). Respondents
were instructed to leave the boxes blank that did not pertain to them.
Weighted ratings were then converted into weighted scores for inter-
pretative and statistical treatment and for comparison.

Activities were ranked by degree of involvement according to
magnitude of the weighted scores thus derived. Responses relative
to "degree of importance" of activities were accorded the same treatment. Tied ranks were each assigned the average of the ranks included in the tie.

Rank order correlation coefficients were then computed to
show relationships between each category of librarians and their
rankings for involvement and importance. In addition to this vertical comparison of the data, column by column, the responses were
compared horizontally, item by item. Correlation coefficients were
computed to show the relationships between the perceptions regarding
involvement and importance for each of the 37 items.

Finally, the matched t-test[4] was used to measure the disparity between the degree of importance and the degree of involvement that were accorded each development activity.

II.   Comparison Based on Rankings of
Importance and Involvement

Relative Importance of Professional Development Activities

The importance of 37 professional growth activities were
ranked by 4 different categories: (1) by the 1956 and 1961 classes
and the entire sample;   (2) by type of librarian--academic, public,
school, and special;   (3) by sex;   (4) by population concentration of
residence.

There was a striking similarity between rankings of importance for all of these categories.   The generally high positive correlations reveal that the librarians agreed significantly in their perception of what activities are important for their own professional
development.   The least agreement, however, was between the academic librarians and the public librarians and between the academic
librarians and the school librarians.

The majority rated the following activities as most important
for their professional development: reading professional literature
in library science and subject speciality, attending library conventions and meetings, participating in library associations, recruiting
for the profession, and visiting other libraries.

The activities considered least important for professional development were: service in political clubs, membership in employee
unions or in honor societies, and formal course work leading to a
sixth-year credential in library science.

There was, however, some disagreement in specific areas.

Special librarians ranked reading in their subject specialty
first, while it was slightly lower with the other groups.   Writing for
the profession rated much higher with the special librarians than
with any of the other groups.

Public librarians ranked in-service training second in importance.   The special librarians rated it 9 and the academic librarians
relegated it to 37, which was last.[5]   Public librarians placed greater
stress (Rank 9) on speaking to community groups than the other

groups, especially the special librarians who rated it 27. Academic librarians were much less interested than the other groups in promoting new materials and equipment.

Academic and special librarians ranked research 11, while the public librarians rated it 27 and the school librarians, 33. Academic librarians ranked employee unions 12, while the other groups relegated this item to their lowest rankings.

Male librarians placed more importance on research, promotion of new materials, and non-library professional associations than the women. The female librarians were more interested in speaking to community groups (Rank 2), formal course work for personal enrichment, participation in church groups, and teaching library science courses.

The librarians from cities of 10,000 to 100,000 considered speaking to community groups and teaching library science courses more important than the other groups did. They also placed greater importance on writing for the profession and on research.

Those from towns of less than 10,000 and the open country considered formal course work for an advanced degree more important. Those from the large cities ranked in-service training 6.5, while those from the medium-sized cities rated it 12.5 and those from small towns 28.5. Those from smaller towns, however, saw a greater importance in library committees setting goals, procedures, and policies. They also ranked workshops and participation in small voluntary study groups higher than the other two groups. Those from the medium-sized towns ranked participation in library associations lower than the other groups.

Relative Involvement in Professional
Development Activities

Actual involvement was ranked in terms of time and energy expended in professional development activities for four different categories: (1) by the 1956 and 1961 classes and the entire sample; (2) by type of librarian--academic, public, school, and special; (3) by sex; (4) by population concentration of residence.

Again, there was a great similarity of degree of involvement indicated by all of these categories.   In general, the degree of involvement did not vary to any statistically significant degree although the least agreement was between the school librarians and the special librarians.

The activities which involved most time, energy, and effort were: reading professional literature in library science and subject specialities, attending library conventions and meetings, participating in library associations, and visiting other libraries.

They generally seemed to be least involved with service in political clubs, membership in employee unions or in honor societies, and formal course work leading to a sixth-year credential in library science.

There was, however, some disagreement in specific areas.

Public librarians spent more of their time in speaking to community groups and with in-service training, which they ranked 2 for involvement.   Both public and academic librarians generally spent more of their time attending staff association activities.

The academic librarians spent more time and energy in recruiting, research, participating in employee unions, and in service to church groups.

Striving for increased accessibility of books and libraries took most of the school librarians' time.   In addition, they were more involved in working for an advanced degree in a subject specialty or in meeting certification requirements.

The special librarians were more involved with writing and editing.   Generally they were least involved with taking formal course work.

Male librarians spent more time working for an advanced degree in their subject specialty or for a Ph. D.   The women participated more in community service groups and in teaching library science courses.

Librarians from medium-sized cities and small towns placed more emphasis on recruitment, service in church groups, participation in non-library professional associations, and research, than did those from cities of 100,000 and over.

Librarians from small towns were more involved than the
others with the promotion of new materials and equipment, visiting
other libraries, and formal course work. However, they spent
much less time and energy than the other two groups in in-service
training.

Relation of Involvement to Importance

The relationship between involvement and importance was
ranked by four different categories: (1) by the 1956 and 1961 classes
and the entire sample; (2) by type of librarian--academic, public,
school, and special; (3) by sex; (4) by population concentration of
residence.

The rank order correlations for involvement and importance
were also very similar, ranging from 0.65 for the academic librarians to 0.96 for the public librarians, with the average for the
total sample, 0.88.

Generally activities which ranked most important also ranked
highest in degree of involvement: professional reading, library conventions and meetings, library associations, and visiting other libraries.   The items which ranked lowest in degree of involvement
were also generally considered of less importance: political clubs;
employee unions; honor societies; and formal course work for a salary increment, certification requirements, or a sixth-year credential in library science.

There were, however, some activities which the sample felt
deserved considerably more time and energy than were being expended:

1. Legislative promotion of librarians' benefits, such as re-
   tirement and tenure, of legal support of intellectual freedom, and of financial support for libraries.
2. Participation in small, voluntary study groups.
3. Writing for the profession.
4. Engaging in research.
5. Formal course work toward a Ph.D. degree in library science or a subject field.

Based on comparative rankings alone, it appeared that the librarians felt the following activities took more time and energy than

they warranted.
1. Participation in non-library professional association.
2. Participation in community groups, especially the church.
3. Participation in staff association activities within the
   library.
4. Promotion of new materials and equipment.

III. Comparison of Items by Degree of Involvement
and Degree of Importance

From the rank-order comparisons used in the previous section it was possible to ascertain the overall relative importance and
degree of involvement for the 37 activities as perceived by different
categories of librarians, but not the gap between what the librarians
thought was important and what they were actually doing about each
activity.   To determine if there were such gaps, a horizontal item
by item analysis, with two different steps, was used.

Statistical Analyses Used

First the correlation coefficients for the relationship between
the involvement response and the importance response were computed for each of the 37 double-entry activity items. [6]
Of these correlations, 31 were not significant for the 1956
class and 21 were not significant for the 1961 class.   The non-significant correlations indicate nothing about the importance of the
item although the amount of time and energy expended is known.
The positive correlations indicate that to the extent that time and
energy are spent on these activities, they seem important to the respondents.
Second, the data were analyzed by the paired t-test to determine if the gap was significant between what the librarian was doing and what he thought he should be doing for each of the 37 activity items.   Although in the previous section the comparisons were
made between several categories of librarians, in this section they
are limited to the 1956 and 1961 classes.

Gaps Between Importance and Involvement
for the 1956 Graduate

The positively significant differences indicated in Table XXIV show that the 1956 librarians were spending less time, energy, and effort on 78 per cent (29) of the activities than they considered important for maximum professional growth.

For the remaining 8 items, the time and energy spent was approximately proportionate to their evaluation of the importance of the activities. The paired t-test revealed no significant gap for the following activities:

Item 3.   Assistance to other librarians in projects related to the profession.
Item 9.   Reading in the area of subject specialization.
Item 10. Visiting other libraries.
Item 25. Participation in staff association for library employees.
Item 26. Participation on committee within the library.
Item 33. Participation in non-library professional association.
Item 34. Participation in honor societies.
Item 36. Service in church groups.

Figure 1 shows the size of the gaps between importance and involvement for those activities that the librarians ranked as most important in the previous section. Three activities showed no significant gaps: professional reading in the area of specialization, visiting other libraries, and library committees. For the remaining 12 items more time and energy was needed. The greatest gaps, which showed that little time and energy were spent on activities ranked the most important, were: legislative promotion of tenure and other benefits, promotion of intellectual freedom, formal course work for enrichment purposes, legislative activity for financial support of libraries, writing for the profession, recruitment, working for the increased accessibility of books and libraries, and participation in workshops and seminars.

Table XXIV
Mean Difference Between Degree of Involvement and Degree of
Importance of Activity Items as Perceived by the Librarians in
the Sample, Based on Application of the Matched t-test: 1967

Activity Concerning Professional Development	Relationship between Involvement and Importance			
	1956		1961	
	N	Mean Diff.	N	Mean Diff.
Individual Activities				
Extra-Library Service:				
1. Speaking to community groups	38	.66**	64	.59**
2. Recruitment for profession	44	.75**	75	.60**
3. Assistance to other librarians	38	.34	61	.62**
4. Promotion of new materials	33	.45**	53	.15
5. Teaching library science courses	37	1.11**	49	.78**
6. Working for increased accessibility	39	.69**	64	.78**
7. Support of promotional campaigns	34	.53**	56	.80**
Personal Activities, such as:				
8. Reading professional literature in Library Science	49	.39*	84	.31**
9. Reading in subject specialization	44	.11	79	.42**
10. Visiting other libraries	49	-.12	76	.33**
11. Writing for the profession	41	.85**	56	1.00**
12. Editing for the profession	33	.64**	47	.57**
13. Research	38	1.00**	56	1.00**
14. Entertaining foreign librarians	36	.78**	48	.44**
Formal Course Work for:				
15. Ph. D. in Library Science or subject speciality	33	1.00**	48	.94**
16. Master's in subject speciality	27	.78*	43	1.19**
17. 6th yr. credential in Lib. Science	16	1.19**	24	.79**
18. Certification requirements	16	.81*	25	.32*
19. Salary increment	23	.96**	34	.56*
20. Enrichment purposes	35	1.11**	54	.81**
Legislative Promotion of:				
21. Financial support for libraries	39	1.03**	65	1.26**
22. Legal support of intellectual freedom	39	1.18**	61	1.28**
23. Librarian's tenure, retire't, etc.	35	1.34**	57	1.19**
Group Activities				
In a Library:				
24. In-service training	38	.53**	58	.28
25. Staff association	34	.24	60	.07
26. Library committees	39	.44	51	.45*
27. Employee unions	18	1.22**	33	.64**
Library Oriented, but Outside Specific Library:				
28. Library Associations	48	.52**	79	.30*
29. Alumni association of my library school	37	.68**	67	.33**

Table XXIV (cont.)

Activity Concerning Professional Development	Relationship between Involvement and Importance			
	1956		1961	
	N	Mean Diff.	N	Mean Diff.
30. Library conventions and/or meetings	50	.62**	79	.22**
31. Workshops, seminars, institutes	44	.68**	66	.68**
32. Small voluntary study groups	30	1.03**	50	1.06**
33. Non-library professional associations	35	.31	53	.21
34. Honor Societies	30	.33	37	.54**
Community Groups:				
35. Community service clubs	33	.82**	50	.46**
36. Church groups	36	.31	58	-.09
37. Political clubs	22	.82**	35	.43*

** Significant at 1% level.
 * Significant at 5% level.

Gaps Between Importance and Involvement
for the 1961 Graduate

Table XXIV, page 141, also shows that the 1961 librarians were spending less time, energy, and effort on 84 per cent (31) of the activities they considered important for maximum professional growth.

For the remaining 6 items, the time and energy spent was approximately proportionate to their evaluation of the importance of the activities. The paired t-test revealed no significant gap for the following activities:

Item 4. Promotion of new materials and equipment.
Item 24. Participation in in-service (on the job) training programs.
Item 25. Participation in staff association for library employees.
Item 30. Participation in library conventions and meetings.
Item 33. Membership in non-library professional associations.
Item 36. Service in church groups.

Figure 1

Gap Between Perceived Importance and Relative Time and
Energy Spent on Professional Development Activities
Ranked Most Important by the 1956 MLS Graduates: 1967

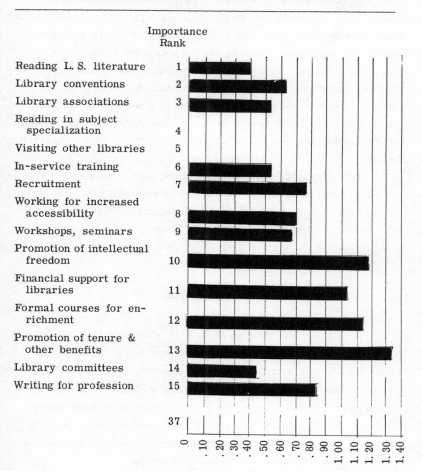

Importance
Rank

Reading L. S. literature	1
Library conventions	2
Library associations	3
Reading in subject specialization	4
Visiting other libraries	5
In-service training	6
Recruitment	7
Working for increased accessibility	8
Workshops, seminars	9
Promotion of intellectual freedom	10
Financial support for libraries	11
Formal courses for enrichment	12
Promotion of tenure & other benefits	13
Library committees	14
Writing for profession	15
	37

Mean Difference Between Importance
and Involvement

Figure 2 shows that of the 15 items ranked most important, there were 13 on which, in actual practice, the librarians felt more time and energy should be spent. Of the 13 rankings, they felt the most additional time and energy should be spent on the following: promotion of intellectual freedom, legislative promotion of increased financial support for libraries, the promotion of tenure and other benefits for librarians, working for the increased accessibility of books and libraries, participation in workshops and seminars, professional assistance to other librarians, and recruitment for the profession. Reading professional literature in a subject specialization and in Library Science ranked as the 2 highest items in importance but the sample felt more time should be devoted to both of these activities.

Two activities showed no significant gap: attending library conventions and in-service training. It is interesting that two activities appear in this list of the 1961 respondents that did not appear for 1956: speaking to community groups, and assistance to other librarians in off-the-job projects related to the profession.

IV. Conclusion

No matter how the librarians were classified they all were generally spending the most time and energy on the same professional development activities and they generally thought that those activities were the ones which would do most for their growth in the profession. However, there was a statistically significant gap between the amount of time and energy they were expending and the amount of time and energy they thought they should be expending on these activities for their maximum development.[7]

The findings in this chapter raise a question which is discussed in Chapter IX. Are the things that the librarians desire the most and think the most important really the things that would upgrade the profession most?

Figure 2

Gap Between Perceived Importance and Relative Time and
Energy Spent on Professional Development Activities
Ranked Most Important by the 1961 MLS Graduates: 1967

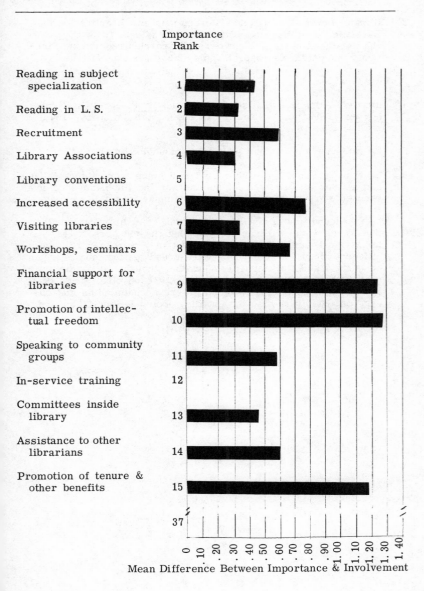

Importance
Rank

Reading in subject specialization	1
Reading in L. S.	2
Recruitment	3
Library Associations	4
Library conventions	5
Increased accessibility	6
Visiting libraries	7
Workshops, seminars	8
Financial support for libraries	9
Promotion of intellectual freedom	10
Speaking to community groups	11
In-service training	12
Committees inside library	13
Assistance to other librarians	14
Promotion of tenure & other benefits	15
	37

0 .10 .20 .30 .40 .50 .60 .70 .80 .90 1.00 1.10 1.20 1.30 1.40

Mean Difference Between Importance & Involvement

Notes

1. Blizzard, Samuel W.   "The Minister's Dilemma"   The Christian Century 73:509 (April 25, 1956).

2. Dillman, Beryl R.   "Teacher Perceptions and Practices in the
   Development of Responsibility for Professional Growth" (paper
   read at the American Educational Research Association, Pick-
   Congress Hotel, Chicago, Illinois, February 25, 1961).

3. Ibid., p. 2-3.

4. Edwards, Allen L.   Statistical Analysis for Students in Psychology and Education   (New York: Rinehart & Company, 1946)
   p. 217-225.

5. The rankings for all four categories ranged from 1 to 37.

6. The N is different for each correlation since those items which
   had neither the involvement column nor the importance column
   checked were eliminated from the computations.

7. The gap found among the librarians was of a different type than
   that found in the Dillman study among the teachers.   The
   former had significant gaps, too, but they were generally of a
   different kind.   The teachers were spending time and energy
   on certain kinds of activities, but they thought for maximum
   growth they should be spending their time on other kinds of
   activities; whereas the librarians were spending time and energy on the things they thought they should be doing, but not
   in sufficient depth.   Dillman, op. cit., p. 13.

Chapter VII

Relationship Between Degree and Kind of Motivation Toward
Professional Development and Selected Variables

Special devices were developed to determine if it is possible
to measure degree and kind of motivation. The results of these
measures were then related to other variables from the study for
increased understanding of what motivates librarians to participate
in professional development activities. The hypotheses tested are
reported in this chapter.

I. Identification of Motivational Variables

This study developed 4 different scores in order to measure
the librarians' motivations for professional development, based on
their answers to Parts 5 and 6 of the questionnaire. The theoretical framework developed by Abraham Maslow[1] and Douglas Mc-
Gregor[2] for the classification of motives according to a hierarchy
of needs, and Swanson's classification of motives in regard to professional development,[3] were used as guides for these measurements. These special scores are as follows:

1. Degree of Professional Improvement Motivation.

2. Kind of Professional Improvement Motivation.

3. Degree of Formal Study Motivation.

4. Kind of Formal Study Motivation.

Each of these measurements was based on rankings assigned
to either 4 or 5 questions of the questionnaire and each respondent
was given a definite score for each of these 4 measurements.[4]
While most of the variables in this study have been based on instruments that compared the librarians in relation to the others in this

study, these 4 motivational variables were measured by a rating system that was intrinsic in itself.   The scores are based strictly on the responses recorded in the questionnaire.

For purposes of analysis, correlation coefficients were computed for each motivational variable on the basis of the actual scores made and a high-low dichotomy.   For the latter, the total sample of 138 was arbitrarily divided at the frequency unit containing the median.   Those who were at the median or above were placed in the high category for that graduating class; the remainder were placed in the low category.   This same method was followed for each of the 4 motivational variables.   In interpreting the statistics according to the scoring system devised, the highest score possible for each variable was 1. 0.   All of the relationships reported between the motivational variables and others in the study are significant at the 5 per cent level.

II.   Professional Improvement Motivation

The two special devices used to give an approximate measurement of the degree and kind of motivation will be presented in turn.   The hypotheses that apply to each, in relation to selected variables, will be either accepted or rejected.   Acceptance of the hypothesis is shown by the statement of no relationship and rejection by the statement that a significant relationship exists.   The hypothesis number as listed in Chapter I is indicated immediately after each variable.

Degree of Professional Improvement Motivation

Of the 1956 respondents, 46. 2 per cent were in the high category (score of 0. 5 and above), as compared with 52. 3 per cent of the class of 1961.   See Table XXV.   The average score for the class of 1956 was 0. 38 as compared to 0. 39 for the 1961 class. See Table XXVI.

The null hypotheses 1-a through 1-k (Chapter I) of no rela-

Table XXV

Distribution of the Librarians in the Sample by Degree and Kind
of Motivation for Professional Improvement: 1967

Motivational Variables	1956[a] No.	%	1961[b] No.	%	Total Sample[c] No.	%
Degree of Professional Improvement Motivation						
High (0.5 and above)	24	46.2	45	52.3	69	50.0
Low (less than 0.5)	28	53.8	41	57.7	69	50.0
Kind of Professional Improvement Motivation						
High (0.6 and over)	26	50.0	37	43.0	63	45.7
Low (less than 0.6)	26	50.0	49	57.0	75	54.3

[a]N for 1956 = 52

[b]N for 1961 = 86

[c]N for Total Sample = 138

tionship between Professional Improvement Degree and selected variables in the study are reported in the following sections.   The null
hypotheses of no relationship between Professional Improvement
Motivation Degree and the variables age (1-a), undergraduate major
(1-c), years between the Bachelor's and MLS degree (1-d), degree
of aspiration (1-f), type of aspiration (1-g), and salary (1-i), were
accepted for both the class of 1956 and the class of 1961.

The other hypotheses were rejected either for the class of
1956 or 1961.   There was a significant relationship between Professional Improvement Motivation Degree and each of the following for
the class of 1961:   sex (1-b), Professional Index Score (1-e), and
years in present institution (1-h); and for the class of 1956:   position in library (1-j) and perceived attitude of administration and supervisor (1-k).   The significant relationships and some of the non-
significant relationships will now be discussed.

150 Professional Development of Librarians

Age (1-a)

There was no significant relationship between age and Professional Improvement Motivation Degree. This would seem to reinforce the finding in Chapter V on encouraging and discouraging factors toward motivation for professional improvement, which indicated that age was considered one of the least important of the 42 factors listed. However, 52.3 per cent of the later graduates (found in Chapter III to be 3.5 years younger on the average) were in the high category concerning professional improvement motivation degree, as compared to 46.2 per cent of the slightly older group in the earlier graduating class.

Table XXVI

Mean and Standard Deviation of Degree and Kind of Professional
Improvement and Formal Course Work Motivation
of the Librarians in the Sample: 1967

Motivational Variables	Mean[a]	
	1956	1961
Degree of Professional Improvement Motivation Score	.38	.39
Kind of Professional Improvement Motivation Score	.20	.28
Degree of Formal Course Work Motivation Score	.30	.37
Kind of Formal Course Work Motivation Score	.46	.42

[a]N for 1956 librarians = 52
N for 1961 librarians = 86

Sex (1-b)

There was no significant relationship between sex and Professional Improvement Motivation Degree for the class of 1956.

For the class of 1961 there was a significant relationship, showing
that there was a slight tendency for the women to have a higher
Professional Improvement Motivation Degree Score than the men.

Professional Index Score (1-e)

There was an association (0. 31 for the class of 1956 and
0. 22 for the class of 1961) between the Professional Index Score
and the score assigned Professional Improvement Motivation Degree.
For the class of 1956 there was also a relationship (0. 34) between
the exact Professional Index Score and the high category of the Professional Improvement Motivation Degree.   In the total of all the
relationships between degree and kind of motivation, for both professional improvement and formal course work, there were not a
great many associations found, but within the constituent parts of
the Professional Index Score there were a number of significant relationships.

The significant positive correlations showed that there was a
tendency for those who had a higher Professional Improvement Motivation Degree Score to have read more library journals, for example, than those who had a lower score.   The negative correlations indicated that those having a higher Formal Course Work
Motivation Degree did less research, for example, than those less
highly motivated toward formal course work.   The relationships
which were not significant indicate that no prediction whatsoever
can be made about these particular professional improvement activities from a knowledge of the persons' Professional Improvement
Motivation Degree Score.

Degree of Aspiration (1-f)

There was no significant relationship between level of aspiration and Professional Improvement Motivation Degree.   This might
indicate that the librarian regarded professional improvement activities as only incidental to his aspirations.   A more precise
measure of aspirations might eliminate this apprehension, but it is

reinforced by the fact that there was also no significant relationship between Professional Improvement Motivation Degree and kind of aspiration in librarianship, satisfaction with career, or career desire to remain in or leave the profession.

It might also imply the reason for this lack of relationship: that the profession has not had offerings in the field of professional improvement which meet the personal needs and aspirations of the librarians and, therefore, they have not felt motivated to participate in them.

Years in Present Institution (1-h)

There was an association (0. 24) between number of years in present library and Professional Improvement Degree for the class of 1961, but not for the class of 1956.   This indicates that those in librarianship 5 years are more motivated toward professional improvement activity than those in longer.

Position in Library (1-j)

There was an association (0. 30) between the respondent who was head or assistant head of his library and Professional Improvement Degree for the class of 1956, but not for the class of 1961. This indicates that those more recent graduates who were already in the top administrative positions tended to have a higher degree of motivation toward professional improvement than the others in the class.

Perceived Attitudes of Administrators
and Supervisors (1-k)

For the class of 1956, but not for the class of 1961, there was a significant relationship (0. 28) between what librarians perceived as the attitudes of their supervisors and the administration toward professional development and their Degree of Professional Improvement Motivation.   Those with higher motivation scores in

the class of 1956 felt their administration or supervisor generally
had a favorable attitude toward formal course work. For this comparison, the attitudes of strongly favorable and mildly favorable
were combined with neutral; mildly opposed and strongly opposed
were grouped.

Conclusion

The findings for this set of hypotheses lead to the conclusion
that the degree of professional improvement motivation was greater
for those 1956 librarians who had a higher Professional Index Score,
who had become head or assistant head of their libraries, and who
perceived the attitude of their administration or supervisor as being favorable toward their development activities. It was also higher for those who worked in libraries with fewer employees.

The degree of motivation toward professional improvement
was greater for those 1961 librarians who were women, who had a
higher Professional Index Score, and who had worked more years
in their present institution.

Kind of Professional Improvement Motivation

As with degree of professional improvement motivation, librarians were classified either as high or low when the distribution
was dichotomized at the median. This provided 50 per cent in the
high group for the class of 1956 and 43 per cent in the high group
for the class of 1961. See Table XXV, page 149. The average
score for the 1956 class was 0.20 as compared with 0.28 for the
later graduates, as indicated in Table XXVI, page 150.

As previously indicated, high Kind of Professional Improvement Motivation refers to the tendency of a person to seek self-
actualization and the highest use of his potential. These are ego-
enhancing motives. Low Kind of Formal Course Work Motivation
refers to the tendency of a person to seek security and to belong
or to be accepted. These are ego-defensive motives.

Specifically referring to hypotheses 2-a through 2-k, the null

hypotheses of no relationship between Kind of Professional Improvement Motivation and age (2-a), sex (2-b), undergraduate major (2-
c), years between Bachelor's and MLS (2-d), degree of aspiration
(2-f), type of aspiration (2-g), years in present institution (2-h),
position in library (2-j), and perceived attitude of administration
and/or supervisor (2-k) were accepted for both the class of 1956
and 1961.

The other two hypotheses were rejected either for the class
of 1956 or 1961. There was a significant relationship between Kind
of Professional Improvement Motivation and each of the following:
Professional Index Score (2-e) for the class of 1956, but the null
hypothesis was accepted for the class of 1961; salary (2-i) for the
class of 1961, but the null hypothesis accepted for the class of 1956.

Professional Index Score (2-e)

There was a significant relationship between Kind of Professional Improvement Motivation and the Professional Index Score of
the 1956 graduate (0.29 when compared with actual score; 0.30
when compared with the high-low dichotomy). Those with a higher
Kind of Professional Improvement Motivation Score tended also to
have a higher Professional Index Score in the class of 1956. Individual components of the Professional Index Score indicated that this
relationship pertained especially to the Occupational Index which
measured attitudes toward the profession rather than actual accomplishments or number of activities engaged in. Therefore, in a
sense this relationship may be inflated because certain elements in
the two measurements may be similar.

Salary (2-i)

There was a significant relationship between Kind of Professional Improvement Motivation and the various measurements of salary for the 1961 graduate both for present salary (-.26) and for difference between current salary and first professional salary (-.23).
The null hypothesis of no relationship between salary and Kind of

Professional Improvement Motivation was accepted for the 1956 graduate, however. These negative correlations for the 1961 graduate show that the librarian with a higher type of professional improvement motivation made less salary than those with a lower Kind of Professional Improvement Motivation Score. It might be hypothesized that being more interested in self-fulfillment and self-actualization than in security, matters of salary were of less concern to him than to those individuals less highly motivated. Such a possibility would reinforce the findings in Chapter V that salary in itself was not a prime motivator toward professional development activity.

Conclusion

The findings in connection with these hypotheses lead to the conclusion that there were few significant relationships between kind of professional improvement and other variables. This lack of statistical significance indicating association may in itself be the most important finding in connection with this type of motivation. It may indicate that kind of professional improvement motivation follows no particular pattern and is related to few, if any, of the characteristics to which it was related here. Or it may simply indicate that the instrument was far too simple to discern basic differences in so complex a concept as kind of motivation.

Two exceptions were that the 1956 librarians with a higher Kind of Professional Improvement Score also tended to have a higher Professional Index Score and 1961 librarians with a higher kind of professional improvement motivation made less salary.

III.   Formal Course Work Motivation

The following paragraphs discuss the relations between Degree and Kind of Motivation for Formal Course Work and selected variables. The hypotheses 3-a through 3-k and 4-a through 4-k presented in Chapter I will be discussed in this section.

Degree of Formal Course Work Motivation

As with professional improvement motivation, librarians were classified into a high or low category. 44.2 per cent of the 1956 class were in the high group as compared to 50.0 per cent of the 1961 class, as indicated in Table XXVII. Comparisons were also made with the actual scores. The mean score for Formal Course Work Degree for the 1956 class was 0.30 as compared to 0.37 for the class of 1961, as shown in Table XXVI, page 150.

Hypotheses 3-a through 3-k are discussed in this section. The null hypotheses of no relationship between Formal Course Work Degree and the variables sex (3-b), undergraduate major (3-c), Professional Index Score (3-e), years in present institution (3-h), and position in library (3-j) were accepted for both the class of 1956 and the class of 1961.

The other hypotheses were rejected in relation to one class, but accepted for the other as indicated. There was a significant relationship between Degree of Formal Course Work Motivation and each of the following: age (3-a) for the class of 1956, but not for the class of 1961; years between Bachelor's and MLS (3-d) for the class of 1956, but not for the class of 1961; degree of aspiration (3-f) for the class of 1961, but not for the class of 1956; salary (3-i) for the class of 1956, but not for the class of 1961; and perceived attitudes of a relevant group (3-k) for the class of 1961, but not for the class of 1956.

Age (3-a)

There was a significant negative relationship between age and Degree of Formal Course Work Motivation for the older class (-0.30). Relatively more of the younger members in the class of 1956 had a high Formal Course Work Motivation Degree and relatively more of the older librarians in the class were low.

Generally those in the class of 1956 had a lower score, 0.30 as compared to 0.37 for the 1961 class.

Table XXVII

Distribution of the Librarians in the Sample by Degree and Kind
of Motivation for Formal Course Work: 1967

Motivational Variables	1956[a]		1961[b]		Total Sample[c]	
	No.	%	No.	%	No.	%
Formal Course Work Motivation Degree						
High (0. 2 and above)	23	44. 2	43	50. 0	66	47. 8
Low (less than 0. 2)	29	55. 8	43	50. 0	72	52. 2
Formal Course Work Motivation Kind						
High (0. 6 and over)	26	50. 0	37	43. 0	63	45. 7
Low (less than 0. 6)	26	50. 0	49	57. 0	75	54. 3

[a]N for 1956 = 52

[b]N for 1961 = 86

[c]N for Total Sample = 138

Years Between Bachelor's and
MLS Degree (3-d)

This variable is related to age and provided much the same
results. When the exact score for the Formal Course Work Motivation Degree was used there was a significant correlation of -0. 31
and when the high-low dichotomy was used the correlation was -0. 27.
This negative significant relationship shows that relatively more of
those members of the class who had a greater time lag (and therefore would currently tend to be older) between Bachelor's and MLS
tended to have a low Formal Course Work Motivation Degree. This
is an important relationship because it indicates that the greater
this time gap the less interest there is among librarians to take
formal course work to avoid obsolescence.

Degree of Aspiration (3-f)

There was a significant positive relationship between Formal Course Work Motivation Degree and level of aspiration for the class of 1961 of 0. 41 when based on actual Formal Course Work Score and 0. 35 when based on the high-low dichotomy. This positive tendency indicates that the 1961 graduate sees formal course work as a means of reaching his aspiration, while a lack of any such relationship would indicate the opposite.

Salary (3-i)

There was a significant negative relationship between Formal Course Work Motivation Degree and salary for the class of 1956, but not for the class of 1961. Those making a lower salary in the class of 1956 tended to have a higher Formal Course Work Motivation Degree than those who were making a higher salary. One possible interpretation is that through the formal course work the 1956 librarian hoped to be able to increase his salary. This is somewhat reinforced by the fact that whereas salary was not considered important as related to professional improvement by the 1956 graduate in the encouraging-deterring list of factors (Rank of 37. 5 out of 42), it did rate considerably higher as related to formal course work (Rank of 17. 5 out of 42). See Table XIII, page 90.

Perceived Attitudes (3-k)

There was a significant relationship between Formal Course Work Degree and perceived attitude of the administration and supervisor for the class of 1961 of -0. 28. This indicates that those members of the class of 1961 who perceived opposition, either strong or mild, toward professional improvement activities tended to have a higher Formal Course Work Motivation Degree Score. Possibly these librarians felt deterred from professional improvement activity and found formal course work the chief way open to them to broaden their knowledge and skills.

Conclusion

The findings in connection with these hypotheses warrant the
conclusion that the Degree of Formal Course Work Motivation is
greater among the 1956 graduates who were younger, who had a
fewer number of years between the Bachelor's and MLS degree, and
who had a lower salary. The degree of motivation was greater for
the 1961 graduates who had a higher degree of aspiration and who
had an administration or supervisor who did not favor professional
improvement activities.

Kind of Formal Course work Motivation

As with degree of motivation, two different bases of comparison were used:

1. High and low with the population arbitrarily divided at
the frequency unit containing the median for the whole sample of
138. This placed 50.0 per cent in the high group in 1956 and 43.0
per cent in the high group for 1961. See Table XXVII, p. 157.

2. The exact scores made regarding Kind of Formal Course
Work Motivation. The average was 0.46 for the class of 1956 as
compared with 0.42 for the class of 1961. See Table XXVI, page
150.

The null hypotheses, 4-a through 4-j, of no relationship between other variables and Kind of Formal Course Work Motivation
will be treated in this section. Only those variables with significant relationships or where special comment is needed will be considered separately.

There was no significant relationship between Kind of Formal Course Work Motivation and any one of the following: age
(4-a); sex (4-b); undergraduate major (4-c); Professional Index
Score (4-e); type of aspiration (4-g); years in present institution
(4-h); perceived attitude of a relevant group (4-k).

The other hypotheses were rejected in relation to one class,

but accepted for the other as indicated. There was a significant relationship between Kind of Formal Course Work Motivation and each
of the following: years between the Bachelor's degree and the MLS
(4-d) for the class of 1961, but not for the class of 1956; degree of
aspiration (4-f) for class of 1961, but not for the class of 1956;
salary (4-i) for the class of 1961, but not for the class of 1956;
position in library (4-j) for the 1956 class, but not for the class of
1961.

Age (4-a)

Although there was no significant positive relationship between age and Kind of Formal Course Work Motivation, and the null
hypothesis was accepted as indicated in the preceding paragraph, it
is interesting to note that those who had been in librarianship longer
(and generally were older) had a higher mean Kind of Formal-Study
Motivation Degree Score than did members of the later graduating
class.   This may mean that older librarians were more likely to
pursue graduate work to make the best use of their own talents
(self-actualization) and to gain prestige rather than to protect themselves or to gain security.

Years Between Bachelor's and MLS (4-d)

There was a significant positive relationship between years
between the Bachelor's and MLS degrees and Kind of Formal Course
Work Motivation for the class of 1961 (.22), but not for the class
of 1956.   This indicates that a larger proportion of those who had
a greater time lag between degrees (and, therefore, were generally
older) had a higher type motivation toward formal course work than
did those who went more directly to library school.   This may indicate that older librarians in the 1956 class who desire to pursue
formal course work would be more likely to do so in order to make
the best use of their own talents (self-actualization) and to gain
prestige rather than to protect themselves or to gain security.

Professional Index Score (4-e)

There was no significant relationship between Professional
Index Score and Kind of Formal Course Work Motivation for either
the class of 1956 or the class of 1961 and, therefore, the null hypothesis of no relationship was accepted. This lack of relationship
might be important in itself, however. If the true professional is
one who seeks to satisfy himself, to achieve self-actualization or
to develop himself to his fullest capabilities, then one might ask if
the librarians questioned had achieved a higher level of professionalization.

In an analysis betweek Kind of Formal Course Work Motivation and several of the constituent parts of the Professional Index,
there were some significant relationships, as indicated in Table
XXVII, page 157. Four of the 5 significant relationships related to
the class of 1961, indicating that those members of the class of
1961 who belonged to more professional associations, and read more
professional literature, tended to have a higher type motive toward
formal course work than those who were less active. The other
significant relationship between Kind of Formal Course Work Motivation and attitude toward employee problems applied to the class
of 1956 and was higher (0. 35). This indicated that those members
in the class who tended to view the employee as a whole person
and to be interested in his on-the-job as well as his off-the-job problems tended to be motivated toward formal course work for reasons
of self-development rather than for reasons of security on the job.

Degree of Aspiration (4-f)

There was a significant positive relationship between degree
of aspiration and Kind of Formal Course Work Motivation (0. 25
when the actual motivation scores were compared with the exact aspiration scores and 0. 23 when the actual motivation scores were
compared with the aspiration high-low dichotomy) for the class of
1961, but not for the class of 1956. This would indicate that those

Professional Development of Librarians

in the class of 1961 who had a high degree of aspiration score
tended to be those who would pursue formal course work to make
the best use of their potential rather than for security.

Salary (4-i)

There was a significant negative relationship between salary
currently received and the Kind of Formal Course Work for the
class of 1961, but not for the class of 1956. This negative correlation of -0.28 indicates that those receiving lower salaries were
motivated more toward formal course work because of a desire for
development of potential than for security.

Position (4-j)

There was a significant positive correlation between those
who were heads or assistant heads of libraries in the class of 1956
and Kind of Formal Course Work Motivation, but not for the class
of 1961.   There was a tendency for those in the 1956 class who
were in the top positions of leadership to be more highly motivated
toward formal course work because of the opportunity it gave them
for self-development than for job security.

Conclusion

The findings in connection with these hypotheses warrant the
conclusion that the Kind of Formal Course Work Motivation is higher
among the 1956 librarians who had more years between the Bachelor's degree and the MLS and who had achieved the position of director or assistant director of their library.   The Kind of Formal
Course Work Motivation was higher for the 1961 graduates who had
a higher degree of aspiration, and who were currently earning a
lower salary.

There were also more correlations between Kind of Formal
Course Work Motivation and the other variables than there were
regarding Kind of Professional Improvement Motivation.   This may

indicate that the Kind of Formal Course Work Motivation follows a more specific pattern than does Professional Improvement Motivation.

IV. Relationships Between Motivational Variables

This section will review the relationship between the motivational variables. The null hypothesis 5, stated in Chapter I, of no relationship between any possible combination of 2 of the 4 motivational variables was only accepted in part. All of the correlation coefficients are shown between all possible combinations of these 4 variables in Table XXVIII. Those that are significant at the 5 per cent level are starred. In making the comparisons for each motivational variable, 2 scores are given: the high-low dichotomy and the actual individual score achieved.

Professional Improvement Motivation
Degree (5a)

The null hypothesis of no relationship between Professional Improvement Motivation Degree and Kind of Professional Improvement Motivation was accepted for both the 1956 and the 1961 class.

The hypothesis of no relationship relative to Professional Improvement Motivation Degree and Formal Course Work Motivation Degree was accepted for the class of 1956, but rejected for the class of 1961. For the 1961 graduates there was a significant relationship (both actual score and high-low dichotomy). Those librarians with high Professional Improvement Motivation Degree Scores also tended to have high Formal Course Work Motivation Degree Scores.

The hypothesis of no relationship relative to Professional Improvement Motivation Degree and Kind of Formal Course Work Motivation was accepted for the class of 1961, but rejected for the class of 1956. Proportionately more 1956 librarians with a higher Professional Improvement Motivation Degree Score tended to have a

Table XXVIII

Summary of Association (Correlation Coefficients) Between the Four Motivational Variables
of the Librarians in the Sample: 1967[a]

Hypothesis No.[b]	Motivation Measurement	P.I.M.D.[a]		K.P.I.M.[a]		F.C.W.M.D.[a]		K.F.C.W.M.[a]	
		Actual Score	High-Low	Actual Score	High-Low	Actual Score	High-Low	Actual Score	High-Low
	1956 MLS librarians (N = 52)								
5a	**P.I.M.D.**								
	Actual score	--	--	.10	.10	-.04	-.08	.29*	.16
	High-low dichotomy	--	--	.11	.10	-.06	-.13	.13	-.00
5b	**K.P.I.M.**								
	Actual score	.10	.11	--	--	.06	.20	-.24	-.22
	High-low dichotomy	.10	.10	--	--	.07	.21	-.17	-.20
5c	**F.C.W.M.D.**								
	Actual score	-.04	-.06	.06	.07	--	--	.47*	.46*
	High-low dichotomy	-.08	-.13	.20	.21	--	--	.42*	.43*
5d	**K.F.C.W.M.**								
	Actual score	.29*	.13	-.24	-.17	.47*	.42*	--	--
	High-low dichotomy	.16	-.00	-.22	-.20	.46*	.43*	--	--

Table XXVIII (cont.)

Hypoth-esis No.[b]	Motivation Measurement	P.I.M.D.[a] Actual Score	P.I.M.D.[a] High-Low	K.P.I.M.[a] Actual Score	K.P.I.M.[a] High-Low	F.C.W.M.D.[a] Actual Score	F.C.W.M.D.[a] High-Low	K.F.C.W.M.[a] Actual Score	K.F.C.W.M.[a] High-Low
	1961 MLS librarians (N = 86)								
5a	**P.I.M.D.**								
	Actual score	--	--	.11	.03	.38*	.40*	.17	.20
	High-low dichotomy	--	--	-.07	-.14	.23*	.29*	.01	.06
5b	**K.P.I.M.**								
	Actual score	.11	-.07	--	--	.17	.08	.09	.16
	High-low dichotomy	.03	-.14	--	--	.09	.02	.19	.21
5c	**F.C.W.M.D.**								
	Actual score	.38*	.23*	.17	.09	--	--	.43*	.43*
	High-low dichotomy	.40*	.29*	.08	.02	--	--	.40*	.39*
5d	**K.F.C.W.M.**								
	Actual score	.17	.01	.09	.19	.43*	.40*	--	--
	High-low dichotomy	.20	.06	.16	.21	.43*	.39*	--	--

* Relationships having a correlation coefficient at 0.05.

[a] P.I.M.D. = Professional Improvement Motivation Degree
K.P.I.M. = Kind of Professional Improvement Motivation
F.C.W.M.D. = Formal Course Work Motivation Degree
K.F.C.W.M. = Kind of Formal Course Work Motivation

[b] Numbers refer to list of hypotheses in Chapter I.

higher Formal Course Work Score.

Kind of Professional Improvement Motivation (5b)

The null hypothesis of no relationship between Kind of Professional Improvement Motivation and other possible combinations of
the motivational variables was accepted for both classes.

Formal Course Work Motivation Degree (5c)

The null hypothesis of no relationship between Formal Course
Work Motivation Degree and Professional Improvement Motivation
Degree was accepted for the class of 1956, but not for the class of
1961. All correlations both by score and high-low dichotomy
showed a significant relationship. Librarians with higher type motives toward formal course work in the class of 1961 were likely
to have a more intense desire to pursue professional improvement
activities.

The null hypothesis of no relationship between Formal Course
Work Motivation Degree and Kind of Formal Course Work Motivation was rejected for both the classes of 1956 and 1961. There was
a significant relationship for both actual scores and high-low dichotomy. Librarians with a high kind of motivation toward course work
(self-actualization and fulfillment) also tended to have a strong degree of determination to pursue formal course work. This was the
strongest intercorrelation between the motivational variables, for
not only were the correlations uniformly the highest (running from
0.39 to 0.47), but they applied to both classes, using both types of
comparative analyses.

Kind of Formal Course Work Motivation (5d)

The null hypothesis of no relationship between Kind of Formal Course Work Motivation and all the other motivational variables
was rejected for Formal Course Work Motivation Degree for both
classes. The hypothesis was accepted for 1961 librarians in regard

to Professional Improvement Motivation Degree, but rejected for
the class of 1956.   There was a significant relationship (based on
actual scores) between Kind of Formal Course Work Motivation and
Professional Improvement Motivation Degree (0. 29).

The hypothesis of no relationship between Kind of Formal
Course Work Motivation and Kind of Professional Improvement Motivation was accepted for both classes.   Table XXVIII, page 164,
gives a summary of all the relationships for Hypotheses 5, a
through d, and indicates the correlation coefficients that were found
to be significant at the 5 per cent level.

Conclusion

The findings in connection with this set of hypotheses warrant the conclusion that for both the 1956 and the 1961 graduates
there was a strong relationship between kind of motivation and degree of motivation for formal course work.

It was also found for both classes that if they had a strong
desire to participate in professional improvement activities they also had a strong desire to take formal course work.

V.   Relationship to Other Variables

The possible association between the motivational variables
and several of the other variables not given in the form of hypotheses were also explored with the following results:

Those 1956 graduates living in a population concentration of
less than 100, 000 tended to have a higher kind of motivation toward
formal course work.   The 1956 graduates who worked in libraries
with a larger number of employees tended to have a lower degree
of motivation toward professional improvement activities and a lower
kind of motivation toward formal course work.   This tendency supports the theory that close colleague associations with other librarians does not enhance professional activity, but rather tends
to foster minimal participation in development activities.

A special analysis revealed no significant relationship between marital status and any of the four motivational variables. There was no significant difference in association between marital status and any of the 8 variables reported in this table that could be detected by chi-square at the 5 per cent level of significance.

VI. Conclusion

It became apparent in proving the hypotheses in this chapter that most of the significant findings applied to one class or the other; few applied to both classes. This leads to the conclusion that length of time in librarianship makes a difference in kind of motivation and degree of motivation toward continuing education. A larger proportion of those who had been in librarianship a longer period of time had a higher kind of motivation toward professional improvement and toward formal course work than those who had been in a shorter period of time. The converse was true for intensity of desire toward professional development. A larger proportion of those who had been in librarianship a shorter period of time had a greater degree of motivation toward professional improvement activity and formal course work.

Two additional individual characteristics that seemed to have particular relationship to degree and kind of motivation toward formal course work were: (1) degree of aspiration; and (2) number of years between the Bachelor's and MLS degree. For the class of 1956, age was also significantly related to degree for formal course work motivation.

The individual measurement that seemed to have the greatest overall relationship to degree and kind of motivation toward professional improvement activities was the Professional Index Score.

Notes
1. Maslow, Abraham H. Motivation and Personality (New York: Harper & Bros., 1954), p. 80-106.

2. McGregor, Douglas The Human Side of Enterprise (New York: McGraw Hill, 1960), p. 35-43.

3. Swanson, Harold B. "Factors Associated with Motivation Toward Professional Development of County Agricultural Extension Agents in Minnesota" (unpublished Doctor's dissertation, University of Wisconsin, 1965), p. 196-199.

4. See Appendix A, Scoring Systems.

Chapter VIII

Responsibility for Professional Development

The concluding section of the questionnaire directed the respondents:

> Think now of the conditions and factors relative to your professional growth as a whole. John Lorenz has put forth the thesis that society has a right to look to the various professions themselves for effective planning and action in developing opportunities for continuing education. One of the key issues is: Whose responsibility is it to provide professional growth activities?
>
> Suppose each of the groups or individuals listed below asked you to develop recommendations for action, and suppose further that you were asked to consider and suggest way-out ideas as well as those which seem practical and appropriate for present conditions as you see them. What recommendations would you address to the following individuals and/or groups?

Seven groups were listed: library administrators, professional library associations, graduate library schools, library planners in the U. S. Office of Education, state library agencies, publishers of library literature, and individual librarians.

The opportunity for the respondents to indicate where the responsibility lay for providing professional development activities came only after 8 pages of intensive inquiry indicating that the librarians sampled had strong feelings they wanted to express on the subject of professional development.

Several benefits accrued from this forum. It was discovered that ideas concerning professional development transcend geographical location, year of graduation, or type of librarianship. The actual scope and complexity of the notion of continuing education was manifested. The respondents' own motivations were revealed through their approach and their sense of values.

Since there were 879 suggestions, they were edited and sum-

170

marized to express only those that appeared to be universal, or
those that were unique.   Many of the librarians feel the same way
about the same things.   On the other hand, some areas were barely
considered.

I. Recommendations to Administrators

Although the respondents were not asked directly where they
thought major responsibility lay in the area of continuing education,
the number and intensity of replies addressed to administrators indicates that major action was needed at this level.   Of the 879 recommendations made to the 7 relevant groups, the largest number
of suggestions (240, or 27 per cent) was directed to the administrators.   It should be noted, also, that in 4 other places in the
questionnaire the respondent had had an opportunity to express his
reaction to this group, but he obviously had much more he wanted
to say.   The tone and spirit of the responses indicate the strength
of the librarians' reactions which substantiate the statistics presented in other parts of this study.

To the administrators, as to the other groups, there were
clusters of ideas common to each set of recommendations.   These
seem worthy of special mention because they indicate major areas
of concern.   As noted in Figure 3, the librarians in the sample
were most universally concerned about encouragement from a conducive environment, availability of time, and the role the administrator should play in regard to continuing education.

The general tenor of the responses showed that the librarians
thought the administrators were fostering organizational conditions
which were less than ideal, even minimal, for the encouragement of
professional growth.   The administrator was urged to develop a climate for professional growth in the library based on the concepts
that professional librarians be given the freedom and time to exercise discretion, to participate in the decisions and goal-setting for
professional development opportunities offered within the library, to
experiment with new ideas, to be used to their full capacity in the

duties assigned to them, to be given varying opportunities for free
exchange of ideas regarding professional development.

The administrator was encouraged to listen, to observe, to
show concern about the employee and his particular needs and capabilities. It was also suggested that the administrator should become
involved in self-development opportunities himself, thus serving as
an example and clearly showing his recognition of the importance of
professional growth, and that he be sensitive to opportunities in the
external environment to which he could direct the staff.

It was also strongly suggested that there should be alterna-
tive rewards for years of professional service to clientele, rather
than the tacit understanding that advancement means only administrative responsibilities. Ruth Warncke stressed the importance of
this when she wrote:

> ... in terms of career progression, it seems to me that
> we should begin to differentiate between two types of li-
> brarianship: that which involves bibliography services
> and guidance and that which involves administration. It
> should be possible to make a career as a cataloger, a
> bibliographer... or any other kind of librarian without ever
> having to become the head of a department or the head of
> a library. It should be possible to have salaries, title,
> and status geared to the growth within the field. [1]

The importance of this concept is also stressed in an article on professionalism by Bundy and Wasserman, who lament that many librarians assume that administration is the "only professional practice. "[2]

The following are grouped samples of the exact statements
of the respondents recommending action:

Encouragement through a Conducive Climate

Encouragement! Encouragement!

Library administrators must develop a place for professional growth. This is the only way to retain the staff, satisfied and
eager, on a level of high professional standards.

Top priority! Administrators should encourage the staff:
to follow their individual needs so they can develop in every pos-

Figure 3

Idea Clusters Represented in the Recommendations to Administrators
Regarding Responsibility for Continuing Education
Made by the 1956 and 1961 MLS Librarians: 1967

Idea Clusters

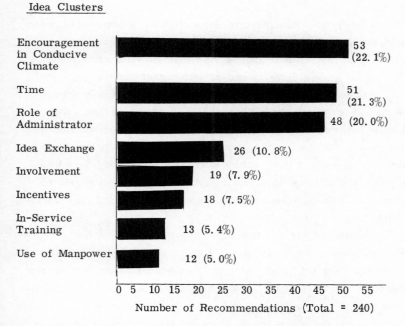

Number of Recommendations (Total = 240)

sible way... to submit articles to professional journals, but warn
them against submitting dull rehashes... to expand their horizons.

Administrators should not sit back on their haunches and
haw, haw when they find one of their staff has been asked to participate in professional association activities.

Time

Time should be given--work time--to be creative, to think.

The library could be a "Teaching Library" if time were given
(not to be made up).

Work schedules should be arranged so that courses could be

taken. Sabbatical leaves should be granted to those who have a
definite program of study or who have a definite research project
they wish to pursue.

The Role of the Administrator

Too many administrators seem opposed to any sort of change.
A "don't rock the boat" philosophy, completely oblivious to the world
about them.   Or a short sighted view that when the employee has
"developed" he will move on and be lost to that job.

Listen! and Observe! Administrators should take a week
off and walk around like a visitor in their own libraries.   How
does it function? How do the librarians function? Are they imaginative or are they in a rut? Are they out in front with new ideas or
always bogged down with routine work? Now that they have taken
a fresh look at their librarians in action, plan for the growth of
every one of them.   Keep the good ones good, and wake up the in-
active ones.

Learn the art of flexibility.

Reverse impersonalization; take an interest in ALL staff
members.   Equity! Distribute opportunities for attending meetings
and other activities among ALL THE STAFF, not just a few department heads.

Learn the processes of administration; an important one is
delegation! Administrators should recognize their need for improved skills and take courses to improve them.   There should be
workshops for administrators conducted by the real leaders in the
profession.

Administrators should demonstrate their belief in continuing
education by active professional development of their own.   One
shouldn't have to guess the administrator's feelings about professional development; they should be stated.

Idea Exchange

There should always be open lines of communication with

the top administrator.

Staff meetings: should be conducted on a plane of growth...
should make a difference... staff should be involved in the planning
and discussion... means for keeping staff abreast of changes in profession... group as a whole should determine which ideas will be
incorporated into the library program.

Some method should be devised so that staff members could
get together for free exchange of ideas and to keep up to date.   In-
house seminars for dialogue among all interested staff members.

The community should be informed of the changes in the profession.   There should be ways to inject the library program in
various areas of the community.

Development through Creative Involvement

Ask more of us, not less!

The best way for the administrator to encourage his staff is
through promoting creativity in his staff.

In making long-range plans, administrators should call on
the young professionals for way-out ideas and allow them to advance
as rapidly as they can.   Let them play with ideas that may seem
silly; something will usually come of them.

Too many administrators overlook the expertise on their own
staffs.   In-system studies of the patrons would determine the library's public; the staff could then seek ways to educate itself to
help that public.   Growth would follow.

Allow us to make mistakes!   This too is a form of development.

Incentives

There should be pay for traveling expenses... financial help
for all professional activities... Materials, such as periodical sub-
scriptions, should be provided by libraries for professional growth.

Supervisors should be rewarded or promoted on the basis of
how well they promote professional growth of those under them.

Administrators should see to it that built-in increments are incorporated into salary schedules for post-Master's credits, whether in library science or in work-related fields.

Professional growth should be demanded or there should be no salary increment or promotion.

In-Service Training

The staff should be allowed to help plan in-service training programs--they might have some very creative ideas!

The budget should provide for top quality in-service training... bring in noted leaders from outside the library... make it special... provide for full exchange of ideas by those taking the program.

Job training in supervision should be constant and unceasing.

Utilization of Manpower

Professionals for professional work, technicians for technical work, clerks for clerical work! Use a classification which falls between clerical and professional--library technician.

There should be two lines of promotion for those who don't want to be administrators... Should be able to be promoted on basis of merit not just because of supervisory responsibilities.

II.   Recommendations to Library Associations

"The professional association is as the professional association does: its manifest and latent social functions, not the structure designed to put these functions into effect, are its social excuse for being."[3]

Houle asserted:

> The professional association crowns all other efforts at
> continuing education and bears the chief collective respon-
> sibility for it... a manifest function of every profession-
> al association is the continuing education of its member-
> ship; indeed, scarcely any other function is more mani-

fest and has a longer tradition than this one.[4]

The importance accorded to the professional association as an agent for professional growth was indicated by the fact that the second largest number of recommendations (160) was directed to this group. Figure 4 details the idea clusters directed to the associations. The most frequent suggestion was that the library associations upgrade the content of their activities. Various means were mentioned: reinforcement through small group discussion or voluntary study groups; an interdisciplinary approach through affiliation with learned societies and other professional associations; using creative ways to keep the profession up-to-date on changes that would affect the library. Several respondents suggested that the activities should be evaluated regularly in order to assure high quality content.

Involvement and innovation were also suggested. Associations should encourage voluntary service for their committees, especially by the eager younger members. Not only would the association benefit, by attracting younger innovators who could develop imaginative approaches to librarianship, but the members would gain new knowledge and experience, and leadership for the profession would be developed. Associations were criticized for being so closed and not spreading the responsibilities to larger numbers.

Several good suggestions were made for redistributing the geographical location of opportunities. One was that State and American Library Association pre-conference programs could be brought to librarians in scattered areas. Another was that library associations raise funds for individual members to engage in research, since it is difficult for an individual to receive a Federal grant.

Content

It's the content that counts! ... More accent on things of the mind!

Don't be afraid to evaluate! Send out forms to members for evaluation of meetings and ask for their suggestions.

Figure 4

Idea Clusters Represented in the Recommendations to Library Associations Regarding Responsibility for Continuing Education Made by the 1956 and 1961 MLS Librarians: 1967

Idea Clusters

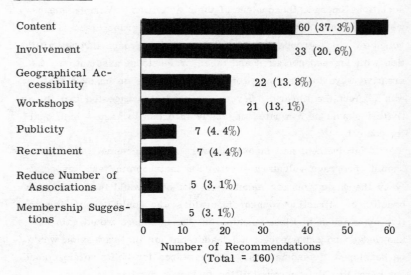

Number of Recommendations
(Total = 160)

There is a desperate need for intelligent planning... planning that represents all the interests and concerns of the meetings... don't be afraid of the newest or most way-out.

Concentrate on solid content--not inspirational speeches.

Key ideas are lost at meetings if there is no opportunity to discuss them afterwards.

Am getting weary of so-called professional associations which have degenerated into social groups or duplication of the type of activity I can get better in other similar groups in community.

Let a professional meeting be just that, a professional meeting.

Library associations should have more liaison with learned societies... less concern with the image and public relations.

Associations should be more aware of their obligations to
society. Take firm stands on anti-censorship, on integration, etc.
American Library Association does it, but not state or local societies as much as they should.

Throw out the claptrap which includes 90 per cent of every
ten papers presented at meetings... if there is nothing solid to discuss at association meetings; dissolve associations... other professions dream up more important things to talk about at their meetings than the stuff we get at meetings.

There should be a two-level program within associations, so
at every meeting members could be challenged at both professional
and sub-professional levels.

Plan program meetings so members will go home "dreaming
big!"

Involvement

Have the guts to permit broader participation by promising
non-tried people. Right now we are dealing with a closed corporation. I have been lucky, but many of my colleagues have been
stifled.

I often wonder how any work gets done, either at the committee level or on the home front, when one person serves on five
or six or even more committees. Until more liberal policies are
adopted to catch the associations up-to-date, not many junior members will become involved in professional library associations.

Do not stifle new members. They have the energy and en-
thusiasm to carry through the problems that the old pros claim as
their birthright and rarely achieve... make new members feel welcome... try harder to incorporate the lesser known into committee
positions... I think most members feel as though they are on the
outside looking in.

Make a place for volunteers to serve on committees; such
service will bring new knowledge and experience to the individuals.

Geographical Accessibility

Library associations should think about access of membership in isolated areas.

If you can't have the big meetings in a small place, at least
you can take small meetings to small places... plan for smaller
groups within state association to meet leaders in smaller areas...
sponsor one or two professional sessions at smaller centers throughout states to follow up and discuss mutual problems.

We are isolated in small towns! Get meetings to us.

Pre-Conference Workshops at American Library Associations
should TRAVEL. So all in country could have a chance at attending them.

Some Miscellaneous Views

Don't compete with library schools in offering training programs; cooperate with them.

Prepare a handbook of helpful hints for new members and
open up to them opportunities possible through association. Publi-
cize research; do research... provide scholarships... and funds so
members can take the sixth year program beyond the Master's.

Take a lead in developing recruitment programs ... bring in
students and others in pilot projects that may interest them to become professionals.

Too many associations; and too much of them is social...
eliminate some of the duplications; have stronger joined associations
... executive councils of all library organizations should concentrate
on coordination.

III.   Recommendations to the Library Schools

Figure 5 shows the idea clusters recommended to library
schools.

Figure 5

Idea Clusters Represented in the Recommendations to Graduate
Library Schools Regarding Responsibility for Continuing
Education Made by the 1956 and 1961 MLS Librarians: 1967

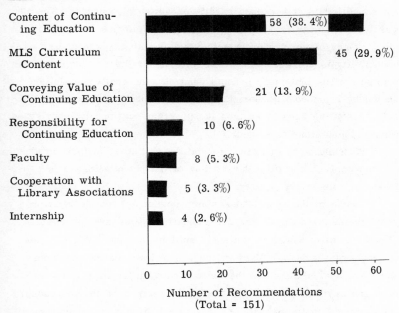

Idea Clusters

Content of Continu-
ing Education   58 (38. 4%)

MLS Curriculum
Content   45 (29. 9%)

Conveying Value of
Continuing Education   21 (13. 9%)

Responsibility for
Continuing Education   10 (6. 6%)

Faculty   8 (5. 3%)

Cooperation with
Library Associations   5 (3. 3%)

Internship   4 (2. 6%)

0   10   20   30   40   50   60

Number of Recommendations
(Total = 151)

The general attitude of the respondents seemed to be that the
library schools should be giving much more serious thought to their
roles in continuing education.   There was a consensus that the
schools should continually adapt the curriculum to behavioral, societal, and technological advances and provide courses needed for present jobs.   Some areas that were stressed were personnel management, human relations, supervision, budgeting, data processing, systems analysis, and also the broad area studies, to give the students
perspective.   If the present faculty could not handle such a wide variety of subjects, the library schools should work out cooperative
programs with other departments in the university.

There was a general feeling that the schools should focus on basic and fundamental programs in the areas needed. These programs should be presented in a series of sessions, in two or three all-day meetings, in institutes, or in a period of residence, especially during the summer. Above all, they should be flexible and not bound by insistence upon credits or advanced degrees. The plea was for knowledge for the sake of doing a better job.

Many of the respondents felt that the library school had a responsibility to upgrade its contacts with its graduates, including the printed notices that many schools send out; the chatty newsletter should be replaced with something in the nature of a scholarly journal. Also, the schools should take program sessions to other cities where alumni were clustered.

Schools were criticized for failing to impart to their graduates an appreciation or understanding of the potentialities of a professional role in our society.

Some of the respondents stated opinions about the MLS program itself, even though the questionnaire did not ask for them. These opinions, however, reflect a split in thinking about the role of the library school. Many of the respondents stated that theory and conceptual skills were the most needed in preparation for the MLS and anything practical that could be learned on the job should not be taught in the school. Others urged the library schools faculties to come down from their ivory tower and teach the practical methods, routines, and procedures that were needed in their jobs.

Every library school faces this problem of balancing the practical need for students of high proficiency with the concern of the university for an intellectual preparation which embodies theory, concepts, issues and scholarly attainment. Apparently few schools had solved the problem to the satisfaction of the respondents.

However, from the total comments submitted it appears that the majority would probably agree with the conviction expressed by Bundy and Wasserman: "To the extent that the details have overshadowed the more fundamental issues, so has education been routinized and stripped of its potential for embodying a content that is intellectually viable."[5]

In summary, the recommendations made by the sample expressed the philosophy stated by William McGloughlin: "The [professional] school must judge itself and be judged on its influence over the full careers of its graduates. Nothing less than endless growth can be considered success. "[6]

The Content of Continuing Education

All library schools should take an active responsibility for providing opportunities for continuing education, especially short courses off the campus.

It's EDUCATION, not CREDITS, that is important.

Find the real needs of alumni and then concentrate on those, not proliferate courses and workshops that are of dubious value anyway.

Develop summer courses of real depth with modern developments that did not appear in the curriculum ten years ago.

Alumni are embarrassed by their failure to keep abreast; they want a chance to get caught up.

I wrote for four library-school catalogs recently and found only one course that a professional person who had been in the field for some time would have been interested in. Such offerings should include psychology of reference questions, job-motivation, literature in special fields, reviews of the structure and parameters of related disciplines.

What we need most after we have been out is courses in human relations, personnel guidance and supervision, also public relations.

Develop a series of non-credit, no-assignment-, no-quiz seminars to produce discussion and exchange of ideas without need for cramming.

Have specially planned seminars or workshops or institutes for those who have been out five to ten years to help gain the knowledge they need as administrators.

Offer a course in how to become professionally involved. Dozens of librarians I know are terrified at the thought of involvement, shy away from leadership, have feelings of inadequacy, and through life are apparently satisfied to let George do it.

Miscellaneous Suggestions

Encourage the graduate to see that continuing education is basically an individual responsibility that one has to plan for.

If students graduate from an MLS program with the attitude that graduate school is a life-time guarantee of professional competence, their minds may never be able to master the growing vastness of today's challenges and problems. They will not be as literate as the people they serve.

Most library school graduates have lost confidence in the library school helping them much with continuing education, because the faculty has not kept up and cannot offer the necessary leadership.

Alumni Associations of library schools should do away with boring reunion teas. Instead, find out what their graduates really need for growth. Don't just guess--use questionnaires or meetings of sample groups in various parts of the country.

Alumni should be involved in planning programs under the guidance of the experts--the faculty.

The alumni newsletter should have a minimum of social news; it should be a scholarly journal, which in itself would be a means of continuing education.

IV.   Recommendations to the Planners in the
U. S. Office of Education

Strong suggestions were made for the Library Services Division's role in continuing education with the stress on long-range planning, workshops and institutes that would travel to every part of the country, and thereby reach isolated areas. Almost every respondent was concerned with the lack of opportunity in remote towns. The respondents, wanting a better understanding of what is being done at the Library Services Division, suggested that a public relations officer be employed to inform the profession of programs being offered by the Division, of funds that were available and how they could be obtained, and to serve as a national clearinghouse for all the various grants, fellowships, and research opportunities.

There was also a suggestion that the Library Services Division should attempt to raise its status in the Office of Education and in this way have more freedom for creative approaches aimed especially at librarians.

There seemed to be general disillusionment with the handling of research funds. Many demanded higher standards so that mediocre projects would not be considered. The red tape involved, the length of time required, and the general lack of information were some discouraging factors that were noted repeatedly. A more equitable distribution of funds, which would include individuals and library associations as well as schools and institutions, was urged. Figure 6 focuses on the main areas of ideas suggested to the Library Services Division.

Long-Range Planning

Engage in long-range planning... plan in terms of the year 2100.

When the Santa Claus of the "over-watered cactus" cycle is over, state agencies will need to know how to create and sustain vital programs without Federal help.

Prepare states for independence and less provinciality by conducting study groups where goals can be projected and experiences shared.

Workshops should be planned at the national level.

Institutes and workshops should meet the needs of every area, cover the subjects really needed. There is lack of evidence that they are a part of a master plan to reach all librarians who want them.

Emphasis on planning should be based on two things--need and cooperation with all agencies who should be involved.

Figure 6

Idea Clusters Represented in the Recommendations to U. S. Office
of Education Regarding Responsibility for Continuing
Education Made by the 1956 and 1961 MLS Librarians: 1967

Idea Clusters

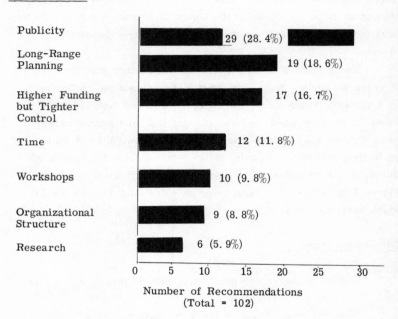

Number of Recommendations
(Total = 102)

    You can't get the picture, if you don't come to the regions
involved. . . come to our libraries and see what is going on before
mapping out programs for us.

    The creative look in workshops. . . set up short courses in a
TRAVELLING SCHOOL. . . take the school all over the country to
areas with the greatest needs.

    Be aware of the value of time for wise spending. . . you give
us more money and less time to spend it.

    The time between the notification and Federal grants have
been approved and the deadline are often just a few days apart.
Money cannot be spent wisely if done hurriedly.

Publication and Publicity

Get a public relations officer!... The picture does not come
through that you know what you are supposed to be doing, the average librarian surely doesn't know ... I'm sure they have people to
help us, but who are they and how do we get their services?

Much money is going for improvement of library services,
but reports are needed so we can learn of progress being made...
if there are such reports they don't reach down to the average librarian.

There should be a mechanism for dynamic dissemination of
new research ideas that presumably the Office is sponsoring... give
ideas to others.

How do you actually get money for research? ... It seems
very mysterious and difficult... issue bibliographies showing what
outstanding programs have done.

The Office should insist that each program get out adequate
promotion material about its offerings.   This material is not widely
enough distributed to make the best use of Federal funds.

Establish a clearinghouse to encourage staff exchange of jobs
throughout the country.

Publish results of studies and special programs and dissemi-
nate more widely... need more publicity on scholarships and fellowships and long-range programs... this should be done on long-range
basis so could be used in recruitment.

Cut the red tape, forms, etc.

Research Funds

Support research but be sure it is coordinated and will really
be of help to the profession.

More funding, but tighter control... relate to ALA Standards
... deny funds when standards are not met... don't give to schools
without adequate faculties... to schools who are not oriented to
newer methods... make the funds a means of upgrading standards,

that is one of their main purposes is it not? ... not so much medi-
ocrity being financed and thus blessed.

Develop higher evaluative criteria for receipt of funds.

V. Recommendations to Statewide Library Planners

Responsibility was given to the state library planners for organizing and initiating statewide plans for continuing education. The
respondents agreed that most important was the publicity of programs and of major accomplishments as indicated in Figure 7.

The state planners were urged to expand their consulting
services. Some of the specific suggestions were: plan and implement more workshops and other training opportunities; take programs to isolated areas of the state where opportunities are limited; visit the individual libraries and assist them in person; develop
programs that meet the specific local needs of the librarians.

There was also a concern for cooperation between the town
and the state, the library association and the state, and between
the other states in the Union and the U. S. Office of Education.

Publicity and Public Relations

Develop a dynamic mechanism for dissemination of new research and ideas within the state. We don't.

The sources of funds available are not widely enough known
so all can take advantage of them.

Get known! Go to all types of library group meetings and
help sponsor all types... can't have much influence unless you are
known... as you travel about state use influence for recruitment.

Invest in publicity.

Without adequate publicity most librarians in state are not
going to have any idea of the opportunities available to them.

Figure 7

Idea Clusters Represented in the Recommendations to State
Library Agencies Regarding Responsibility for Continuing
Education Made by the 1956 and 1961 MLS Librarians: 1967

Idea Clusters

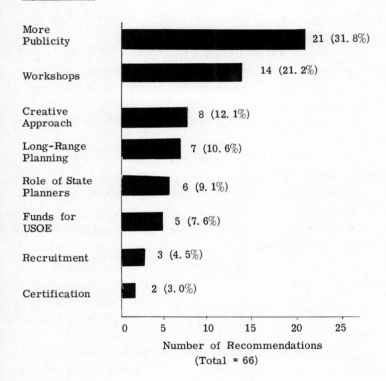

More
Publicity   21 (31. 8%)

Workshops   14 (21. 2%)

Creative
Approach   8 (12. 1%)

Long-Range
Planning   7 (10. 6%)

Role of State
Planners   6 (9. 1%)

Funds for
USOE   5 (7. 6%)

Recruitment   3 (4. 5%)

Certification   2 (3. 0%)

0   5   10   15   20   25

Number of Recommendations
(Total = 66)

Consulting Services

Provision so that those at state level could be used for individual consultation.

Establish a consulting service for all in state who wish it.

Learn to do more than count! ... avoid unnecessary bureauc-
racy!

Go out into the field... nothing is more important than visiting the actual libraries in the state... get into the hinterlands!

Influence will never carry much weight unless all in state programs are real leaders.

Take the initiative in organizing student associations through the State and see that they get to professional meetings and start growing professionally, early.

Work out ways and means and plans of how to improve library administration throughout the state.

Use methods that will really be of help. For example, develop comparative charts showing what is done elsewhere in state in order to stimulate interest and help libraries of similar size see what is possible.

Enough workshops for top administrators; too few for lower level people.

Take the workshops to the people, don't expect the people in isolated places to go there.

A state office should have an itinerant program that is constantly on the road.

Put in state-wide training courses taught by dynamic specialists in related disciplines.

Cooperation

Reach all librarians in the state--not just country ones or city ones.

Concentrate on all libraries and all library groups gaining a perspective... the individual does not know where he fits into the overall system.

Seems to be no connection between university, public, and school libraries or the librarians.

Abandon county and regional library systems. Declare entire state just one big library system with all cooperation from its central branch.

Be sure to include non-professionals. If an interest is taken in them they are more apt to become professionals.

Spend more time working out programs and long-range planning with other states.

Interstate planning should be a key emphasis... join forces with other states... with the U.S. Office of Education.

Don't go it alone. Sponsor programs with library schools... with library associations.

VI. Recommendations to Publishers of Library Literature

Many of the respondents felt that library literature was totally lacking in quality and therefore was of little value in professional development. Figure 8 reflects this concern.

There was agreement that the publishers could actually stimulate worthwhile research and writing by suggesting interesting subjects and topics. The respondents were generally weary of articles that seemed to be arguing for argument's sake alone.

Cut the nit-picking clap-trap, emphasize quality over quantity in the publication.

I must restrain my candid comments here!

Cut out the pseudo-scientific jargon approach to perfectly ordinary library problems... recover some of the humaneness of the profession.

Publish only the good technical, or the learned--the garbage for the proper refuse pile--trash burner--but not for our valuable stack space.

Stop making our journals a mockery in comparison to the learned journals of other professional groups.

Publish articles that will encourage individual librarians to do individual research... if research is published, more will be interested in making the effort.

Publishers should see that they have a major role to perform ... publications should be tools for continuing education.

Consolidate journals... most worthwhile library literature could easily be published in one scholarly journal.

Seek out those who can write... don't rely on material sent

Figure 8

Idea Clusters Represented in the Recommendations to Publishers
of Professional Library Literature Regarding Responsibility
for Continuing Education Made by the 1956 and 1961
MLS Librarians: 1967

<u>Idea Clusters</u>

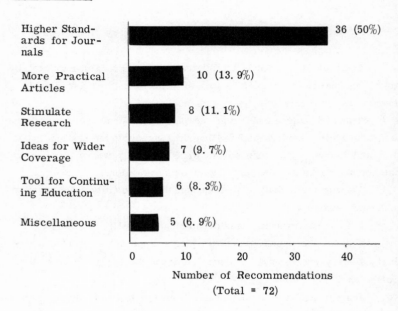

Number of Recommendations
(Total = 72)

in on volunteer basis.

VII.   Recommendations to the Individual Librarian

The ultimate responsibility for continuing education was
placed by the librarians on the individual. The suggestions dealt
largely with the urgency of a self-directed program if one hopes to
keep up at all.

The major concern was for obsolescence. Suggested strategy for combating this was to read; to take further courses, both

formal and informal; and to participate in group activities, as indicated in Figure 9.   Although books and printed material were still the primary source for self-directed learning, a few other media were also mentioned.

The barriers to self-development noted most often were lack of time, lack of encouragement and conducive environment, and geographic isolation.   This study has treated these deterring factors in depth.

The respondents seemed to realize great personal value from their professional development activities.   They were also convinced that continuing education was necessary for better service to their clientele, improved performance on their job, and a better professional image.   Many of the recommendations in this section stressed the importance of remembering that the ultimate in professionalism is client orientation.

Goals

The primary responsibility for the individual's continuing growth rests with the individual himself... try to learn more constantly... decide on goals.

No matter what opportunities are made available by societies or government, they are useless without individual initiative.

Classify impediments and favorable conditions... seek avenues of growth... plot a course of action and stick to it.

From now on if you have been remiss, plan your time to include professional growth, even if it means starting with such a simple thing as a chat with another librarian.

Strategies for Learning

Read! Widely! ... continue professional reading... reading outside of professional literature extends and fills in and contributes background to my professional life.

Great opportunities for professional growth and leadership are available if you participate in professional organization activi-

Figure 9

Idea Clusters Represented in the Recommendations to Individual
Librarians Regarding Responsibility for Continuing Eduation
Made by the 1956 and 1961 MLS Librarians: 1967

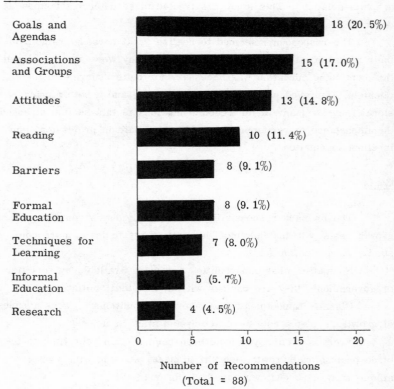

Idea Clusters

Goals and Agendas	18 (20. 5%)
Associations and Groups	15 (17. 0%)
Attitudes	13 (14. 8%)
Reading	10 (11. 4%)
Barriers	8 (9. 1%)
Formal Education	8 (9. 1%)
Techniques for Learning	7 (8. 0%)
Informal Education	5 (5. 7%)
Research	4 (4. 5%)

0   5   10   15   20

Number of Recommendations
(Total = 88)

ties and learn to communicate with others.

Librarians should get involved in non-library activities in the
community... be active and alive, the rest of us are being judged
by you.

Formal instruction in government, economics, information

retrieval, education, public administration, sociology, all would be
helpful.

I'll suggest individual discussion groups to my colleagues.

Attitudes

Study when you can, but remember that the library exists
only to serve its clientele so keep procedures as simple as possible.

Get involved in every activity you possibly can... participation... become less passive and more active.

Encourage staff to take advantage of all opportunities for
self-education; do so yourself.

Specialize if you like, but don't be afraid to be a generalist
in an age gone mad with specialization.

Don't be afraid of innovation and change. We see fear every-
where that the non-book material is going to gain supremacy. Fear
is nurtured by ignorance. Go to every workshop and meeting you
can.

Be creative, be alert, but above all don't lose sight of the
fact that we are a service profession.

Read and know your materials. Our best public relations is
public contact; share whatever ideas you have freely with others.

Professional growth is formal, also informal. How you grow
depends upon you alone; but any growth should be based upon a considered view that the growth enables you to serve your clientele
(not yourself) better.

VIII.   Conclusion

The scope of these recommendations illustrated that the librarians sampled hold all of the relevant groups accountable for
providing favorable conditions for their professional improvement
activities and formal course work. In addition, the answers appeared to reveal insights about the respondents' own motivation for
professional growth.

This chapter concludes the report on the data obtained from the questionnaire.

Notes

1. Warncke, Ruth "Careers in Librarianship" ALA Bulletin 60: 808 (September, 1966).

2. Bundy, Mary Lee, and Wasserman, Paul "Professionalism Reconsidered" College and Research Libraries 29:17 (January 1968).

3. Merton, Robert "The Function of the Professional Association" American Journal of Nursing 63:50 (1958).

4. Houle, Cyril O. "Continuing Education: Purpose, Principles and Trends" (paper read before American Library Association, New Orleans, Louisiana, January 11, 1967).

5. Bundy and Wasserman op. cit. , p. 20.

6. McGloughlin, William J. The Professional Schools (New York: Center for Applied Research in Education, 1964) p. 29.

Chapter IX

Conclusions and Recommendations

This study was basically exploratory and descriptive. The
data suggests certain recommendations to the librarian for individual
action; to library leaders for administrative policy and decision; and
finally, to the entire profession for its formulation of a concept of
career development.

I. Action on the Part of the Individual Librarian

The present character of librarianship became apparent from
the Professional Index Scores and from the findings which showed a
significant disparity between what the librarians were doing and what
they thought they should be doing for maximum professional development. The entire sample seemed to regard activities that were
somewhat informal and which provided social contacts with other professionals as more important. These were also the activities in
which they were most involved. The librarians were less involved
with activities which call for independent action. Most of their time
was devoted to library association work; meetings and conventions;
visiting other libraries; recruiting for the profession; and reading
professional literature, particularly library journals.

This was evidenced by the following statistics: 77.5 percent
of the total sample had not engaged in any research projects since
receiving their MLS; 53 percent had not published any articles nor
delivered any papers at professional meetings during the last five
years; 92 percent had not published any books in library science or
in their subject specialization; 24.6 percent had not read any books
in library science during the past year; 21.7 percent had not read
any books during the past year in their subject speciality; 55.8 per-

cent did not read non-library professional journals regularly; 81. 2
percent did not belong to any learned societies and 65 percent did
not belong to a non-library professional association.

Of the total sample, 53. 6 percent received no score on the
question that tested concern for the problems of fellow workers both
on and off the job; 78. 3 percent were not participating in a voluntary study group; 67. 4 percent did not have a self-learning agenda
worked out for their professional development; 94. 2 percent had not
completed an advanced degree since receiving their MLS degree.
Finally, during the last 5 years, three-fifths of a day per year was
the median time spent in attendance at workshops or short courses.

This study did not attempt to state what the ideal character
of librarianship should be. But the collected data did suggest some
objective norms by which an individual librarian can compare his
position within the profession and a supervisor can gain an understanding of where his employees are in relation to such a norm.
The norms that were derived, however, fall short of what would
seem to be an ideal representation for the profession. [1]

If an ideal is to be achieved, it should require, among other
things, more advanced study, both formal and informal, in areas
which did not appear to be of major concern to the librarians in
this study. More formal preparation would be particularly necessary
in such subjects as the behavioral sciences, government and finance,
adult education, public administration, and social problems.

Relative to the data presented, there would seem to be two
basic dilemmas that the profession faces. One, how to span the
gap between what the librarians are actually doing for their professional development and what they think they should be doing. Two,
how to upgrade the type of activities that the librarian considers
most important for his professional development.

The gap can be closed only if the individual librarian is motivated to action, for the success of any program depends upon the
action of its participants. To encourage effective staff development,
library administrators, educators, and association leaders should be
aware of the factors that motivate participation when planning professional development activities. The next section, "Possible Ad-

ministrative Strategy," deals in some depth with this approach.

Before the type of activities that the librarian considers most important can be upgraded, the individual must realize that continuing education is something he should do for himself. John Gardner asserted that the ultimate goal is "to shift to the individual the burden of pursuing his own education."[2] But Samuel Rothstein found that "continuing professional education is essentially a peripheral activity with librarianship."[3]

Based on the findings of this study, it seems that the individual librarian could do much to enhance his own professional development. Such attention could determine the means by which the profession as a whole might be upgraded. To do this would involve:

1. Re-examination of his attitude toward professional development and assumption of more personal responsibility. Realization that he has entered a client-oriented profession which makes life-long learning mandatory if he is to serve his clients effectively.

2. Careful analysis of his own needs and development of a plan for long-term professional growth. Realization that he has an obligation to learn new truths in order to share in solving information problems.

3. Recognition that he must also study the basic disciplines which support librarianship so that he will be able to judge the applicability of their findings to his own work.

4. Realization that as he assumes broader responsibilities he must acquire special knowledge to meet these increased demands effectively.

5. Ability to develop his skills in a rapidly changing society in which he needs social understanding to do his work well.

6. A concern for ethical values, and a sensitivity to human values and to the development of each individual in his library.

7. A scholarly concern which will lead him to solve problems through his own research activity or to interpret and apply research of others.

8. Regard for the importance of publishing his ideas and findings in a scientific manner, and of making his materials visible to as wide a reading audience as possible.

Speaking at the 1967 Midwinter meeting of the American Library Association, Houle expressed his belief that a profession could be improved only through the action of its members:

> While continuing education will not cure all the problems of the professions, without it no cure is possible. The task for this generation is to work, amid all the distractions and complexities of practice, to aid the individual, either alone or in his natural work groups, constantly to refine his sensitivities, to enlarge his conceptions, and to increase his capacity to discharge the responsibilities his work requires as that work is seen in the larger contexts of his own personality, and the society of which he is a part. In all such efforts the ultimate aim--seldom sought directly but always present--is to insure that the active members of a profession exercise the self-discipline and the dedication which their preferred positions impose upon them. [4]

The question arises as to where the responsibility should lie for developing these concepts and attitudes of professionalism, including responsibility of the profession to society. This responsibility may best be undertaken by the library schools, emulating other professions, such as medicine and law. This requires a clear and precise model of what one should be to qualify as a professional librarian. If the library school does not instill this concept, it is unlikely that it will be developed within the individual practitioner.

Although the individual is ultimately responsible for his own continuing education and most of his effort must be self-directed, the librarian needs support and assistance from outside sources. The next section deals with the responsibility of administrators in the employing institution, in the library association, in the library school, and in State and Federal positions concerned with library planning.

II.   Possible Administrative Strategy

It is not uncommon to hear a library administrator, educator or leader ask: We have provided opportunities for continuing education, but how do we get the librarians to take advantage of them? How do we get them to see that they should be concerned about their

professional development for a lifetime? Why plan for more opportunities when they seem indifferent to the opportunities that already
exist?

      This study was made on the assumption that increased in-
volvement in professional development activities could be achieved
if library leaders knew the types of factors that encourage the individual librarian to participate in professional development activities and the types of factors that deter him. The findings imply
certain recommendations for administrative strategy.

      In planning professional development activities, top priority
should be given to those factors which are strong motivators. Perhaps of major value for administrative strategy were these findings:
(1) generally the reasons a librarian engages in professional development activities are different from, and not merely opposite to, the
reasons which deter him from participating; and (2) factors that deal
with the content of the development opportunity which can be related
to the librarian's actual job were the most influential in motivating
participation. These highly motivating factors tended to give the librarian a feeling of growth in job competence.

      It is recommended, therefore, that the administrator planning
professional improvement activities give top priority to those sources
of encouragement which were found to be the major motivators:

    1. The quality of the professional improvement activity itself.

    2. The chance to be exposed to new and creative ideas.

    3. The opportunity to use new knowledge on the job.

      Leaders concerned with planning formal course work should
give top priority to the following factors which were found to be the
major sources of motivation:

    1. The opportunity to use new knowledge on the job.

    2. High quality of the course work itself.

    3. Opportunity to be exposed to new and creative ideas.

      The deterring forces were found to be primarily associated
with extrinsic conditions: lack of time, inconvenient location, library policy and administration, supervision, interpersonal relationships, the costs of continuing education, salary, requirements, leadership, publicity, security.

Factors which were major sources of determent to the librarians in their professional improvement activities were:

1. Inferior quality of professional improvement activity itself.
2. The remoteness or inconvenience of the professional improvement opportunity.
3. The lack of available time and difficulty of fitting activities into schedule.

Factors which were major sources of determent to the librarians participating in formal course work were:

1. Lack of available time and the difficulty of fitting activities into schedule.
2. The remoteness or inconvenience of the formal course work.
3. Inferior quality of the formal course work itself.

Figures 10 and 11 indicate that content factors were the primary cause of encouragement, and that context factors were the primary cause of determent in formal course work and professional improvement activities. The relationships are not perfect, but the trends are substantial.

Figure 12 shows that 87 per cent of all the factors contributing to encouragement toward formal course work were related to content and that 70 per cent of all the factors contributing to determent were concerned with context. Figure 13 shows that 79 percent of the factors that encouraged professional development activities were related to content; 61 percent of the factors that deterred were concerned with context.

It should be understood, however, that even if all the contextual factors are satisfactory they alone generally will not influence librarians to a high level of participation. If, however, they are unsatisfactory, they will produce negative side effects and will discourage the librarians from participation. Awareness of this distinction should contribute to greater success in encouraging participation in professional development activities.

An example of this circumstance was the effect of the administrator's and supervisor's attitude toward the respondent's development activities. The study showed that when the management was

Figure 10

A Comparison of Major Positive and Negative Forces, as Perceived by Sample Librarians, that Affect Motivation Toward Professional Improvement: 1967

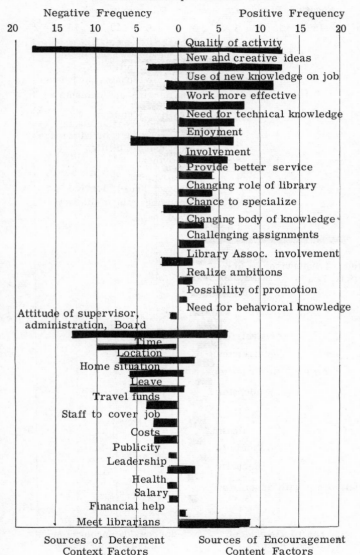

Negative Frequency					Positive Frequency		
20	15	10	5	0	5	10	15	20

Quality of activity
New and creative ideas
Use of new knowledge on job
Work more effective
Need for technical knowledge
Enjoyment
Involvement
Provide better service
Changing role of library
Chance to specialize
Changing body of knowledge
Challenging assignments
Library Assoc. involvement
Realize ambitions
Possibility of promotion
Need for behavioral knowledge
Attitude of supervisor, administration, Board
Time
Location
Home situation
Leave
Travel funds
Staff to cover job
Costs
Publicity
Leadership
Health
Salary
Financial help
Meet librarians

Sources of Determent   Sources of Encouragement
Context Factors   Content Factors

Figure 11

A Comparison of Major Positive and Negative Forces, as Perceived
by Sample Librarians, that Affect Motivation Toward
Formal Course Work: 1967

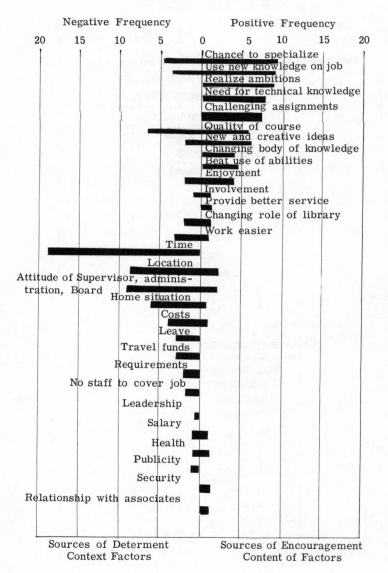

Sources of Determent   Sources of Encouragement
Context Factors   Content of Factors

Figure 12

Relationship Between Sources of Encouragement and Determent and
Characteristics of Formal Course Work as Perceived
by All Librarians in the Sample: 1967

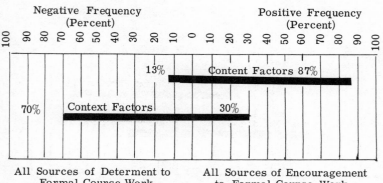

Negative Frequency
(Percent)

Positive Frequency
(Percent)

13%   Content Factors 87%

70%   Context Factors   30%

All Sources of Determent to   All Sources of Encouragement
Formal Course Work   to Formal Course Work

hostile or indifferent, the librarian would be restrained from participating in development activities.   In addition, the librarian com-
plained about this lack of support, as evidenced by the open-end responses.   But when the supervisor, administration and board were
favorable, this support of itself was not a highly motivating factor.
Similarly, improvements in scheduling, convenience of location, provision of transportation costs will not of themselves be prime motivators.   Something more is needed: content that can be related to
the work-process.

An administrator should realize that people who have jobs
that offer opportunity for growth, achievement, responsibility and
recognition will, in general, have little concern for the peripheral
issues.   The employee becomes involved in his work and in a sense
becomes a manager of himself.   His interest in his job will help
give him a sense of identification with the library and will help
prompt him to develop his professionalism in order to attain a high
level of creative performance.

Figure 13

Relationship Between Sources of Encouragement and Determent and
Characteristics of Professional Improvement Activities as
Perceived by All Librarians in the Sample: 1967

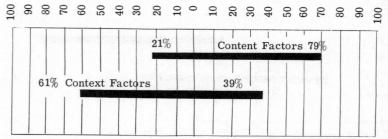

Negative Frequency   Positive Frequency
(Percent)   (Percent)

All Sources of Determent to   All Sources of Encouragement
Professional Improvement Activity   to Professional Improvement
                                              Activity

Since motivation was found to be related to the opportunity to
grow in job competence, it seems important to provide for job enrichment. [5] The changes brought about through job enrichment should
make the challenge of the job equal the skill for which the librarian
was hired.   Those who have even more ability will be able to demonstrate it and should be promoted to jobs which make full use of
their ability.

The librarians sampled asked for more responsibility to encourage them to grow professionally.   Job enrichment seems to be
particularly necessary for those with high Professional Index Scores,
as they were generally more motivated by content factors than those
with low Scores.

Herzberg makes a forceful argument for job enrichment:

> If you have someone on a job, use him.   If you can't use
> him on the job, get rid of him, either via automation or
> by selecting someone with lesser ability.   If you can't use

him and you can't get rid of him, you will have a motivation problem on your hands. [6]

Programs should be adjusted to the needs and characteristics
of the individual. The administrator should understand the variables
of each employee in order to stimulate him to develop his own
unique capabilities. McGregor states:

> Any useful scientific knowledge consists in (1) identifica-
> tion of the factors, characteristics, or variables that are
> sufficient and necessary "causes" of a given set of phe-
> nomena, and (2) statements about the relationships among
> these factors that are associated with changes in the phe-
> nomena. Thus the performance (P) of an individual at
> work... is a function of certain characteristics of the in-
> dividual (including his knowledge, skills, motivations, at-
> titudes) and certain aspects of the environmental situation
> (including the nature of his job, the rewards associated
> with his performance, the leadership provided him). [7]

By creating the proper relationships, it seems possible to release
the individual's energy so that he can develop professionally.

This study has concluded that the characteristics, aspirations, needs and conditions reported in the following paragraphs are
connected with the motivation of the librarian and, therefore, de-
serve the careful attention of the administrator. In certain instances the lack of significant relationships was also important and
these instances are also noted.

1. Age. In general, the respondents themselves indicated
that age was of minimal importance, either as an encouragement or
as a determent to professional development activity. When correlations were made between age and other variables, however, age appeared to make a difference in several instances. For example, it
was found that generally the older librarians in both classes had
less job mobility: they had been employed in fewer libraries and
had been in their present positions without advancement for a longer
period of time than their younger counterparts. Also, they tended
to have a greater time span between receiving the Bachelor's and
MLS degrees than the younger librarians in the sample.

In the 1961 class there was a strong relationship between
age and degree of aspiration which indicated that the older the li-

brarian, the lower his degree of aspiration tended to be. Similarly, the older 1956 librarian did not generally aspire to a position very different from the one he had. Older librarians had a less intense desire to take formal course work. There was, however, no significant correlation between age and the degree of professional improvement motivation.

The administrator needs to recognize that the older librarian may require special incentives to become interested in continuing education activities, especially since there were indications that the average age of the entering librarian was gradually increasing. The overall implication is, however, that learning can and should be continuous throughout one's professional life and the administrator should encourage the older as well as the younger members in professional development activities. Such stimulation is of especial importance to the librarians in the age brackets represented in this study because they are not so old that retirements will soon deplete their numbers and the major decisions influencing library services in a drastically changing society will be made by these librarians who are already in the field.

2. Sex. There was no correlation between sex and the Professional Index Score. Nearly as many women as men in the sample were heads or assistant heads of libraries (37.9 percent were men; 26.3 percent were women). Library literature frequently refers to "a young man (or an occasional young woman) who wishes to become an administrator," but there was no evidence that women were less motivated than men in becoming top administrators. The implication is that men and women are equally capable of being challenged toward professional growth.

3. Family status. Whether a librarian was married or not, whether he had children or not, seemed to bear little relationship to any of the variables in this study. This would indicate to the administrator that large family responsibilities, or singleness, should not predetermine or prejudice his attitudes about an employee's potential.

4. Salary and financial aid. Factors dealing with costs or with salary did not appear as strong motivators. Also, there was

no significant correlation between the Professional Index Score and salary, either the current one or the increase since the first library position. It appears that salary was not the type of incentive that would determine the amount of professional development activities of the librarian.

5. Formal course work beyond the MLS degree. Only 5.8 percent of the entire sample had obtained an additional advanced degree following the MLS. However, 38.4 percent had taken some courses for credit after the MLS degree. Only one significant relationship appeared between having taken courses and other variables in the study: the 1961 respondents who aspired to a different type of position than the one they had at the time of the study were likely to have taken formal course work. The administrator should know that taking formal course work in itself is not a significant motivator.[8]

When asked what form of continuing education they preferred, 11.1 percent of the 1961 respondents chose formal course work alone as compared to 6.8 percent of the 1956 respondents. The majority of both classes (75 percent of the 1956 class and 69.1 percent of the 1961 class) favored a combination of formal course work and professional improvement activities as their means of continuing education. These statistics urge a greater exposure of employees to professional development activities beyond the library's conventional in-service training efforts.

6. Degree of aspiration. A number of significant associations were found between the degree of aspiration and other variables in the study. Those who had a high degree of aspiration tended to have a high Professional Index Score, were generally younger, were more apt to have gone directly from college to library school, and seemed to take a more professional outlook toward their work as indicated by a higher Occupations Index Score. The more recent graduates also had a higher kind and degree of motivation for formal course work.

Knowledge that possibly one-third of the staff are likely to have a high level of aspiration presents an opportunity for management to capitalize on further staff development. The manager should endeavor to identify and assist those librarians who have high aspirations and help them develop their unique capabilities for growth rather than stand as a control over their activities.

The correlation between degree of aspiration and age should also receive the administrator's attention. Generally, the younger the librarian the higher the degree of aspiration and the more likely he is to take advantage of continuing education opportunities. The administrator should consider the potential for managerial development for the librarian who has a high degree of motivation for formal course work and a high degree of aspiration. Although additional training would be needed, the necessary motivation would most likely be present.

The findings of this study suggested that professionalism might be enhanced by providing some incentives within the library for participation in professional development activities. For example, the administration could take such participation into account whenever promotions were made. Some of the respondents suggested in their open-end remarks that no one should be promoted unless he had engaged in such activities. This strategy might be particularly effective with those employees who had a high degree of aspiration. These people also tended to have a high degree of motivation for formal course work.

Such an incentive, however, would probably have maximum effectiveness only for those with high aspiration, since the sample as a whole ranked the outlook for promotion low, both as an encouragement or as a determent to professional development activity which at present is not one of the criteria for promotion. The respondents, therefore, may not have seen any relation between them.

It is recommended that administrators give more attention to helping employees realize their full potential. Chapter VIII measured the sample's kind and degree of motivation for professional development, based on a concept which Maslow labeled self-actualization, the ability and the desire of an individual to achieve full realization. The findings indicated that the professional index was associated with the degree of motivation for professional development for the total sample, and, for the 1956 class, with the kind of mo-

tivation. It seems important, therefore, that administrators and
supervisors learn how to gauge their employees' motivations and ad-
just their strategy to the librarian's individual needs and differences.
McGregor pointed out that supervisors and managers fail to
motivate their employees' higher needs. Most employees can fulfill
their physiological needs. But their attempts to seek fulfillment by
the exercise of ingenuity, creativity in problem solving, acceptance
of responsibility, and the development of knowledge, skill, and judg-
ment are often thwarted by their superiors and end in frustration and
apathy. Evidence in this study supported this theory.

The librarians sampled reported substantial opposition from
their management to their continuing education. There were other
indications that library management has underestimated the potential
capabilities of its human assets: (1) 17 percent of the sample stated
they wanted to leave for an occupation that would make better use of
their unrealized potential; (2) many of the librarians wanted to be
more fully used in their jobs and believed they were capable of more
creative and responsible performance.

For those librarians who are not striving for self-actualization, either this need is lacking in the individual at the time, or it
has had no opportunity to express itself. The latter may be due to
an organizational climate which has conditioned the individual to expect little intellectual fulfillment from his work. Often he has sought
realization of his ambitions outside the work situation. Such a situation is most likely to exist in a library where there is great disparity between what a librarian is doing and what he feels he should be
doing as a professional person.

It is difficult for any library manager to assess correctly the
diverse and changing needs of his employees, which requires a manager to emphasize his role as teacher and leader, along with his
traditional management functions. It may also call for special training of managers, possibly through motivation seminars, and the provision of competent guidance for supervisors who want to fulfill their
responsibilities to their subordinates.

Strategy that recognizes the desire of the individual to fully
realize his potential could be a way for the library to tap resources

212 Professional Development of Librarians

of creativity, skill and knowledge that are otherwise unavailable. Two practices seem to merit special consideration. First, there might be a constructive developmental approach to performance appraisal in which the librarian is encouraged to take greater responsibility for planning and appraising his own contribution to organization objectives. Second, the administrator might require that every supervisor actively promote the growth of all librarians under his direction and regularly report what he had accomplished.

It is recommended that library managers exercise a developmental style of leadership. The general tenor of responses showed that the librarians sampled thought the administrators were fostering organizational conditions which were less than ideal, even minimal, for the encouragement of professional growth. The manager should see important implications in the fact that the entire sample, with both high and low Professional Index Scores, perceived substantial opposition to their development efforts from their administration, supervisor, or library board. The respondents, however, did not just offer criticism, but presented many constructive suggestions concerning management-employee relations.

The respondents described the type of leader who could best stimulate them to participate in professional development activities. He should be approachable, open-minded, sensitive, and as concerned about the individual's goals as the library's objectives and have the ability to relate personal goals to library goals. They wanted management to keep them informed on all library matters, to recognize their performance, to encourage innovation, to be willing to accept mistakes and to let them take risks, and to expect a high level of performance from each individual librarian. They wanted to work under the supervision of administrators who were capable of organizing clear and efficient work systems.

This describes the type of developmental leadership that recent behavioral research has shown furthers the professional growth of employees.

The respondents also stressed the positive influence of the administrators who themselves participated in continuing education activities. There was a consensus that administrators should both create an atmosphere within the library hospitable to professional growth, and suggest various possibilities for staff development outside the library.

It is recommended that the individual be allowed to participate in the decisions that are made concerning continuing education. The study also revealed that librarians would be more likely to participate in activities when they had been involved in the decision making. This seems to agree with the psychological concept that when a person participates actively in a learning situation he tends to acquire the response more rapidly and more stably than when he remains passive.

The librarians sampled did not want library leaders at any level, whether in the library, the library school, or the association, to decide what programs were needed and then establish them. They wanted to be consulted and involved in the planning and implementation.

Based on the premise that all librarians are equals as professionals and should, therefore, work together in planning for professional development, some means for implementing wider involvement were suggested: regular staff meetings in which the entire staff would participate; involvement in policy formation embracing both development opportunities and the library goals in general; freedom of dialogue in the library and library association, with opportunity for feedback and the assurance that suggestions would be considered; encouragement of volunteer service for library association committees; small group discussions following large association and staff meetings from which recommendations would be sent to those responsible for the planning programs.

It is recommended that creative experimentation and innovation be encouraged. A study of business and education literature indicated willingness in these fields to spend large sums of money for experimenting with new approaches to staff development. Generally the investigators in these fields have taken research findings from the behavioral sciences and experimented with their application.

The manager should look to behavioral scientists not to solve his problems, but only to provide needed informa-

tion about them.   To ask the scientists to do more
robs the manager of his charter and violates the very
principle which he is expected to implement through job
enlargement.

However, the behavioral scientist is operating within his
proper realm of responsibility if he serves as a change
agent by assisting managers in planning the application of
theories and principles and by giving visibility to their
achievements. [9]

Suggestions from respondents relating to innovation clustered
in two areas: (1) objectivity and open-mindedness of the administration to creativity and experimentation; and (2) flexibility regarding
method, time, and place of scheduling.

The respondents expressed the desire for encouragement to
experiment with innovative ideas in their work assignments.   They
felt that growth would come more readily if staff members were allowed to experiment with research-based concepts learned from their
reading or other contacts.   This would be a means of realizing a
long-held goal that library practice and research go hand in hand.
In this way continuing education would be an integral part of library
life.

It seems important that library leaders and planners concentrate on methods for extending opportunities for continuing education
to areas where they are now absent or inadequate.   The study showed
that respondents in the heavily populated areas were more involved
in professional development activities than those in sparsely populated areas.   The respondents suggested that library schools and associations, as well as Federal and state planners, distribute programs and meetings geographically to compensate for the unequal opportunity created by population density.   In addition, they advocated
a master plan that could determine the greatest need at any given
period in time.

Time was isolated as an important element of continuing education.   It was suggested that the library could become a "teaching
library" where a part of the librarian's work load would include
practical aspects of in-service training.   This in itself would encourage the employees toward development activities if the administration
felt they were important enough to warrant this attention.   The col-

lege and university librarians in the sample felt that sabbatical leave should be granted to librarians for research and study in the same manner that it was to professors. Again, the respondents were expressing the concept that continuing education should not be something tacked on or separate, but that it should be an integral part of the organizational climate of the library.

In summary, the profession should make more effort to insure the use of new and creative ideas in staff development. Bundy and Wasserman recognized the pith of the problem: "Progress in librarianship is made by only a relatively small number. Innovation remains on trial when it should be encouraged. The field stands conservative and deeply rooted in the past at a time when such a stance exposes it to danger."[10]

It is recommended that administrators encourage qualified librarians to engage in research. The respondents felt that for those librarians who did research, growth would follow automatically, and they offered many suggestions for stimulating such activity. They also stressed making the results of research more visible to the profession at large in the belief that this would promote more scholarly work and would indirectly add stature to librarianship. The consensus was that promotion of research by the employing library and the library association would serve as a general stimulus for professionalism.

It could be surmised from this study that the profession does not sufficiently honor or recognize those who engage in research to make the effort seem worthwhile. Respondents in both classes who had published were generally dissatisfied with their career progress to date. Also, there was no correlation between career advancement (based on those who were directors and assistant directors) and publication or research. Among academic and special librarians (where research seems to be given more recognition), research was rated 11, out of 37 items, in importance as a development activity. On the other hand, it was ranked 27 by public librarians and 33 by the school librarians.

III. Formulation of a Concept of Career Development

The improvement of continuing education requires the formulation of a clear concept of career development. Such a policy
would help to increase librarians' desire to continue their learning
and to extend their competence. This would place increased responsibility on the library administrator, educator, association leader,
and state and Federal planners.

Findings Indicating Absence of a
System of Career Development

1. The study indicated a rapid rate of advancement. It was
noted in Chapter III that 67. 4 percent of the graduates who had been
in library work 5 years had achieved administrative responsibility
either as a library director, associate or assistant librarian, department or division head, or branch head; 25. 6 percent of these
graduates were the directors or assistant directors of libraries.
Of those who had been out of library school for 10 years, 78. 8 percent were in administrative posts; 40. 4 percent were directors or
assistant directors of libraries.[11] The 1956 graduate was supervising an average of 15 library employees: the 1961 graduate, 11.

On the basis of the MLS degree and experience gained on the
job, had these librarians acquired a solid grasp of the administrative skills necessary to direct these people? From the data collected, specific training for administrative positions was not apparent. This statement is based on the fact that 70. 3 percent of the
sample had entered library school with an undergraduate major in
the humanities or social sciences. In library school, their instruction was largely centered on technical functions with only an introduction to administration, as revealed by curriculum content in catalogs. Those graduates who did take post-MLS courses for credit
generally concentrated on the humanities and social sciences, which
would not presumably contribute directly to their managerial
skills.[12]

The training activities for administrative development that were reported would not appear to give the depth necessary for sound practice, even though this area ranked third in the total number of days spent in workshops. The median number of days spent in workshops and short-term courses of all types during the last 5 years was three-fifths of a day a year. The respondents considered nearly 20 percent of the training courses taken in administration of little or no help. Only 4 research projects were reported in the area of administration, and only 8 respondents had participated in voluntary study groups in this area.

2. Similarly, full utilization of the new data-processing technology will require that librarians be more rigorously trained in automation of library services. If the librarians are not trained in this field, the engineers and scientists will inherit the positions of leadership. True, the respondents recognized the importance of this knowledge since automation was a substantial favorite of the workshops and short training courses, both by days in attendance and also by times listed by subject area. Of these activities, however, 19 per cent were considered of little or no help, and the number of days, when distributed over the sample, were so few that training in depth would appear to be improbable. Only 3, or 2.2 percent of the entire sample, had taken formal course work for credit in automation.

3. Seventeen percent of the sample, all with high participation in professional development activities, expressed a desire to leave librarianship for a profession that would make fuller use of their capabilities and potential. Of the 24 librarians who indicated this attitude, all but 3 thought they had made good progress in the profession to date.

4. Actual opposition was perceived by some of the librarians from their superiors. Of the total sample, 33.4 percent felt that their supervisors opposed their taking further formal course work; 31.2 percent felt this from their administrators, and 18.8 percent from their governing boards. Regarding participation in professional improvement activities, 16.7 percent felt opposition from their administrators, 15.2 percent from their supervisors, and 8.8 per-

cent from their governing boards.

5. When the librarians were asked what position they hoped
to achieve in 10 years, 55. 7 percent said they wanted a high administrative position. This points to the need for additional training in
this area. But what of the other librarians who did not aspire to
management?

Of the total sample, 15. 9 percent indicated dissatisfaction
with the progress of their careers to date. However these respondents had been active in professional development activities.

6. It is possible that in his attempts to improve himself, the
librarian has concentrated on the field in which he specialized and
cannot rise to the higher echelons unless he adds to his specialized
knowledge the skills and concepts of supervision and management.
These respondents felt they were ready for promotion. From the
administration's point of view they may have lacked the necessary
skills of management and supervision and so were held back. In
any event, dissatisfaction was expressed with the present system
which allows for advancement only by the single avenue of increased
management responsibilities. The suggestion was made that there
should be career advancement along two routes: bibliographic services and guidance to clients, and administration. In this way, comparable salaries, titles, and status would be possible along either of
these two routes.

Fifty-three percent of the sample entered librarianship from
a previous occupation. For 6. 5 percent, librarianship was a third
career rather than the second. In most cases there were noticeable
time gaps between the individual's undergraduate degree and his MLS
degree. For the women in the sample there was an average gap of
10. 7 years between the Bachelor's degree and MLS; for the men
there was an average gap of 6. 8 years. The average age at which
the women in the sample received their professional degree was 37;
the average age for the men was 31. 4.

When the profession is overbalanced by those who come from
other professions, it means that the age of the entering librarian is
increased and elsewhere in this study it has been shown that age has
a significant relationship to several aspects of professionalism. In

general, the older the librarian, the less his job mobility, the lower
his salary, the slower his advancement to other positions, the lower
his degree of aspiration, the lower his degree of motivation to formal study, and the less likely he is to aspire to a different kind of
job. From the economic as well as the qualitative standpoint, it
seems reasonable that in general those persons should be selected
who can profit most from preparation and who plan to make it a life-
time career, or at least give 15 to 20 years of professional service
along with family-rearing and homemaking. It is questionable that
librarianship should welcome sizeable numbers of persons who look
upon their preparation as an easy means of security, as an escape
from contemporary realities, or as a solution to boredom after other careers.

7. There were indications of unequal availability of continuing
education opportunities throughout the country. Those in population
centers of 100,000 and larger were more involved in professional
development activities than those in sparsely populated areas; those
living west of the Mississippi were more deeply involved than those
living east of the Mississippi.

8. The wisdom of Carleton Joeckel's observation that librarians would do well to seek models for comparative study in other disciplines still holds. [13] The soil is richer today than when
Joeckel wrote in 1939, but unfortunately the library profession has
not made extensive use of his sound advice. The present findings
indicate an indifference to current research in the behavioral sciences. For example, only 60 percent of the 1956 class and 38 percent of the 1961 class showed concern for the personal as well as
the professional problems of fellow workers. This suggests that respondents were not fully aware of the importance of the supervisor
knowing the whole man and his needs. Since the more recent graduates showed considerably less interest than the older graduates, this
implied that those in the sample probably left library school without
conceptual skill in this area. [14]

Librarianship is related to such fields as business, public
administration, political science, communications, and education,
but none of these are being explored to any substantial degree in li-

brary literature or research. Bundy warned: "Librarians need to
be mindful of the danger to any group whose members limit their
contacts only to their own group."[15] These views suggest that the
interdisciplinary approach to librarianship should receive greater
emphasis, both in the library school and in the administrator's approach to library problems.

     9. It is a waste of manpower to have trained librarians who
are not being fully used. Unless the profession provides and en-
courages opportunities for career development, libraries will probably lose their most talented professional staff at an increasing rate.
Witness the 17 percent of the sample who expressed a wish to leave
librarianship, although the majority of them were satisfied with the
progress they had made since graduation.

     Libraries compete with enterprises that invest large sums of
money in training methods and employ some of the nation's best
teachers. Perhaps even more important, such enterprises frequently provide funds for continuing experimentation with programs for
professional growth, including competent assistance to managers who
want to fulfill their responsibilities for the development of their subordinates.

Recommendations for Improving the
Process of Career Development

     1. Library school administrators should carefully consider
the evidence in this study of the need for more training in administration. This study reinforces data found in earlier studies: that a
large percentage of MLS graduates achieved administrative and supervisory positions rapidly, yet one of the most neglected aspects of
librarianship is administration. There was also some evidence that
supported recent affirmations in library literature that one of the
greatest--if not the greatest--obstacles to professionalism is the administrative pattern that prevails in libraries.[16]

     This dearth of administrative knowledge has been brought to
the attention of the profession repeatedly by such authors as Joeckel,
in 1939; Martin, in 1945; Wheeler and Korb, in 1946; Bryan, in

1952; Wasserman, in 1958; and Bundy and Wasserman in 1968.[17]

In his study of 676 academic librarians, Perry Morrison found that the supervisory qualities among librarians were very low --the most disturbing part of his whole study. He found that the outlook of library supervisors was entirely different from supervisors in other occupations and believed that this had a direct influence on the recruitment of new librarians.[18]

Based on the findings to date, it seems that the systematic preparation of librarians as managers should be initiated in the library school at the MLS level. Such training should emphasize theory and conceptual skill taught from an interdisciplinary point of view. Rather than dropping them, as noted in some recent library school catalogs, the core course or courses in administration should be strengthened and enriched in every possible way. Joeckel considered improved training in administration a major need of the profession in 1939. How much more important it should be considered today when libraries have become big business operations, as more and more systems are created, and as the supportive staff increases drastically.

If library schools refuse to acknowledge their responsibility in this area, more and more institutions will probably select non-librarians as directors. In fact, this was strongly recommended by a regional director of the American Library Trustee Association at the Annual ALA conference in 1967. Lettie Gay Carson questioned the advisability of having library directors who were librarians.

> Why insist that librarians perform a job for which they have little training--or aptitude? Why not follow the pattern in many a business and hire trained and experienced administrators--graduates of the Maxwell School of Business... or the Harvard Graduate School of Business Administration--and get directors who can put into effect established principles of efficient administration--and let librarians concentrate on what they know how to do? Service for which there is a tremendous demand? ... I am suggesting that a thorough examination of library training and library attitudes in the light of present-day needs might lead to an entirely new era of service--and that trustees, responsible for library service, should apply themselves to... these issues.[19]

This force of outside intervention to influence needed administrative changes has also been noted in a number of university libraries where top library administrators have been relieved of their responsibilities or where outside insistence has resulted in the addition of more expert non-library personnel to the staffs of the libraries.

2. Special attention should be given to certain recruitment needs.

a. A regular forecasting of the number of people needed for the different kinds of positions in librarianship so that people with varying educational backgrounds and skills can be provided to meet the needs of the profession.

b. A more aggressive method of attracting both those with special talents who can be trained to fill top-level career positions and those who see librarianship as a client-oriented public service.

c. Provision for lateral entry into the profession by mature well-trained individuals from other professions who are needed in librarianship, such as the business manager, the systems analyst, the statistician, or the public relations expert.

d. Willingness to experiment with new and creative approaches to recruitment, with a realistic picture of the librarian's actual role as a professional.

e. Recognition that librarianship deserves status as a profession only when those who prepare for it plan to make it a lifetime career.

Without minimizing the importance of recruitment, it must be realized that recruitment in itself cannot be the principal answer to the library manpower shortage. Even if it were possible to do a perfect job of recruiting there are other conditions, indicated in sections of this study, which should be remedied. One is the fuller utilization of the manpower already recruited.

3. A rationale should be developed for the requirements of different career progressions in librarianship. The individual should be aware of the requirements for his advancement in the profession,

whether he chooses his career in bibliographic services and guidance or in administrative positions.

For example, if he chooses to advance as an administrator, he will need the ability to direct others; an understanding of the processes of management; a respect for the importance of motivation; a thorough understanding of the library's internal system; and an understanding of the library's environment, particularly in the light of major social and technological changes.

4. A policy of career development should be established for acquiring the competencies needed. Opportunities for special training should be easily available to the librarian through the cooperative efforts of the employing library, the library school, library associations, and library planners at the state and Federal levels. In addition, there is need for regularly examining and improving the processes of selection, assignment, and promotion. The library profession could profitably study the programs of industry, business and the Federal government, where the concepts of the behavioral sciences are being used to motivate employees.

5. Career development and continuing education could be a major responsibility of a central organization. Developing a visible policy of career development may best be undertaken by the American Library Association, as is done by other professional organizations. In 1965, Rothstein urged that the American Library Association should "move to establish offices for continuing professional education with paid secretaries and field workers comparable to, say, the ALA Recruitment Office."[20]

Such an office could follow up the National Education Association's effort to focus attention of the whole profession on continuing education. That initial effort consisted of 8 regional conferences conducted in different sections of the country to discuss continuing education through 101 individual study groups. The problems and central ideas about continuing education were identified and recommendations for action made which were studied and are now being implemented by the National Education Association.[21]

In addition to developing a career policy, promoting profession-wide interest in continuing education, and seeking sources of support, Rothstein suggested that a secretariat for continuing education might design a formal program of courses leading to definite objectives, perhaps similar to the plan for advanced studies worked out by the Medical Library Association. [22] For those not wishing to engage in or to be certified in any way for having taken formal courses, the office could offer numerous aids to self-study or small independent study groups.

Such a central office could also offer consultant services. State library associations could be assisted with their plans and programs for the continuing education of their members. In an address given in 1966, Sarah Reed emphasized the important role that library associations should play in continuing education for the profession. She stated:

> Only as associations make the soundest possible provision for the education of its most precious resource--its membership--will they have fulfilled one of their primary obligations as professional library associations. [23]

Even if a state association considers itself "the mainspring of library development in the State," [24] the constantly changing, often inexperienced, leadership needs assistance in long-range planning. A central office at the Headquarters of the American Library Association would also be the natural promoter of administration workshops to train the volunteer leaders in every section of the country.

This suggestion for a central headquarters office does not mean that all continuing education activity should be centered there but that it could serve as the coordinating agent and resource center for all of the groups responsible for continuing education.

IV. Some Possible Research Projects
Stemming From This Study

The central purpose of this study has been to identify some of the factors that motivate or deter librarians in various professional development activities. In this process a general picture has been presented which, in some instances, indicated possible relationships. It would now seem valuable to do more detailed analyses in those specific areas where significant associations were found based on broader populations for verification. The following suggestions are offered:

1. A future study, perhaps 5 years from now, could test the reliability of this study by comparing the 1961 group with a 1966 group. A longer time span between the groups might reveal differences due to the greater maturity of one group rather than to any intrinsic difference between them. Such a study might concentrate on the content versus context factors which influence motivation. The measurements for the professional index and for the degree of aspiration seemed to be satisfactory devices and could also be recommended for use in such a study.

2. It is important to identify, clarify, and delineate the knowledge, skills, and attitudes that are essential to library service and that make one truly a professional. Such knowlege would be of great value in building library school curricula and provide valuable criteria in developing continuing education programs. A related important study would investigate the professional status of information science in relation to librarianship.

3. Many special studies of career development are needed. Ideally these might emanate from a research center where the changing requirements and needs of librarians could be followed and the results of related studies synchronized.

Two groups of respondents would make particularly interesting subjects of research. One was the group with a high Professional Index Score. Identifying the critical incidents which influenced their career development would presumably be significant to anyone creating programs of professional development. The other group would be those who wished to leave librarianship for another profession, although they appeared to be successful. Such a study could look more deeply into their reasons, determine if they had any common characteristics, and offer recommendations for keeping well-qualified librarians within the profession. It might also offer some helpful guidelines to the admission officers of library schools.

Another study which might lead to helpful admission policy would be to investigate ability patterns which are characteristic of

226 Professional Development of Librarians

successful students in library science curricula.

4. The various types of activity could be evaluated to identify the most effective approaches to professional development.

5. The findings reported here indicated that many library managers need to be made aware of their own importance in the professional development of their staff. It would be valuable to discover what type of supervisors and managers are successful and whether those managers who had formal training or course work in administration, beyond that received in library schools, were more effective in stimulating their employees.

6. Research should be done to show library managers how they can use the findings from the behavioral sciences in their continuing education program. Areas where a great deal might be accomplished are job enrichment, a developmental approach to employee appraisal, sensitivity training, involvement of librarians in decision making in their professional activities, and the creation of a climate conducive to growth within the library.

7. In order to upgrade the library profession's image in the eyes of other occupations, a questionnaire could be submitted to educators, doctors, ministers, lawyers, politicians, technicians, even unskilled laborers. While the librarians may regard certain activities as extremely important for professional growth, persons in other occupations may consider other activities of more importance.

8. Much of the data gathered in this study has not been analyzed in detail and further research could be done using the material already collected, for example, to compare relationships by types of library. Another example would be that respondents from the 1961 class with a higher level of aspiration generally tended to be younger than those with a lower aspiration score. How did age difference affect their participation in professional development activities? This might lead to some considerations for admission to library school.

In conclusion, no area of investigation is more important to the individual librarian and to the well being of the entire profession than valid, reliable inquiries into the entire field of education and utilization of staff. The findings reported here attest to the complexity and the importance of maintaining effective programs of professional development. The only sound basis for such programming is well planned and successfully implemented programs of research, experimentation, and evaluation.

Notes

1. In 1924 Learned described an ideal public librarian as follows:
   They must indeed understand their several fields of knowledge, but they must understand the world of men as well or better; their excellence is measured by their power to connect the two. They must have sensitized minds that in addition to a good education possess quick insight into new relations and novel applications. They must... discover how knowledge in books may be selected and arranged the better to meet the changing demands or a shifting point of view. They should work beneath the surface in terms of truth and a wiser world.
   Learned, William S. The American Public Library and the Diffusion of Knowledge (New York: Harcourt, Brace and Company, 1924), p. 17.

2. Gardner, John Self-Renewal (New York: Harper & Row, 1963), p. 12.

3. Rothstein, Samuel "Nobody's Baby: A Brief Sermon on Continuing Professional Education" Library Journal 90:2226 (May 15, 1965).

4. Houle, Cyril O. "The Role of Continuing Education in Current Professional Development" ALA Bulletin 41:261 (March, 1967).

5. Herzberg, Frederick "One More Time: How Do You Motivate Employees?" Harvard Business Review 46:59 (January-February, 1968).

6. Ibid., 62.

7. Bennis, Warren G., and Schein, Edgar H. (eds.) Leadership and Motivation: Essays of Douglas McGregor (Cambridge: The Massachusetts Institute of Technology Press, 1966), p. 201.

8. In his study of the motivation of agricultural agents for professional development, Swanson found that if the respondent had taken some graduate work this was one of the four factors most closely related to greater professional development motivation. Harold B. Swanson, "Factors Associated with Motivation Toward Professional Development of County Agricultural Extension Agents in Minnesota" (unpublished Doctor's disser-

228   Professional Development of Librarians

tation, University of Wisconsin, 1965), p. 164-65.

9. Gomersall, Earl R. , and Myers, M. Scott "Breakthrough in
    On-the-Job Training" Harvard Business Review 44:71 (July-
    August, 1966).

10. Bundy, Mary Lee, and Wasserman, Paul "Professionalism Re-
    considered" College and Research Libraries 29:25-26 (Janu-
    ary, 1968).

11. Chapter III, p. 45. These percentages do not include 3 other
    groups also needing administrative skills: first-line super-
    visors, coordinators, and those operating one or two man li-
    braries.

12. Fields of specialization for formal course work following the
    MLS listed were: 32. 1 percent in the humanities and 30. 2
    percent in the social sciences. Two other subjects studied
    were education and library science. Automation accounted
    for 5. 7 percent of the formal courses taken; none were listed
    for the natural sciences.

13. Joeckel, Carleton B. (ed.) Current Issues in Library Adminis-
    tration: Papers Presented before the Library Institute at the
    University of Chicago, August 1-12, 1938 (Chicago: Uni-
    versity of Chicago Press, 1939), p. vii-ix.

14. The difference between the two classes was statistically signifi-
    cant: Chi square = 5. 88; P = . 01.

15. Bundy, Mary Lee "Public Library Administrators View Their
    Professional Periodicals" Illinois Libraries 43:418 (June,
    1961).

16. Smith, Eldred "Libraries and Unions: The Berkeley Experi-
    ence" Library Journal 93:718 (February 15, 1968).

17. Joeckel, op. cit. ; Lowell Martin "Shall Library Schools Teach
    Administration?" College and Research Libraries 6:335-340
    (September, 1945) Joseph L. Wheeler Progress and Problems
    in Education for Librarianship (New York: Carnegie Corpora-
    tion, 1946); George M. Korb " 'Successful' Librarians as Re-
    vealed in 'Who's Who in America' " Wilson Library Bulletin
    20:603-604, 607 (April, 1946); Alice I. Bryan The Public Li-
    brarian: A Report of the Public Library Inquiry (New York:
    Columbia University Press, 1952); Paul Wasserman "Devel-
    opment of Administration in Library Service: Current Status
    and Future Prospects" College and Research Libraries 19:
    283-294 (July, 1958); Bundy and Wasserman College and Re-
    search Libraries 29:5-26 (January, 1968).

18. Morrison, Perry D. "The Personality of the Academic Li-
    brarian" College & Research Libraries 24:366 (Sept. 1963).

19. Carson, Lettie Gay "Remarks at ALA Meeting, Region VII" (paper read at the American Library Association Annual Conference, San Francisco, California, June 25, 1967), p. 3. (Mimeographed.)

20. Rothstein Library Journal 90:2227 (May 15, 1965).

21. National Education Association of the United States, National Commission on Teacher Education and Professional Standards, The Development of the Career Teacher. Professional Responsibility for Continuing Education (Washington: National Education Association, 1964).

22. Rothstein, loc. cit.

23. Reed, Sarah R. "Education Activities of Library Associations" (paper read at the Drexel Institute of Technology Library Association Administration Workshop, Philadelphia, Pennsylvania, November 10, 1966), p. 14. (Mimeographed.)

24. Warncke, Ruth "State Libraries, Library Associations and Library Schools: Partners in Library Development" South Dakota Library Bulletin 51:119 (October-December, 1965).

Bibliography

A. Books

American Association of School Librarians and the National Commission on Teacher Education and Professional Standards
The Teachers' Library: How to Organize It and What to Include Washington: National Education Association, 1966.

American Library Association National Inventory of Library Needs
Chicago: American Library Association, 1965.

American Library Association, Office for Library Education Continuing Education for Librarians--Conferences, Workshops,
and Short Courses 1967-68 Chicago: American Library
Association, 1967.

---- Continuing Education for Librarians--Conferences, Workshops,
and Short Courses 1968-69 Chicago: American Library
Association, 1967.

Argyris, Chris Integrating the Individual and the Organization
New York: John Wiley and Sons, 1964.

---- Personality and Organization: The Conflict Between System
and the Individual New York: Harper and Row, 1957.

Ash, Lee (ed.) Who's Who in Library Service: A Biographical
Directory of Professional Librarians in the United States and
Canada Ed. 4 New York: Shoe String Press, Inc., 1966.

Asheim, Lester E. (ed.) The Core of Education for Librarianship:
A Report of a Workshop Held under the Auspices of the
Graduate Library School of the University of Chicago, August
10-15, 1953 Chicago: American Library Association, 1954.

---- Library Manpower: Needs and Utilization. A Conference Co-
sponsored by The Office for Library Education and The Library Administration Division of the American Library Association with the Cooperation of the National Book Committee, March 9-11, 1967, Washington Chicago: American Library Association, 1967.

Atkinson, John W. Motives in Fantasy, Action, and Society
Princeton, N. J.: D. Van Nostrand Company, Inc., 1958.

230

Barnard, Chester I.   The Functions of the Executive   Cambridge: Harvard University Press, 1938.

Bennis, Warren G.   Changing Organizations   New York: McGraw-Hill Book Co., 1966.

----, and Schein, Edgar H. (eds.)   Leadership and Motivation: Essays of Douglas McGregor   With the collaboration of Caroline McGregor   Cambridge: The Massachusetts Institute of Technology Press, 1966.

Blake, Robert R., and Mouton, Jane S.   The Managerial Grid: Key Orientations for Achieving Production Through People   Houston: Gulf Publishing Company, 1964.

Bryan, Alice I.   Public Librarian: A Report of the Public Library Inquiry   New York: Columbia University Press, 1952.

Carr-Saunders, Alexander M., and Wilson, P. S.   The Professions   Oxford: Clarendon Press, 1933.

Clark, Harold F., and Sloan, Harold S.   Classrooms in the Factories: An Account of Educational Activities Conducted by American Industries   Rutherford, N. J.:   Institute of Research, Fairleigh-Dickinson College, 1958.

Conant, James G.   The Education of American Teachers   New York: McGraw-Hill Book Co., 1963.

Corson, John J., and Paul, R. Shale   Men Near the Top   Baltimore: The Johns Hopkins Press, 1966.

Danton, J. Periam, and Merritt, LeRoy C.   "Characteristics of the Graduates of the University of California School of Librarianship"   University of Illinois Library School Occasional Papers No. 22   Urbana, Ill.:   University of Illinois, 1951.

Doby, John T. (ed.)   An Introduction to Social Research   Harrisburg: Stackpole Books, 1954.

Drennan, Henry T., and Darling, Richard L.   Library Manpower: Occupational Characteristics of Public and School Librarians   Washington: Government Printing Office, 1966.

Edwards, Allen L.   Statistical Analysis for Students in Psychology and Education   New York: Rinehart and Company, 1946.

Ennis, Philip H., and Winger, Howard W. (eds.)   Seven Questions About the Profession of Librarianship   The 26th Annual Conference of the Graduate School, June 21-23, 1961   University of Chicago Studies in Library Science   Chicago: University of Chicago Press, 1962.

231

Flexner, Abraham   Universities: American, English, German
    New York: Oxford University Press, 1930.

Garceau, Oliver   Political Life of the American Medical Associa-
    tion   Cambridge: Harvard University Press, 1941.

Gardner, John W.   Excellence: Can We Be Equal and Excellent
    Too?   New York: Harper and Row, 1961.

----   Self-Renewal: The Individual and the Innovative Society
    New York: Harper and Row, 1964.

Gellerman, Saul W.   Motivation and Productivity   New York:
    American Management Association, Inc., 1963.

Good, Carter V.   Essentials of Educational Research: Methodology
    and Design   New York: Appleton-Century-Crofts, 1966.

Goode, William J.   "The Librarian: From Occupation to Profes-
    sion?"   Seven Questions About the Profession of Librarian-
    ship   Philip H. Ennis and Howard W. Winger, editors
    Chicago: University of Chicago Press, 1961.

Guilford, Jay P.   Fundamental Statistics in Psychology and Educa-
    tion   Ed. 3   New York: McGraw-Hill Book Co., 1956.

Haggerty, M. E.   The Faculty   Volume II of The Evaluation of
    Higher Institutions   Chicago: The University of Chicago
    Press, 1957.

Haire, Mason   Psychology in Management   Ed. 2   New York:
    McGraw-Hill Book Co., 1964.

Harvey, John Frederick   The Librarian's Career: A Study of Mo-
    bility   ACRL Microcard Series No. 85   Rochester, N. Y.:
    University of Rochester Press, 1957.

Havighurst, Robert J.   Developmental Tasks and Education   New
    York: David McKay, Inc., 1962.

Herzberg, Frederick; Mausner, Bernard; Peterson, Richard, and
    Capewell, Dora F.   Job Attitudes   Pittsburgh: Psychologi-
    cal Service of Pittsburgh, 1957.

Herzberg, Frederick; Mausner, Bernard and Snyderman, Barbara
    The Motivation to Work   Ed. 2   New York: John Wiley and
    Sons, Inc., 1959.

Homans, G. C.   The Human Group   New York: Harcourt, Brace,
    1950.

Houle, Cyril O.   The Inquiring Mind   Madison, Wisc.: The Uni-
    versity of Wisconsin Press, 1961.

232

Houston, George C. Manager Development: Principles and Perspectives Homewood, Ill. : Richard D. Irwin, 1961.

Hyman, Herbert Survey Design and Analysis Glencoe, Ill. : Free Press of Glencoe, 1955.

Joeckel, Carleton B. (ed.) Current Issues in Library Administration: Papers Presented Before the Library Institute at the University of Chicago, August 1-12, 1938 Chicago: University of Chicago Press, 1939.

Jones, Marshall R. (ed.) Nebraska Symposium on Motivation: 1955 Lincoln, Nebr. : University of Nebraska Press, 1955.

Kellogg Foundation Continuing Education: An Evolving Form of Adult Education Battle Creek, Mich. : W. K. Kellogg Foundation, n. d.

---- Toward Improved School Administration: A Decade of Professional Effort to Heighten Administrative Understanding and Skills Battle Creek, Mich. : W. K. Kellogg Foundation, 1961.

Keppel, Francis The Necessary Revolution in American Education New York: Holt, 1966.

Kortendick, James J. The Library in the Catholic Theological Seminary in the United States Washington: The Catholic University of America Press, 1963.

Landis, Benson Y. Professional Codes New York: Teachers College, Columbia University, 1927.

Learned, William S. The American Public Library and the Diffusion of Knowledge New York: Harcourt, Brace and Company, 1924.

Leavitt, Harold J. Managerial Psychology Chicago: The University of Chicago Press, 1958.

Lee, Robert E. Continuing Education for Adults Through the American Public Library, 1833-1964 Chicago: American Library Association, 1966.

Leigh, Robert D. The Public Library in the United States: The General Report of the Public Library Inquiry New York: Columbia University Press, 1950.

Lester, Richard Manpower Planning in a Free Society Princeton, N. J. : Princeton University Press, 1965.

Lewin, Kurt Resolving Social Conflict New York: Harper, 1950.

233

Lieberman, Myron Education as a Profession Englewood Cliffs,
  N. J. : Prentice-Hall, 1956.

Likert, Rensis The Human Organization: Its Management and
  Value New York: McGraw-Hill Book Company, 1967.

---- "A Motivational Approach to a Modified Theory of Organization and Management" Modern Organization Theory Mason
  Haire, editor New York: John Wiley, 1959, p. 184-217

---- New Patterns of Management New York: McGraw-Hill Book
  Co. , 1961.

Lindsley, Donald B. "Psychophysiology and Motivation" Nebraska
  Symposium on Motivation: 1957 Lincoln, Nebr. : University
  of Nebraska Press, 1957.

Lindzey, Gardner Assessment of Human Motives New York:
  Rinehart, 1958.

McClelland, David The Achieving Society Princeton, N. J. : Van
  Nostrand, 1961.

---- Studies in Motivation New York: Appleton-Century-Crofts,
  1955.

McGlothin, William J. The Professional Schools New York: The
  Center for Applied Research in Education, Inc. , 1964.

McGregor, Douglas The Human Side of Enterprise New York:
  McGraw-Hill Book Co. , 1960.

Madsen, K. B. Theories of Motivation Cleveland, Ohio: Howard
  Allen, 1961.

Maslow, Abraham H. Motivation and Personality New York:
  Harper and Bros. , 1954.

Maxwell, Albert E. Analyzing Qualitative Data New York: Wiley,
  1961.

Mayo, Elton The Social Problems of an Industrial Civilization
  Boston: Harvard Business School, 1945.

Metcalf, Henry C. , and Urwick, L. (eds.) Dynamic Administration: The Collected Papers of Mary Parker Follett New
  York: Harper and Brothers, 1940.

Murphy, Gardner "Social Motivation" Handbook of Social Psychology Vol. II Gardner Lindzey, editor Cambridge: Addi-
  son-Wesley Publishing Co. , 1954.

National Education Association, National Commission on Teacher

Education and Professional Standards   The Development of
the Career Teacher: Professional Responsibility for Continuing Education   Washington: National Education Association,
1964.

---- A Position Paper on Teacher Education and Professional
     Standards   Washington: National Education Association, 1963.

---- What You Should Know About New Horizons: A Condensation
     of New Horizons for the Teaching Profession, a Report of
     the Task Force on New Horizons in Teacher Education and
     Professional Standards   Washington: National Education As-
     sociation, 1962.

National Manpower Council   Manpower Policies for a Democratic
     Society   New York: Columbia University Press, 1965.

National Society for the Study of Education   Education for the Pro-
     fessions   Chicago: University of Chicago Press, 1962.

Presthus, Robert V.   The Organizational Society   New York:
     Knopf, 1962.

Professional Librarians: An Inventory of Personnel and Personnel
     Needs in Wisconsin in College, University, School, Public
     and Special Libraries   Madison: University of Wisconsin
     Library School, 1965.

Public Opinion Research Corporation   How to Improve Your ...
     Trade and Professional Association   Research Report of
     the Public Opinion Index for Industry   Princeton, N. J. :
     Opinion Research Corporation, 1966.

Reece, Ernest   The Task and Training of Librarians: Report of a
     Field Investigation   New York: Kings Crown Press, 1949.

Reed, Sarah R. (ed.)   Continuing Education for Librarians--Confer-
     ences, Workshops and Short Courses, 1964-1965.   Washing-
     ton: Office of Education, U. S. Department of Health, Educa-
     tion, and Welfare, 1964.

---- Continuing Education for Librarians--Conferences, Workshops,
     and Short Courses, 1966-1967.   Washington: Office of Educa-
     tion, U. S. Department of Health, Education, and Welfare,
     1966.

---- (ed.)   Problems of Library School Administration: Report of
     an Institute, April 14-15, 1965, Washington, D. C.   Washing-
     ton: U. S. Department of Health, Education, and Welfare,
     1965.

---- and Toye, Willie P.   Continuing Education for Librarians--
     Conferences, Workshops and Short Courses, 1965-1966

Washington: Office of Education, U. S. Department of Health, Education, and Welfare, 1965.

St. John, Francis R.   "In-Service Training" Personnel Administration in Libraries: Papers Presented before the Library Institute at the University of Chicago, August 27-September 1, 1945, Lowell Martin, editor   Chicago: The University of Chicago Press, 1946, p. 131-147.

Scates, Douglas E.   "Analysis of a Professional Organization: The American Educational Research Association in 1948" Growing Points in Educational Research, 1949   Official Report of the American Educational Research Association   Washington: The American Educational Research Association, 1949.

Schein, Edgar H.   Organization Psychology   Englewood Cliffs, N. J. : Prentice-Hall, 1965.

Schreier, Fred T.   Human Motivation, Probability, and Meaning   Glencoe, Ill. : Free Press of Glencoe, 1957.

Scott, William G.   Human Relations in Management: A Behavioral Science Approach: Philosophy Analysis and Issues   Homewood, Ill. : Richard D. Irwin, Inc. , 1962.

Selltiz, Claire, and others   Research Methods in Social Relations   Revised 1 volume edition   New York: Holt, Rinehart and Winston, 1959.

Selznick, Philip   Leadership in Administration   Evanston, Ill. : Harper, 1957.

Simon, Herbert A.   Administrative Behavior   Ed. 2   New York: Macmillan, 1957.

Spurr, William A. ; Kellogg, Lester S; and Smith, John H.   Business and Economic Statistics   New York: Richard D. Irwin, 1961.

Stahl, O. Glenn   Public Personnel Administration   Ed. 6   New York: Harper, 1964.

Standards for Statistical Surveys   Exhibit A, Circular No. A-46 Washington: Executive Office of the President, Bureau of the Budget, March 28, 1952.

Stevenson, Charles L.   Ethics and Language   New Haven: Yale University Press, 1944.

Stogdill, Ralph   Individual Behavior and Group Adjustment   New York: Oxford University Press, 1959.

Stone, Elizabeth W.   An Analysis of the Core Administration Course of the Library Schools Accredited by the American Library Association ACRL Microcard Series No. 138: M. S. Thesis, Department of Library Science, The Catholic University of America, 1961 Rochester, N. Y. : University of Rochester Press for Association of College and Research Libraries, 1962.

---- Training for the Improvement of Library Administration Urbana, Ill. : University of Illinois, 1967.

Swank, Raymond C. "The Graduate Library School Curriculum" Problems of Library School Administration: Report of an Institute, April 14-15, 1965, Washington, D. C. Washington: Office of Education, U. S. Department of Health, Education, and Welfare, 1965.

Tannenbaum, Robert, and others Leadership and Organization: A Behavioral Science Approach New York: McGraw-Hill, 1961.

Tippett, L. H. C. (ed.) Random Sampling Numbers No. XV in Tracts for Computers London: Cambridge University Press, 1952.

Toops, H. A. "Questionnaire" Encyclopedia of Educational Research W. S. Monroe, editor New York: Macmillan, 1941.

Ulich, Robert Crisis and Hope in American Education Boston: The Beacon Press, 1951.

Vieg, John A. "The Growth of Public Administration" Elements of Public Administration Fritz Morstein Marx, editor New York: Prentice-Hall, 1946.

Viteles, Morris S. Motivation and Morale in Industry New York: W. W. Norton and Company, 1953.

Vroom, Victor Work and Motivation New York: John Wiley, 1964.

Ward, Patricia Layzell Women and Librarianship London: The Library Association, 1966.

Wasserman, Paul The Librarian and the Machine Detroit: Gale Publishing Company, 1965.

Wheeler, Joseph L. Progress and Problems in Education for Librarianship New York: Carnegie Corporation, 1946.

---- and Goldhor, Herbert Practical Administration of Public Libraries New York: Harper and Row, 1962.

Whitehead, Alfred North Adventures of Ideas New York: Macmillan Co. , 1933.

237

Williamson, C. C. Training for Library Service: A Report Prepared for the Carnegie Corporation of New York New York: Carnegie Corporation, 1923.

Zaleznik, A. ; Christensen, C. R. ; and Roethlisberger, F. J. The Motivation and Productivity of Workers Boston: Harvard University, Research Division, Graduate School of Business Administration, 1958.

B. Articles and Periodicals

Allport, Gordon W. "The Trend in Motivational Theory" American Journal of Orthopsychiatry 23:107-119 (January, 1952).

Andrews, Kenneth R. "Is Management Training Effective? I. Evaluation by Managers and Instructors" Harvard Business Review 35:85-94 (January-February, 1957).

---- "Is Management Training Effective? II. Measurement, Objectives, and Policy" Harvard Business Review 35:63-72 (March-April, 1957).

---- "Reaction to University Development Programs: As Reported by More Than 6,000 Executives Who Went Back to School" Harvard Business Review 39:116-34 (May-June, 1961).

Anshen, Melvin "Better Use of Executive Development Programs" Harvard Business Review 33:67-74 (November-December, 1955).

Argyris, Chris "Executive Development Programs: Some Unresolved Problems" Personnel 33:33-41 (July, 1956).

Asheim, Lester "Education for Librarianship" Library Quarterly 25:76-90 (January, 1955).

---- "Manpower: A Call for Action" Library Journal 92:1795-97 (May 1, 1967).

Barber, Bernard "Some Problems in the Sociology of the Professions" Daedalus 92:669-688 (Fall, 1963).

Barry, F. Gordon, and Coleman, C. J. , Jr. "Tougher Program for Management Training" Harvard Business Review 36: 117-125 (November-December, 1958).

Ben-David, Joseph "The Professional Role of the Physician in Bureaucratized Medicine: A Study in Role Conflict" Human Relations 2:255-274 (August, 1958).

---- "Professions in the Class System of Present-Day Societies: A Trend Report and Bibliography" Current Sociology 12(3): 245-330 (1963-1964).

238

Berninghausen, David K. "Teaching a Commitment to Intellectual Freedom" Library Journal 92:3601-3605 (October 15, 1967).

Bird, J. "A New Look at Library Literature--or Why Write About Information Work?" Association of Special Libraries and Information Bureaus Proceedings 7:74-82 (1955).

---- "The Role of Professional Periodicals in Education for Library and Information Work" Association of Special Libraries and Information Bureau Proceedings 8:55-67 (1956).

Blake, Robert R., and others "Breakthrough in Organization Development: A Large-Scale Program that Implements Behavioral Science Concepts" Harvard Business Review 42:133-155 (November-December, 1964).

Blizzard, Samuel W. "The Minister's Dilemma" The Christian Century 73:509-510 (April 25, 1956).

Boaz, Martha "Continuing Education" Drexel Library Quarterly 3(2):151-157 (April, 1967).

---- "More Than Deliberate Speed" American Library Association Bulletin 60:286-288 (March, 1966).

Boyd, Robert D. "A Model for the Analysis of Motivation" Adult Education 16:23-33 (Autumn, 1965).

Bradford, Leland P. "Toward a Philosophy of Adult Education" Adult Education 7:83-93 (Winter, 1957).

Brayfield, Arthur H., and Crockett, Walter H. "Employee Attitudes and Employee Performance" Psychological Bulletin 52(5):396-422 (1955).

Brickman, William W. "Obstacles Impeding Professional Reading" Phi Delta Kappan 38:369-373 (June, 1957).

Brodman, Estelle, and others "Continuing Education of Medical Librarians" Bulletin Medical Library Association 51:354-383 (July, 1963).

Bundy, Mary Lee "Public Library Administrators View Their Professional Periodicals" Illinois Libraries 43:397-420 (June, 1961).

---- and Womack, Hilda "Librarians as Readers" Illinois Libraries 42:427-435 (September, 1960).

---- and Wasserman, Paul "Professionalism Reconsidered" College and Research Libraries 29:5-26 (January, 1968).

Burton, Howard A. "Maximum Benefits from a Program for Staff

Reading" College and Research Libraries 15:277-280 (July, 1954).

Butler, Pierce "Librarianship as a Profession" Library Quarterly 21:234-247 (October, 1951).

Byrd, Cecil K. "School for Administrators: The Rutgers Carnegie Project" College and Research Libraries 20:130-133, 153 (March, 1959).

Chalupsky, Albert "Incentive Practices as Viewed by Scientists and Managers of Pharmaceutical Laboratories" Personnel Psychology 17:385-401 (Winter, 1964).

Clark, James V. "Motivation in Work Groups: A Tentative View" Human Organization 19:199-208 (Winter, 1960-61).

Clarke, Alfred C. "The Use of Leisure and Its Relation to Levels of Occupational Prestige" American Sociological Review 21: 301-307 (January, 1956).

Coch, L., and French, J. R. P. "Overcoming Resistance to Change" Human Relations 1:512-532 (August, 1948).

Cogan, Morris L. "The Problem of Defining a Profession" Annals of the American Academy of Political and Social Scientists 297:105-111 (January, 1955).

---- "Toward a Definition of Professionals" Harvard Educational Review 23:33-50 (Winter, 1953).

Coleman, James; Katz, Elihu, and Menzel, Herbert "The Diffusion of an Innovation Among Physicians" Sociometry 20:253-270 (December, 1957).

"The Computer and Educational Research: A Symposium" Harvard Educational Review 31:235-263 (Summer, 1961).

Conant, Ralph W. "Sociological and Institutional Changes in American Life: Their Implications for the Library" ALA Bulletin 61:528-536 (May, 1967).

Cooke, Morris L. "Professional Ethics and Social Change" American Scholar 15:487-497 (1946).

Cornell, Francis C. "Sample Surveys in Education" Review of Educational Research 24:363 (December, 1954).

Corson, John J. "Equipping Men for Career Growth in the Public Service" Public Administration Review 23:1-9 (May, 1963).

Danton, J. Periam "Doctoral Study in Librarianship in the United States" College and Research Libraries 20:435-453 (November, 1959).

Davies, Don "Professional Standards in Teaching: Moving from Ideas to Action" Journal of Teacher Education 13:191ff (June, 1962).

Dill, William R. , and others "Strategies for Self-Education" Harvard Business Review 43:119-130 (November-December, 1965).

---- "How Aspiring Managers Promote Their Own Careers: Why Do Some Young Men In Business Progress Rapidly to Top Management Jobs While Others, with the Same Educational Background, Reach a Stalemate?" California Management Review 2:9-15 (Summer, 1960).

Dillman, Beryl R. "Teacher Activities and Professional Growth as Perceived by Physicians, Lawyers, Clergymen and Educators" Journal of Teacher Education 15:386-392 (December, 1964).

Dimock, Marshall E. "The Administrative Staff College: Executive Development in Government and Industry" American Political Science Review 50:166-176 (March, 1956).

---- "Executive Development After Ten Years" Public Administration Review 17:91-97 (Spring, 1958).

Doherty, Victor W. "The Carnegie Professional Growth Program: An Experiment in the In-Service Education of Teachers" Journal of Teacher Education 18:261-268 (Fall, 1967).

Drucker, Peter F. "Is Business Letting Young People Down?" Harvard Business Review 43:49ff (November-December, 1965).

Duchac, Kenneth F. "Manpower: A Proposal" Library Journal 92:1797-1798 (May 1, 1967).

Duncan, W. G. K. "A Librarian's First Loyalty" ALA Bulletin 56: 509-519 (June, 1962).

Eckland, Bruce K. "Effects of Prodding to Increase Mail-Back Returns" Journal of Applied Psychology 49:165-169 (June, 1965).

"Educating Executives: Social Science, Self-Study, or Socrates?" Public Administration Review 18:275-305 (Autumn, 1958).

Ferguson, Lawrence L. "Better Management of Managers' Careers" Harvard Business Review 44:139-153 (March-April, 1966).

Flexner, Abraham "Is Social Work a Profession?" School and Society 1:901-911 (June 26, 1915).

241

Frarey, Carlyle "Forum on Education for Special Librarianship" Special Libraries 56:517-519 (September, 1965).

Friedlander, Frank "Job Characteristics as Satisfiers and Dissatisfiers" Journal of Applied Psychology 48:388-392 (December, 1964).

---- "Relationships between the Importance and the Satisfaction of Various Environmental Facts" Journal of Applied Psychology 49:160-164 (June, 1965).

---- "Underlying Sources of Job Satisfaction" Journal of Applied Psychology 47:246-250 (August, 1963).

---- and Walton, Eugene "Positive and Negative Motivations Toward Work" Administrative Science Quarterly 9:194-207 (September, 1964).

Gomersall, Earl R., and Meyers, M. Scott "Breakthrough in On-the-Job Training" Harvard Business Review 44:62-72 (July-August, 1966).

Hall, O. "The Stages of a Medical Career" American Journal of Sociology 53:327-336 (March, 1948).

Harvard University "The School's Executive Development Programs: The Advanced Management Program; Objectives of Training for Top and Middle Managers and What Makes Program Tick" Harvard Business School Bulletin 41:7-9 (May-June, 1965).

Harvey, John F. "Advancement in the Library Profession" Wilson Library Bulletin 36:144-147 (October, 1961).

Havighurst, Robert J. "Educational Changes: Their Implications for the Library" ALA Bulletin 61:537-543 (May, 1967).

Herzberg, Frederick "One More Time: How Do You Motivate Employees?" Harvard Business Review 46:53-62 (January-February, 1968).

Hickman, C. Addison "Managerial Motivation and the Theory of the Firm" The American Economic Review 45:544-554 (May, 1955).

Hodges, J. B. "Continuing Education: Why and How" Education Leadership 17:330-346 (March, 1960).

Houle, Cyril O. "Education for Adult Leadership" Adult Education 8:3-17 (Autumn, 1957).

---- "The Role of Continuing Education in Current Professional Development" ALA Bulletin 41:259-267 (March, 1967).

Hulin, Charles L., and Smith, Patricia A. "An Empirical Investigation of Two Implications of the Two-factor Theory of Job Satisfaction" Journal of Applied Psychology 51(5):396-402 (October, 1967).

Hunervager, S. G. "Re-Education for Executives: Many Organizations Are Sending Their Executives Back to School" Personnel Administration 24:5-9 (January-February, 1961).

Hurt, Peyton "Staff Specialization: A Possible Substitute for Departmentalization" American Library Association Bulletin 29:417-421 (July, 1935).

"In-Service Training and Intramural Communication for Supervisors: An Institute Sponsored by the School of Library Science, U. S. C." News Notes of California Libraries 56:377-399 (Fall, 1961).

Katz, Robert L. "Human Relations Skills Can be Sharpened" Harvard Business Review 34:61-72 (July-August, 1956).

Kent, Charles Deane "What Is a Professional?" Ontario Library Review 40:89-91 (May, 1957).

Klass, Alan A. "What Is a Profession?" Continuous Learning 1: 234-240 (September-October, 1962).

Knox, Alan B., and Sjogren, Douglas "Motivation to Participate and Learn in Adult Education" Adult Education 12:238-242 (Summer, 1962).

Knox, Margaret Enid "For Every Reference Librarian--A Development Program" Southeastern Librarian 11:303-310, 320 (Winter, 1961).

Kohn, Robert D. "The Significance of the Professional Ideal" The Annals 110:1-5 (May, 1922).

Korb, George M. "'Successful' Librarians as Revealed in 'Who's Who in America'" Wilson Library Bulletin 20:603-604, 607 (April, 1946).

Kortendick, James J., S. S. "Continuing Education and Library Administration" ALA Bulletin 61:268-271 (March, 1967).

---- "Curriculum--Administration" in "Guide to Library Education, Part I" Drexel Library Quarterly 3:92-103 (January, 1967).

---- "The Supervisor as Leader" Virginia Librarian 7:56-69 (Winter, 1961).

Kraus, Joe W. "The Qualifications of University Librarians, 1948 and 1933" College and Research Libraries 11:17-21 (January, 1950).

243

Labb, June "Librarians in 'Who's Who in America'" Wilson Library Bulletin 24:54-56 (September, 1950).

Lauwerys, J. A. "Definition and Goals of Professional Reading" Phi Delta Kappan 38:365-368 (June, 1957).

Levine, Sol and Gordon, Gerald "Maximizing Returns on Mail Questionnaires" Public Opinion Quarterly 22:568-575 (Winter, 1958-1959).

Lorenz, John G. "The Challenge of Change" PNLA Quarterly 29:7-15 (October, 1964).

Lundy, Frank A. "Philosophical Concepts of Professional Organization" College and Research Libraries 20:487-495 (November, 1959).

McClelland, David C. "Achievement Motivation Can Be Developed" Harvard Business Review 43:6ff (November-December, 1965).

McJenkin, Virginia "Continuing Education for School Librarians" ALA Bulletin 61:272-275 (March, 1967).

"Manpower and the Library Profession" Wilson Library Bulletin 41:793-822 (April, 1967).

Marshall, J. D. "Southeastern Librarians in 'Who's Who in the Southland'" Southeastern Librarian 8:5-9 (Spring, 1958).

Martin, Lowell A. "Shall Library Schools Teach Administration?" College and Research Libraries 6:335-340 (September, 1945).

Maslow, A. H. "Theory of Human Motivation" Psychological Review 50:370-396 (July, 1943).

Mead, Margaret "Changing Patterns of Trust and Responsibility: The Need for New Canons of Professional Ethics" The Journal of Higher Education 37:307-311 (June, 1966).

---- "Redefinition of Education" National Education Association Journal 48:15-17 (October, 1959).

---- "Why is Education Obsolete?" Harvard Business Review 36: 23-37, 164-70 (November-December, 1958).

Medical Library Association, Committee on Continuing Education "Continuing Education for Medical Librarianship: A Symposium" Bulletin Medical Library Association 48:404-423 (October, 1960).

---- "Continuing Education of Medical Librarians" Bulletin Medical Library Association 51:354-383 (July, 1963).

Merritt, Leroy C. "Doctoral Study in Librarianship--A Supplement" College and Research Libraries 23:539-540 (November, 1962).

Metcalfe, John "The Standards of Librarianship and the Status of the Library Profession" Australian Library Journal 8:171-180 (October, 1959).

Meyer, Herbert H., and others "Split Roles in Performance Appraisal" Harvard Business Review 43:123-129 (January-February, 1965).

Monroe, Margaret E. "Variety in Continuing Education" ALA Bulletin 61:275-278 (March, 1967).

Morrison, Perry D. "The Personality of the Academic Librarian" College and Research Libraries 24:365-368 (September, 1963).

Myers, Charles A. "Behavioral Sciences for Personnel Managers" Harvard Business Review 44:154-162 (July-August, 1966).

Myers, M. Scott "Conditions for Manager Motivation" Harvard Business Review 44:58-71 (January-February, 1966).

---- "Who Are Your Motivated Workers?" Harvard Business Review 42:73-88 (January-February, 1964).

"New Horizons in Teacher Education and Professional Standards" NEA Journal 50:55-68 (January, 1961).

Opinion Research Corporation "How to Improve Your Trade and Professional Associations: A Survey of Members and Association Heads--Main Report" Public Opinion Index for Industry 24 (January, 1966).

Pound, Roscoe "The Professions in the Society of Today" New England Journal of Medicine 241:351-357 (September, 1949).

Powell, Reed M. "Two Approaches to University Management Education: Today Forty Universities in the United States Offer Major Educational Programs for Executives; Here is a Research Report Contrasting Two Approaches, the Intensive Live-In Programs and the Part-Time Development Courses" California Management Review 5:87-104 (Spring, 1963).

"Professionals in Organizations" Administrative Science Quarterly 10 (June, 1965).

Ready, William B. "The Rutgers Seminar for Library Administrators" College and Research Libraries 18:281-283 (July, 1957).

Reed, Sarah R. "Trends in Professional Education" in "Guide to Library Education, Part I" Drexel Library Quarterly 3: 1-24 (January, 1967).

Roethlisberger, F. J. "Training Supervisors in Human Relations" Harvard Business Review 29:47-57 (September, 1951).

Rogers, Carl R. "Significant Learning: In Therapy and In Education" Educational Leadership 16:232-242 (January, 1959).

Rothstein, Samuel "Nobody's Baby: A Brief Sermon on Continuing Professional Education" Library Journal 90:2226-2227 (May 15, 1965).

Schein, Edgar H. "Forces Which Undermine Management Development" California Management Review 5:23-24 (Summer, 1963).

Schick, Frank L. "Professional Library Manpower" ALA Bulletin 58:315, 317 (April, 1964).

Schiller, Anita R. "Survey of Salary Surveys" ALA Bulletin 58: 279-286 (April, 1964)

Schoenfeld, C. "On Defining Adult Education" School and Society 81:69-70 (March 5, 1955).

Shank, Russell "In-Service Training in Libraries" ALA Bulletin 55:38-41 (January, 1961).

Shostrom, Everett L. "An Inventory for the Measurement of Self-Actualization" Educational and Psychological Measurement 24:207-218 (Summer, 1964).

Slager, Fred C. "What are the Characteristics of an Effective Professional Growth Program?" Proceedings of the Thirty-Eighth Annual Convention National Association of Secondary School Principals Bulletin 38:206-209 (April, 1954).

Smith, Eldred "Librarians and Unions: The Berkeley Experience" Library Journal 93:717-720 (February 15, 1968).

Smith, Patricia Cain, and Cranny, C. J. "Psychology of Men at Work" Annual Review of Psychology 19:467-496 (1968).

Solla Price, Derek J. de, and Beaver, Donald de B. "Collaboration in an Invisible College" American Psychologist 21:1011 (November, 1966).

Special Libraries Association "A Study of 1967 Annual Salaries of Members of the Special Libraries Association" Special Libraries 58:217-254 (April, 1967).

Spencer, Howard C. "Continuing Liberal Education Through Independent Study" Adult Education 15:91-95 (Winter, 1965).

Stevenson, Grace T. "Training for Growth--the Future for Librarians" ALA Bulletin 61:278-286 (March, 1967).

Stewart, Nathaniel "Library In-Service Training. Part I--General" Library Journal 72:16-18 (January 1, 1947).

---- "Library In-Service Training. Part II--The Solution" Library Journal 72:146-148 (January 15, 1947).

---- "Library In-Service Training. Part III--The Records" Library Journal 72:200-203 (February 1, 1947).

Stogdill, Ralph M. "The Sociometry of Working Relationships in Formal Organizations" Sociometry 12:276-286 (November, 1949).

Stolz, Robert K. "Executive Development--New Perspective" Harvard Business Review 44:133-143 (May-June, 1966).

Stone, Elizabeth W. "Methods and Materials for Teaching Library Administration" Journal of Education for Librarianship 6: 34-42 (Summer, 1965).

Strauss, George, and others "Professionalism and Occupational Associations" Industrial Relations 2:7-31, 33-65 (May, 1963).

Strout, Donald R. , and Strout, Ruth B. "Salaries Stronger: More Positions" Library Journal 82:1597-1604 (June 15, 1957).

---- "Story Is the Same" Library Journal 87:2323-2329 (June 15, 1962).

Stumpf, Felix F. "Continuing Legal Education: Its Role" American Bar Association Journal 49:248-250 (March, 1963).

Thompson, J. W. "The Bi-Polar and Undirectional Measurement of Intelligence" British Journal of Psychology 52:17-23 (1961).

Thornton, Luanne "A Scale to Measure Librarians' Attitudes Toward Librarianship" Journal of Education for Librarianship 4:15-26 (Summer, 1963).

Towle, Charlotte "General Objectives of Professional Education" Social Service Review 25:427-440 (December, 1951).

Troxel, Wilma "Continuing Education for Medical Librarianship: A Symposium" Bulletin Medical Library Association 48:404-407 (October, 1960).

Tweed, Harrison "Continuing Legal Education: New Conference to

Chart Broader Goals" American Bar Association Journal 49:470-474 (May, 1963).

Uterberger, S. Herbert "The Lawyer's View of Continuing Legal Education" The Practical Lawyer 10:4-21, 89-104 (February, 1964).

Waldo, Dwight "The Administrative State Revisited" Public Administration Review 25:5-37 (March, 1965).

Warncke, Ruth "Careers in Librarianship" ALA Bulletin 60:806-808 (September, 1966).

---- "State Libraries, Library Associations and Library Schools: Partners in Library Development" South Dakota Library Bulletin 51:112-115 (October-December 1965).

Wasserman, Paul "Development of Administration in Library Service: Current Status and Future Prospects" College and Research Libraries 19:283-294 (July, 1958).

Wight, Edward A. "Standards and Stature in Librarianship" American Library Association Bulletin 55:871-875 (November, 1961).

Wilensky, Harold "The Professionalization of Everyone?" American Journal of Sociology 70:137-158 (September, 1964).

Williamson, Charles C. "Some Present-Day Aspects of Library Training" Bulletin of the American Library Association 13: 120-126 (July, 1919).

C.   Unpublished Material

Allen, Lawrence A. "The Evaluation Schema--The Community Librarian's Training Courses" Unpublished nondegree study, Library Extension Division, New York State Library, Albany, N. Y. [n. d.]

Alvarez, Robert Smyth "Qualifications of Heads of Libraries in Cities of Over 10,000 Population in the Seven North-Central States" Unpublished Doctor's dissertation, Graduate Library School, University of Chicago, 1939.

Anderson, Frederic "Factors in Motivation to Work Across Three Occupational Levels" Unpublished Doctor's dissertation, University of Utah, 1961.

Ayres, S. F. "Report of an Eleven-Month Internship in the Library of Yale University, July 1959 to June 1960" Unpublished Master's thesis, University of Texas, 1961.

Ballard, Robert Melvyn   "A Job History of the Atlanta University School of Library Service Graduates, 1948-1959" Unpublished Master's thesis, School of Library Service, Atlanta University, 1961.

Bentley, B.   "Report of an Internship Served in the Abilene (Texas) Public Library, February 1 to August 1, 1960" Unpublished Master's thesis, University of Texas, 1961.

Calkins, Robert D.   "Business Education: Goals and Prospects" Paper read before the American Association of Collegiate Schools of Business.   Chicago, Illinois, April 30, 1964. (Mimeographed).

----   "Education for Business--Changing Perspectives and Requirements" Paper read before the International Society of Business Education.   New York University, New York, August 25, 1965.   (Mimeographed).

Carson, Lettie Gay   "Remarks at ALTA Meeting, Region VII" Paper read at the American Library Trustee Association Annual Conference, San Francisco, California, June 25, 1967. (Mimeographed).

Clegg, Denzil   "The Motivation of County Administrators in the Cooperative Extension Service" Unpublished Doctor's dissertation, University of Wisconsin, 1963.

Colley, Louise A.   "Relationship of Ego Development to Re-Creation" Unpublished Doctor's dissertation, University of Wisconsin, 1965.

Dillman, Beryl R.   "The Professional Growth of Teachers as Perceived by Members of Other Professions--Physicians, Lawyers, Clergymen" Unpublished research paper presented at the American Educational Research Association National Annual Convention, Atlantic City, N.J. , February 21, 1962. (Mimeographed).

----   "Teacher Perceptions and Practices in the Development of Responsibility for Professional Growth" Unpublished research paper presented at the American Educational Research Association National Annual Convention, Pic-Congress Hotel, Chicago, Ill. , February 25, 1961.   (Mimeographed).

Douglas, Robert Raymond   "The Personality of the Librarian" Unpublished Doctor's dissertation, Graduate Library School, University of Chicago, 1957.

Dow, June Barth   "Characteristics of Non-Credit University Extension Students" Unpublished Doctor's dissertation, University of California, 1965.

249

Drennan, Henry T. and Reed, Sarah R. "Library Manpower" A paper prepared for the ALA Special Presidential Program on "Crisis in Library Manpower: Myth and Reality" June 25, 28, 29, 1967, San Francisco, California.

Fitch, Vera E. "In-Service Training in Public Libraries" Unpublished research report, School of Library Science, The University of Southern California, 1957.

Friedlander, Frank   Personal letter, dated October 9, 1967.

---- "Two Questionnaires, Two Analyses of Variance Tables, and Two Multiple Range Test Tables" American Documentation Institute Document No. 8027. Washington: ADI Auxiliary Publications Project, Photoduplication Service, Library of Congress.

Gardner, John W. "The Purpose of Our Efforts" Paper read at the First Health, Education, and Welfare Forum, HEW Auditorium, Washington, D. C., Wednesday, December 6, 1967.

Giles, Fleetwood, Jr. "Texas Librarians: A Study Based on 'Who's Who in Library Service,' Third Edition, 1955" Unpublished Master's thesis, Graduate School, University of Texas, 1958.

Goodman, Charles H. "Employee Motivation" Paper read at Seminar on Middle Manager Development in Libraries, The Catholic University of America, Washington, D. C., June 17, 1964.

---- "Target Setting: The New Look in Performance Appraisal" Paper read at DCLA Workshop, The Catholic University of America, Washington, D. C., March 11, 1967.

Griffin, Virginia R. A. "Model of the Developmental Career of the Work-Life of County Agents" Unpublished Doctor's dissertation, University of Chicago, 1965.

Gross, Edward and Grambsch, Paul V. "Academic Administrators and University Goals: A Study of the Center for Academic Administration Research, University of Minnesota" Questionnaire used for this study sponsored by the United States Office of Education, 1965.

Hanzas, Barbara "On-the-Job Training Procedures for Library Assistants" Unpublished Master's thesis, Western Reserve University, 1953.

Harper, Dee W. "Some Factors Related to Role Stress and Motivation: A Study in the Sociology of Adult Education" Unpublished Master's thesis, Louisiana State University, 1965.

250

Houle, Cyril O. "Continuing Education: Purpose, Principles and Trends" Paper read before the American Library Association. New Orleans, La. , January 11, 1967. (Mimeographed).

Jones, W. H. "Report of an Internship Served at the Dallas Public Library" Unpublished Master's thesis, University of Texas, 1958.

Kittle, Arthur T. "Management Theories in Public Library Administration in the United States, 1925-1955" Unpublished Doctor's dissertation, Columbia University, 1961.

Knapp, Mark L. "Analysis of Motivational Factors of Adults in University and College Adult Speech Education Courses in the Greater Kansas City Area" Unpublished Master's thesis, University of Kansas, 1963.

Knox, Alan B. "Continuing Legal Education of Nebraska Lawyers" Unpublished nondegree study, Nebraska State Bar Association, 1964.

---- "Nebraska Adult Interests Study" Unpublished nondegree study, Adult Education Research, University of Nebraska, 1965.

----, and Alan Booth "Decisions by Scientists and Engineers to Participate in Educational Programs Designed to Increase Scientific Competence" Unpublished nondegree study, National Science Foundation, 1966.

----, and Sjogren, Douglas "Achievement and Withdrawal in University Adult Education Classes" Unpublished nondegree study, Adult Education Research, University of Nebraska, 1964.

Knox, Margaret Enid "Professional Development of Reference Librarians in a University Library: A Case Study" Unpublished Doctor's dissertation, University of Illinois, 1957.

Lamborn, Robert Louis "Guidance in Independent Secondary Schools for Boys: The Practices and Policies Reported by 227 Schools in the New England and Middle Atlantic States" Unpublished Doctor's dissertation, The Johns Hopkins University, 1951.

Leathers, Chester "Educational Backgrounds, Professional Experience, Role Conceptions and Career Aspirations of Conference Coordinators" Unpublished Master's thesis, University of Chicago, Studies and Training Program in Continuing Education, 1965.

Leyman, Jean Murphy "Types of Induction Training for Library Service: An Historical Survey" Unpublished Master's thesis, Kent State University, 1951.

251

McCreedy, Sister Mary Lucille, C. D. P.   "Questionnaire for Students in Graduate Library Schools and Students in Selected Undergraduate Library Science Departments" Unpublished questionnaire used in preparation for a Ph. D. dissertation, School of Library Service, Columbia University, 1963.

---- "The Selection of School Librarianship as a Career" Unpublished Doctor's dissertation, School of Library Service, Columbia University, 1964.

Maddox, Lucy Jane   "Trends and Issues in American Librarianship as Reflected in the Papers and Proceedings of the American Library Association, 1876-1885" Unpublished Doctor's dissertation, University of Michigan, 1958.

Martin, R. M.   "Report of an Internship Served at the John Crerar Library, February-December, 1954" Unpublished Master's thesis, University of Texas, 1958.

Morrison, Perry David   "Career of the Academic Librarian: A Study of the Social Origins, Educational Attainments, Vocational Experience, and Personality Characteristics of a Group of American Academic Librarians" Unpublished Doctor's dissertation, University of California, 1960.

Morrow, Evelyn   "Long Range Integrated Programming for Adult Education" Unpublished Doctor's dissertation, University of Chicago, 1957.

Myers, M. Scott   "Management Attitude Questionnaire" Unpublished questionnaire developed at Texas Instruments Incorporated, Dallas, Texas, 1964.

National Science Foundation and Center for Applied Linguistics   "National Register of Scientific and Technical Personnel in the Field of Linguistics and Allied Specialties" Questionnaire used for the study, 1966.

Noonan, Fannie Sheppard   "In-Service Training in Catalog Departments of Public Libraries" Unpublished Master's thesis, Columbia University, 1948.

Ore, Stanley H., Jr.   "The Development of an Internship Program in Adult Education" Unpublished Master's thesis, University of Wisconsin, 1964.

Osteen, P. L.   "In-Service Training of Executives" Unpublished Master's thesis, Columbia University, 1947.

Papanestor, William   "A Study of Job Satisfaction as Related to Need Satisfaction Both on the Job and Off the Job" Unpublished Doctor's dissertation, University of Cincinnati, 1957.

Penland, Patrick Robert "Image of Public Library Adult Education as Reflected in the Opinions of Public Library Supervisory Staff Members in the Public Libraries of Michigan Serving Populations over 25,000" Unpublished Doctor's dissertation, University of Michigan, 1960.

Preston, James M. "Characteristics of Continuing and Non-continuing Adult Students" Unpublished Doctor's dissertation, University of California, 1957.

Ranta, Raymond R. "The Professional Status of the Michigan Cooperative Extension Service" Unpublished Doctor's dissertation, National Agricultural Extension Center for Advanced Study, University of Wisconsin, 1960.

Reagan, Agnes Lytton "A Study of Certain Factors in Institutions of Higher Education Which Influence Students to Become Librarians" Unpublished Doctor's dissertation, The University of Illinois, 1957.

Reaves, Alice Cameron "A Study of the Graduate Students Who Received Master's Degrees from the School of Library Science, University of North Carolina, 1953-1962" Unpublished Master's thesis, School of Library Science, University of North Carolina, 1964.

Reed, Sara R. "Education Activities of Library Associations" Paper read at the Drexel Institute of Technology Library Association Administration Workshop, Philadelphia, Pa. , November 10, 1966. (Mimeographed).

Schiller, Anita "Survey of Professional Personnel in College and University Libraries" Questionnaire used for project "Characteristics of Professional Personnel in College and University Libraries" Urbana, Ill. : Library Research Center, University of Illinois, 1967.

Simmons, Gloria Mitchell "A Study of Professional Librarians in the Southwestern Region of the United States as Indicated in 'Who's Who in Library Service,' 1955" Unpublished Master's thesis, School of Library Service, Atlanta University, 1957.

Stone, M. H. "Report of an Internship Served at the Enoch Pratt Free Library, Baltimore, September 16, 1957-July 11, 1958" Unpublished Master's thesis, University of Texas, 1958.

Stonecipher, Charles L. "Characteristics of Adults Who Utilize University Educational Activities in Columbia County, Wisconsin" Unpublished Master's thesis, University of Wisconsin, 1964.

253

Swanson, Harold B. "Factors Associated with Motivation Toward Professional Development of County Agricultural Extension Agents in Minnesota" Unpublished Doctor's dissertation, University of Wisconsin, 1965.

Sykes, Christa "Report of an Internship Served at the Rudolph Matas Medical Library, New Orleans, January 1-June 30, 1956" Unpublished Master's thesis, Graduate School, University of Texas, 1956.

Taylor, Edward B. "An Analysis of the Educational Needs of Nebraska Lawyers in Relation to Career Cycle" Unpublished Doctor's dissertation, University of Nebraska, 1966.

Taylor, Gerry M. "Vocational Interests of Male Librarians in the United States" Unpublished Master's thesis, University of Texas, 1955.

Thomas, Mary Ellen "A Study of the Graduates of the School of Library Science, University of North Carolina, 1951-1957; An Analysis of the Careers in Librarianship of Recipients of the Bachelor of Science in Library Science" Unpublished Master's thesis, School of Library Science, University of North Carolina, 1964.

Tough, Allen M. "The Teaching Tasks Performed by Adult Self-Teachers" Unpublished Doctor's dissertation, University of Chicago, 1965.

Tucker, Harold W. "In-Service Training in Large Public Libraries" Unpublished Master's thesis, University of Chicago, 1941.

University of Southern California, School of Library Science "Alumni Personnel Questionnaire" Unpublished questionnaire sent to alumni of the School of Library Science of the University of Southern California, 1965.

---- "Library Rating of Recent Graduates of the School of Library Science, University of Southern California" Unpublished questionnaire sent to employers of alumni of the School of Library Science of the University of Southern California, 1965.

"Washington D. C. Teacher Study" Unpublished questionnaire, New York: Bureau of Applied Social Research, Columbia University, 1967.

Wasserman, Paul, and Bundy, Mary Lee "Manpower for the Library and Information Professions in the 1970's; An Inquiry Into Fundamental Problems" Unpublished proposal for the U. S. Department of Labor, Office of Manpower, Automation and Training. School of Library and Information Services, University of Maryland, 1966. (Mimeographed).

Appendix A

Scoring Systems

This section describes and explains the scoring systems used
in this study.

I.   Professional Index Score

Thirty-nine items in the Questionnaire concerned with professional criteria were used to compile a Professional Index Score:
Items 1 through 36 and Item 47 in Part 2, and Items 33 and 34 in
Part 3.   Table A shows the 39 questions, indicates the criteria reflected, and the scoring system used for each item.

The purpose of the first 23 questions in Part 2, "Some of
Your Ideas About Yourself and Your Work, " was to identify certain
attributes and attitudes that characterize a professional person.
Weighted scores were given for the answers to 10 of these questions considered indicative of professionalism.   By design, 13 questions did not apply to the information sought and were omitted from
the tabulations.   These 10 questions are concerned with characteristics of occupations in general, not just librarianship, and are referred to as the Occupations Characteristics Index.

The questions used and the professional criteria to which
they were related are indicated in Table B.

The respondent was asked to check the designation which
best expressed the importance to him of each of these occupations
characteristics.   Each item of "major importance" received 2
points; each item "fairly important" received 1 point.   If a characteristic was of no importance the respondent was instructed to leave
a blank.   No points were given if the item was of "little impor-

Table A

Summary of the Scoring System Used to Compute the Professional Index Score for Librarians in the Sample: 1967

Questionnaire Item No.	Subject of Question	Professional Criteria Reflected	Scoring System	Highest No. of Points Possible
Part 2				
1 through 23	Occupational characteristics	Criteria numbered 1, 2, 3, 4, 5, 8, 10, 11, 12[a]	2 points for major importance 1 point for fairly important Only 10 questions included in tabulation: 2, 4, 6, 9, 12, 13, 16, 20, 22, 23	20
24	Concern for colleague's problems	Concern for improvement of colleague's welfare	2 points for both personal and on-the-job problems; no points for any other answer.	2
25	Number of books read in Library Science in the past year	Familiarity with professional literature	Mean = 4; 1 standard deviation = 1.5 3-4 books read = 0.5 points 5, 6, or 7 books = 1.0 points 8, 9, 10, or 11 books = 1.5 points 12 or more books = 2.0 points	2
26	Number of books read in area of specialization in last year	Familiarity with professional literature	Mean = 5 Scoring system same as in #25	2

Table A (continued)

27	Professional articles published in last 5 years	Interchange of information	Mean = 1; standard deviation = 1 1 article = 1.0 points 2 articles = 1.5 points 3 or more articles = 2 points	2
28	Professional books published in last 5 years	Interchange of information	Mean = .25; S.D. = 0.1 1 book = 1.0 points 2 books = 1.5 points 3 or more books = 2 points	2
29	Number of Library Science periodicals edited	Interchange of information	Mean = 0.8; S.D. = 1 1 periodical edited = 1 point 2 periodicals edited = 1.5 points 3 or more edited = 2 points	2
30	No. of library associations in which currently a member	Continuous improvement of profession with other colleagues	Mean = 2.5; S.D. = 1.3 1 or 2 memberships = 0.5 points 3 memberships = 1.0 points 4 or 5 memberships = 1.5 points 6 or more memberships = 2 points	2
31	No. of non-library professional associations in which currently a member	Continuous search for knowledge	Mean = 2.0; S.D. = 1 1 membership = 0.5 points 2 memberships = 1.0 points 3 memberships = 1.5 points 4 or more memberships = 2 points	2
32	No. of learned societies in which currently a member	Continuous search for knowledge	Mean = 1; S.D. = 1 1 membership = 1 point 2 memberships = 1.5 points 3 or more memberships = 2 points	2

Table A (continued)

Questionnaire Item No.	Subject of Question	Professional Criteria Reflected	Scoring System	Highest No. of Points Possible
33	No. of offices held in professional associations	Continuous improvement of profession with other colleagues	Mean = 2; S.D. = 1.8 1 office = 0.5 points 2 or 3 offices = 1.0 points 4 or 5 offices = 1.5 points 6 or more offices = 2 points	2
34	No. of days attended workshops in last 5 years	Continuous search for knowledge	Mean = 4.8; S.D. = 5.8 3 or 4 days = 0.5 points 5 through 8 days = 1.0 points 9-12 days = 1.5 points 13 or more days = 2 points	2
35	No. of periodicals in Library Science regularly read	Familiarity with professional literature	Mean = 4; S.D. = 2 2 or 3 periodicals = 0.5 points 4 or 5 periodicals = 1.0 points 6 or 7 periodicals = 1.5 points 8 or more periodicals = 2 points	2
36	No. of non-library professional periodicals read regularly	Familiarity with professional literature	Mean = 1.7; S.D. = 1 1 periodical = 0.5 points 2 periodicals = 1.0 points 3 periodicals = 1.5 points 4 periodicals = 2.0 points	2
47	Self-learning agenda consistent with probable course of career	Continuous search for knowledge	Yes = 2 points No = 0 points	2

Table A (continued)

Part 3			
33	No. of research projects since MLS	Continuous search for knowledge	Any projects = 2 points No projects = 0 points	2
34	Membership in small voluntary study group	Interchange of information	Membership in a group = 2 points No membership = 0 points	2
			Total of highest possible points for 39 questions	52

[a]#1 - Service to others higher than personal gain
#2 - Strong sense of public responsibility
#3 - Skillful and proficient in work
#4 - Dedicated to job and what it stands for
#5 - Basically direct own program or work independently

#8 - Work with acceptable ethical standards
#10 - Willingness to change methods of job procedure when new information based on research is received
#11 - Belief in inter-exchange of information
#12 - Utilization and understanding of the specific language employed in specialization

tance. " The highest score possible for these 10 questions was 20 points.

Question 24 reflected the individual's professional orientation toward the welfare of his colleagues. A respondent received points only if he felt he should be concerned with "both personal problems and on-the-job problems of fellow workers. "

Questions 25 and 26, 35 and 36 reflect a knowledge of and familiarity with professional literature in their field. For each of these questions, the mean was found for the 138 respondents and a scoring system was worked out based on this mean and the standard deviations. For example, the mean number of library science books read was 4 per year and one standard deviation was 1.5. Scores were assigned as indicated in Table A.

For Question 26, books read in the area of specialization, the mean number read per year was 5. The scoring system was the same as for Question 25. For Question 35, periodicals read regularly, the mean was 4, but the standard deviation was 2. The resulting score was: under 2 periodicals, no points; 2 or 3 periodicals, 0.5 points; 4 or 5, 1 point; 6 or 7, 1.5 points; 8 or more, 2 points.

For Question 36, periodicals read outside of library science, the mean was 1.7 and the standard deviation was 1. The scoring system devised was: 1 other periodical read regularly, 0.5 points; 2 periodicals, 1 point; 3 got 1.5 points; and 4 or more, 2 points.

The highest number of points possible for the 4 questions (25, 26, 35, and 36 was 8.

Questions 27, 28, 29 reflect the belief in the interchange of information. The highest number of points for each was 2 and the total 6.

The mean number of articles published was 1. One article published got 1 point; 2 articles, 1.5 points; and 3 or more, 2 points. The mean number of books published, as revealed from Question 28, was 0.25 and the standard deviation was 0.1. One book published got 1 point; 2, 1.5 points; 3 or more, 2 points.

Question 29 dealt with the number of library periodicals edited. Here the mean was 0.8 and the standard deviation was 1.0. One publication edited got 1 point; 2 got 1.5 points; and 3 got 2.

points.

Questions 30, 31, 32 and 33 reflect active participation with colleagues in developing conditions for the continuous improvement of the profession. The mean number of library associations to which the sample belonged was 2. 5 and the standard deviation was 1. 3. Membership in 1 or 2 associations got 0. 5 points; membership in 3, 1 point; membership in 4 or 5, 1. 5 points, and 6 or more received 2 points.

The mean number of non-library professional associations (Question 31) was 2 and the standard deviation was 0. 5. Membership in 1 association got 0. 5 points; 2 got 1 point, 3 got 1. 5 points; and 4 or more got 2 points. The mean number of learned societies was 1 and the standard deviation was 1. Membership in 1 learned society received 1 point; 2 got 1. 5 points; and 3 got 2 points.

Question 33 dealt with the number of offices held. The mean was 2 and the standard deviation was 1. 8. One office held got 0. 5 points; 2 or 3 offices, 1 point; 4 or 5 offices, 1. 5 points; and 6 or more, 2 points.

Question 34, Part 2, on workshop attendance, Question 33, Part 3, on research, Question 34, Part 3, on independent study groups, and Question 47, Part 2, on self-learning agenda, reflected the respondents' continuing search for new knowledge and skill.

The mean number of days spent in workshops during the last 5 years was 4. 8 and the standard deviation was 5. 8. Days spent under 3 days received no points; 3 or 4 days, 0. 5 points; 5 through 8 days, 1 point; 9 through 12 days, 1. 5 points; and 13 or more days, 2 points.

If the respondent had engaged in research, was a member of an independent study group, or had a self-learning agenda, he got 2 points; if not, he got none.

As a check on the reliability of these scores, those who received top scores were checked by their code numbers. It was found that they were leaders in the profession who were nationally known for their professional outlook and contributions.

Table B

Summary of Questions Used and Professional Criteria Reflected in Computing the Occupations Index Score for Librarians in the Sample: 1967

Item No. in Part 2 of Questionnaire	Occupational Characteristic	Criteria No.	Professional Criteria Reflected (abbreviated)
2	Opportunity to be helpful to others or useful to society	1	Service to others higher than personal gain
4	A chance to exercise civic leadership	2	Sense of public responsibility
6	Opportunity to work with people who are proficient and effective in their work	3	Skillful and proficient in work
9	Relative independence in doing my work	5	Basically direct their own programs of work independently
12	Opportunity to work with people who are dedicated to the work at hand	4	Dedicated to job and what it stands for
13	Opportunity to be original and creative and try new ideas on the job	5	Never-ceasing quest for learning
16	Opportunity to share common knowledge with co-workers	11	Believe in the inter-change of information

Table B (continued)

20	Opportunity to work in a setting in which changes of methods and procedures are accepted when new information based on research is received	10	Will change methods of job procedure when new information based on research is received
22	Opportunity to work with people who understand and speak the language of the profession	12	Utilize and understand the specific language employed in their field of work
23	Opportunity to work where acceptable ethical standards are a continuing standard	8	Work with acceptable ethical standards

II.   Degree of Aspiration

Questions 37 through 43, Part 2, of the Questionnaire were
used to obtain the total Degree of Aspiration Score. These 3 answers were possible for each question about the respondent's plans
and goals for the future: (1) I definitely want to; (2) I have some
desire to; and (3) I do not want to. Each answer was given a
weighted score: 2 points for wanting to pursue a particular plan
and 1 point for some desire to follow a plan for the future.

Assuming the 7 goals to be of equal importance, the highest
possible Degree of Aspiration Score was 14 points. The higher the
total score, the higher the level of aspiration. These scores were
divided into high and low aspiration for comparison in addition to
ranking by the actual scores.

The questions in the schedule were adapted from the type of
Level of Aspiration Score used by Ranta.

III.   Relative Influence of Various Groups

The librarians indicated their perception of the attitudes of
several groups toward professional improvement and formal course
work. The following five responses were possible for each group:
(1) strongly favorable; (2) mildly favorable; (3) neutral; (4) mildly opposed; and (5) strongly opposed. Each answer was given a
score comparable to its place in the range indicated. Thus "strongly favorable" was given a score of 1, "mildly favorable" a score of
2, through to a score of 5 for "strongly opposed."

All of the weighted scores for each of the groups were to-
taled and the mean was determined for each. The lower the mean,
the higher the rank of the group was in its perceived influence.

IV. Kind and Degree of Professional Improvement
and Formal Course Work Motivation

There were 4 scores for kind and degree of motivation, each
the result of a ranking of the possible choices of statements based
on those used by Swanson and adapted for librarians by a panel of
2 library educators. Another panel of 5 librarians then ranked the
statements in order from high to low and those for which there was
perfect agreement were used in the questionnaire. In each of the
4 measures, the scores were based on the ranking given by the respondents in relation to the established order that had been set. A
perfect correlation for all questions in a set yielded a score of 1.
Minus correlations got zero.

Kind of Professional Improvement Motivation

Computation of this score was based on a system derived
from Maslow's hierarchy of needs. Four statements were given designed to reflect: (1) security or safety, (2) acceptance, (3) prestige, status, etc., and (4) self-actualization in Maslow's hierarchy.
The first 2 were regarded as ego-defensive motives and the latter
2 as ego-enhansive motives. Self-actualization was considered the
higher motive and security the lower. Prestige and status was
higher than the desire to belong. After the scores from each of
the 138 respondents were computed, the median was determined, and
the sample was split into a dichotomy. The scores thus differenti-
ated between the individuals and their relative pattern of values in
the safety to self-actualization continuum. The 4 classes as established are shown in Table C.

The specific instructions to each respondent was: Please
number in rank order with 1 meaning most agreement and 4 meaning least agreement. The highest possible score was 1.0, meaning
perfect correlation between rankings chosen and model established.

Table   C

Scoring System Measuring Kind of Motivation Toward Professional
Improvement for Librarians in the Sample: 1967

Question No. in Part 6	Hierarchy of Needs	Ranking From Low to High	Statement used. I feel that professional improvement activities will:
3	Security or safety	4	... be necessary for me to keep abreast of the rapid changes in librarianship and enable me to keep my present position.
1	Acceptance	3	... help me to keep on the same level and be accepted by my colleagues.
2	Prestige, status	2	... enable me to exercise more leadership in the profession.
4	Self-actualization	1	... give me a feeling of self-fulfillment (that is, the feeling of being able to use my own unique capabilities, of realizing my potentialities).

Degree of Professional Improvement Motivation

Five statements ranging on a scale from little motivation to
great motivation toward professional improvement were given.

My attitude toward professional improvement activities is:
(Please number in rank order with 1 meaning most agreement
and 5 least...)

___5   [2]   I hope to devote more time to professional improvement
in the future, and feel I must be more regular in devot-
ing some time each week to this end.

___6   [3]   Keeping up to date through attendance at professional
meetings undoubtedly would be helpful, but my own job
is so demanding that I cannot afford the time.

___7   [1]   Librarianship is my profession and I am aware that I
must constantly improve myself; I frequently use my own
time and my own funds to cover expenses.

___8   [4]   I do some professional reading, but my time is too
limited to do much more than to scan the major professional journals.

__9 [5] No one can deny the importance of professional improve-
         ment, but in my case adequate resources just are not
         available.

The highest possible score was 1, meaning perfect correlation between rankings chosen and model established.

Kind of Formal Course Work Motivation

The rationale and computation of the score for kind of formal course work motivation is the same as for kind of professional
improvement motivation.

The following are the statements as given in the Questionnaire with the number in brackets corresponding to the kind of motivation: (1) security or safety, (2) acceptance, (3) prestige, status,
(4) self-actualization.

Even though I already have a MLS degree, I feel that addi-
    tional formal course work
(Please number in rank order with 1 meaning most agreement
and 4 least agreement.)

__1 [1] is necessary to satisfy myself that I'm keeping up to
         date and that I'm learning about things I ought to know.

__2 [4] will enable me to earn the kind of salary that will meet
         my obligations and enable me to live comfortably.

__3 [2] will probably place me in line for more responsible
         positions.

__4 [3] will be necessary to keep on the same level as my fellow
         librarians. Many are considering formal study.

The highest possible score was 1, meaning perfect correlation between rankings chosen and model established.

Degree of Formal Course Work Motivation

Five statements ranging on a scale from little to great motivation toward formal course work were given.

268

In general, my attitude toward formal course work beyond the MLS is:

(Please number in rank order <u>1</u> meaning most agreement and <u>5</u> least...)

___5 [5] In my situation, further formal course work would not help me so I don't anticipate pursuing it further.

___6 [3] With some encouragement and help, I'd be willing to try taking some formal course work again.

___7 [4] Further formal course work may be useful, but there are too many personal and other factors that make it impossible or impractical for me.

___8 [1] Further formal course work is a must so far as I'm concerned. I want to go back to school and am planning it.

___9 [2] I feel further formal course work would be desirable, and I plan to return to school when conditions are right.

The highest possible score was 1, meaning perfect correlation between rankings chosen and model established.

Index

Prepared by Gladys Sellers Hedstrom

270

156-59, 166, 167, 267-68,
kind 18, 159-62, 163, 166-67,
267
Formal course work since MLS,
as variable 19, 43, Table V
45, Table VI 52, 104-8, 114,
116, 209
Formal Study Motivation Degree
Score, Table IX 60
Formal Study Motivation Type
Score, Table IX 60
Foundation grants 79
Friedlander, Frank
ascription of importance of
variables 86
theory of dual motivation 84,
85, 101, 121
work process and work-context 109

Gardner, John W. , on individual's
responsibility for education
80, 199
Gellerman, Saul W. , definition of
motivation 20
Geographical accessibility 180,
214
Geographical area 27, Table II
38, 46, Table VI 52
Ghiselli "Self-Descriptive Inven-
tory" 17
Ghosh, D. N. ,
on sample size 34
statistical procedures checker
34
Goals, See Aspirations
Gomersall, Earl R. , on behavior-
al scientists 213
Goodman, Charles H. , on em-
ployee motivation 35
Governing board 51, 54
Government (field of study) 198
Group-centered forces 86, 110,
114
Group discussions 213
Guide card, questionnaire aid 30

Haggerty, M. E. , on intellectually active teacher 72
Harvey, John Frederick, on
mobility of librarians 17
Heads of libraries,
as aspiration 59

background characteristics,
Table IV 42
desiring to leave librarianship 62, 66-67
in relation to Kind of Formal
Course Work Motivation 162
membership in associations
49
salaries 47
sex, 39, Table III 40, Table
IV 42, 208
studied by
Alvarez 17, 75
Harvey 17
years since MLS 47
Health 95, 106
Herzberg, Frederick,
conceptual framework 108
critical incident technique 86
on job enrichment 206
theory of dual motivation 84,
85, 101, 122
High-low dichotomy,
approach to variables 32, 148,
163
attitude of supervision 54
degree of aspiration 58
density of population 44
membership in professional
organizations 72
Professional Index Score 65,
66, 67
salary 49
Home situation 94, 106
Honor societies 135, 137, 138
Horizontal analysis of
forty-two factors of encouragement and forty-two of
determent 87
importance and involvement
items 134
Houle, Cyril O. , on continuing
education 176, 200
Human values 199
Humanities (field of study) 43,
44, Table V 45, Table VI
52, 61, 216
Hygiene, factors of 108
Hypotheses tested 18-20
One 148-153
Two 153-155
Three 155-159
Four 159-163

273

275

Positive forces, formal course
work and professional im-
provement 116-18
Practices for professional
growth 15
Pre-testing of questionnaire 30
Price, Bronson, on basics for
true sample 26
Probability sample 26
Professional, defined 63
Professional assistance to other
librarians 144
Professional associates, influence of 94, 98, 106
Professional associations, See
Memberships in profes-
sional organizations
Professional books read, See
Reading of professional
literature
Professional growth equated with
professional development
21, 30
Professional improvement 111,
114
defined 21
responsibility for 170-95
Professional improvement activities 21, 51, 54, 87,
Table XIV 92-93, 94-96,
104-6, 108, 167
importance of 135-6
involvement 136-38
negative motivations 129
per cent listing workshops
and short-term courses,
Table IV 42
positive motivation 128
quality of 201, 202
suggested research project
226
Professional improvement characteristics, measurement
of 57-81
Professional improvement motivation 18, 19, 28, 116,
147-55, 163, Table XXVIII
164-65, 166, 167, 264, 266
Professional Index 64-67
twelve criteria of Ranta 64
Professional Index Score 18, 19,
27, 57, Table IX 60, 61,
65-67, Table XI 68-69, 70,

116, 255-311
actual scores 65
high-low dichotomy 65
in relation to
Degree of Professional Improvement Motivation 149,
151, 168
Degree of Formal Course
Work Motivation 156
Kind of Formal Course
Work Motivation 159, 161
Kind of Professional Im-
provement Motivation 154,
168
number of offices held 73
opposition from supervisor 67
research 79
self-learning agenda 80
voluntary study groups 80
Professional journals read, See
Reading of professional
literature
Professional librarian, defined
25
Professional Orientation Score
67
Professionalism 15, 17, 37, 57,
62, 220
in allied groups 16, 17
indexes of 63-81
Profile of librarians
by indexes of professional development, Table XI 68-69
relative to background characteristics, Table VI 52-53
Profile of librarians' education
and professional training,
Table V 45
Profile of male and female librarians, Table IV 42
Programs of continuing education 16, 17
Promotion aids 95, 98
Promotion of new materials as
activity of importance 136,
138, 139, 142
Promotion policy 210
Psychological arrangement 30
Public administration (field of
study) 198
Public librarians 17, 26, 227
on relative importance of professional development ac-

277

Public librarians (cont.)
   tivities 135-36, 137
Publication and publicity of U. S.
   Office of Education, Library Services Division
   185, 187
Publication by librarians 46, 50,
   57, 61, 62, 65, 77, 79,
   199
   as an area of involvement
      137, 140, 197
   as important to professional
      development 135
   in relation to
      self-learning agenda 80
      voluntary study groups 80
Publications 76-78
   See also reading of profes-
      sional literature
Publicity 201
Publicity and planning help in
   professional development
   104, 106
Publicity and public relations,
   statewide 188-89
Publishers of library literature,
   recommendation to 170,
   191-92
Purpose of the study 15-16

Quality of professional improvement activity 95, 96, 98,
   201
Questionnaire,
   activity items 133
   description of seven parts 30-
      31
   development of 29-32
   for others than librarians 226
   mailing 31
   positive-negative nature of
      85-86
   pre-test 29-30, 86
Questions,
   arranged in six classes 109-
      10
   asked in study 15-16
   concerning professional cri-
      teria 255-311
   questions, inapplicable 70

Rank order 32
Rankings of importance and in-

volvement 135-39
Ranta, Raymond, twelve criteria
   of professionalism 27, 64-
   65, 264
Reading of professional literature 74-78, 197
   area of most involvement 137
   as criteria of professionalism
      57
   as most important in profes-
      sional development 135,
      138
   in area of specialization 140,
      144, 197
   in library science 144, 197
   in relation to
      attitude of supervisors 54
      concern for fellow worker
         71
      desire for change of situa-
         tion 61
      membership in non-library
         professional organization
         72
      number of offices held 73
      salary 50
      self-learning agenda 80-81
      time spent in workshops
         74
      voluntary study groups 80
Reasons to leave librarianship
   62-63
Recommendations from li-
   brarians 31, 51, 170-195
Recruiting 135, 137, 140, 144,
   197, 222
Reed, Sarah R. ,
   on associations' responsibili-
      ties to membership 224
   on continuing education oppor-
      tunities 16-17, 46
   on workshops 74
Religion (field of study), Table
   V 45
Requirements for professional
   improvement activities 97,
   106, 201
Research, as activity of importance 136
   involvement in 137, 138
Research by librarians 48, 54,
   57, 62, 78-79, 197, 199,
   215, 219

Research funds 185, 187
Research projects 224-227
Residence, region of 27, 46
Response to questionnaire 31
Responsibility for professional
    growth 132-144, 199-200,
    212, 220
Responsibility of librarianship
    to society 200
Retirments 36
Rothstein, Samuel,
    on ALA as continuing educa-
    tion sponsor 223-24
    on education as peripheral
    activity 199

Salary,
    as determent factor 201
    as variable 18, 19, 27, 116,
    208-9
    in relation to
        age 37
        Degree of Formal Course
        Work Motivation 156, 158
        Degree of Professional Im-
        provement Motivation 149
        density of population 46
        favorable supervisory atti-
        tude on continuing education
        53
        Kind of Formal Course
        Work Motivation 160, 162
        Kind of Professional Im-
        provement Motivation 154-
        55
        membership in non-library
        associations 72
        number supervised 48
        professional reading 76
        satisfaction with career 61
        sex 39
    incentive to leave librarian-
    ship 62
    no relation to Professional In-
    dex Score 67
Salary data 49-50, Table VI 53
Sample, determination of 24-27
Sample design 26-27
Satisfaction with career, See
    Career satisfaction
Satisfiers 108-9
School librarians 26, 37
    on relative importance of pro-

fessional development ac-
    tivities 135
    on relative involvement in pro-
    fessional development ac-
    tivities 136
School librarianship as workshop
    subject 74
Science (field of study) 44,
    Table V 45
Scoring systems 57, 65, 255-
    316
Security on job 94, 98, 201
Self-learning agenda 80-81, 198
    as criteria for professional-
    ism 57
    in relation to
        desire for change in situa-
        tion 61
        number supervised 48
        voluntary study groups 80
Sex 18, 27, 35, 135, 136, 208
    as background characteristic,
    Table VI 52
    distribution by, Table II 35,
    39, Table III 40, 41, Table
    IV 42
    in relation to
        Degree and Kind of Profes-
        sional Improvement Motiva-
        tion 149, 150-151
        Degree of Formal Course
        Work Motivation 156
        Kind of Formal Course
        Work Motivation 159
    no relation to Professional In-
    dex Score 67, 208
Situation-centered forces 86-87,
    109, 110, 111
Sixth-year certificates in library
    science 43, Table V 45,
    135, 137
Social problems (field of study)
    198
Social sciences (field of study)
    43, Table V 45, Table VI
    52, 216
Solla Price, Derek J. de, See
    de Solla Price, Derek J.
Span between MLS classes in
    survey 24-25
Speaking to community groups
    135-36, 137, 144
Special librarians 26, 37

Date Due